I0810499

IMAGES
of America

SILER CITY

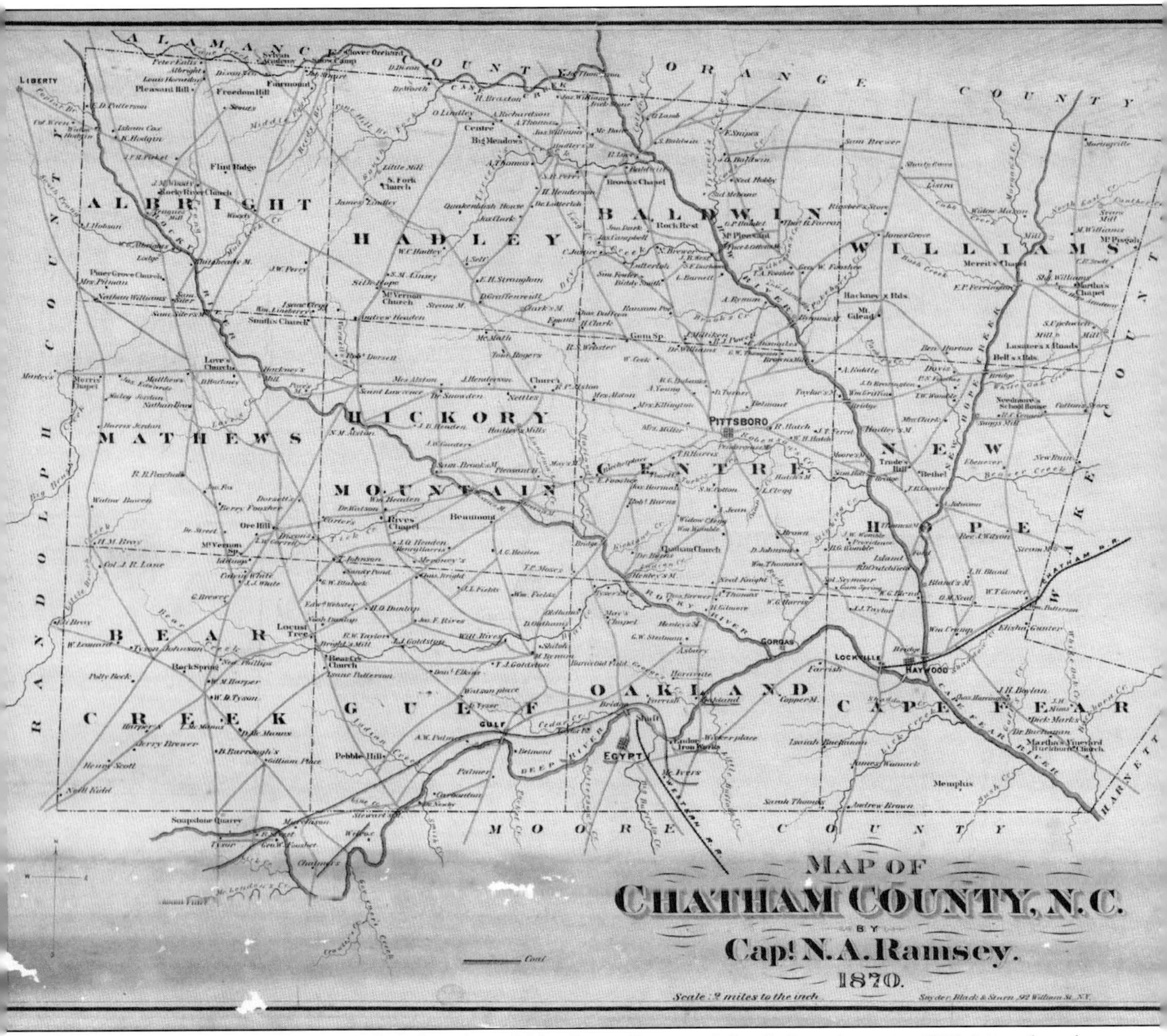

Capt. N.A. Ramsey completed a map of Chatham County, North Carolina, in 1870. Listed within the map are all the counties during that period. Matthews was later renamed Matthews Crossing and then Siler City, North Carolina. (Courtesy of the Town of Siler City.)

On the Cover: Pictured in 1920 at Elders Motors are, from left to right, unidentified, P.J. Reitzel, E. Bray, and two unidentified men. The one-story, brick Elder Motor Company building was constructed for H.H. Elder at 134 East Raleigh Street and was first occupied by his local Ford dealership and service department. Reitzel went on to become involved in the Kennedy and Reitzel Motor Company, which was established in January 1932. Hamp Vestal soon joined them in the business, and the name was later changed to Reitzel Motor Company. Reitzel continued to operate it at the original location of 124 East Second Street until around 1985. The H.H. Elder building was occupied until 1968 by Welford Harris Inc., also a Ford dealer. In 1995, the building was in use by Siler City Mini Storage. This photograph shows the men's dignity, respect, nobility, and appreciation of formality when representing oneself in communal labor. (Courtesy of Duane Hall's historical collection.)

IMAGES
of America

SILER CITY

Marian Rogers-Lindsay

ARCADIA
PUBLISHING

ISBN 978-1-4671-2197-2

Published by Arcadia Publishing
Charleston, South Carolina

Printed in the United States of America

Library of Congress Control Number: 2013955123

For all general information, please contact Arcadia Publishing:
Telephone 843-853-2070
Fax 843-853-0044
E-mail sales@arcadiapublishing.com
For customer service and orders:
Toll-Free 1-888-313-2665

Visit us on the Internet at www.arcadiapublishing.com

To my parents, Austin and Delsia Rogers.
Also to Jacqueline and Trevor (my children), who encouraged me to follow my dreams—I pray they do.

Contents

ACKNOWLEDGMENTS

The overwhelming love and generosity of photographs and stories that came to life from so many people made this book a reality. I will forever be thankful to Gary T. Tyson, the first Siler City African American chief of police, for spending countless hours sharing stories with me and for his devotion to ensuring all the right people were interviewed. I am indebted to my new friend Nancy Tysor, manager of Farmers' Alliance Store, Inc., one of the oldest businesses in Siler City, for sharing her photographic collection and history and for brightening my days with Nehis. Nancy, you are a warm and wonderful woman. Thank you Bryan Thompson, town manager, for your support. Thank you Mayor John Grimes and wife Cecilia Budd Grimes for your photographic collection and stories. Thank you Edward Murray for support and encouragement. Thank you Mike Cowell, Siler City Wren Library manager, for allowing access to the library resources and the building used for research and meetings. Thank you to the Wren Library librarians; your big hearts and time meant a great deal to me. Thank you Barbara Pugh, president of the Chatham County Historical Association, for sharing the organization's photographic collection.

Thank you to Duane R. Hall, Siler City's historian, for your guidance, leadership, opinions, and in-depth, eloquent research about Siler City—which provided the beacon of light for this book—and for providing the oldest photographs. A very special thank you goes to Mrs. Carol Hall for sharing her and Duane's amazing history and opening her heart and home to a complete stranger. Thank you Mary Craven and Norma Boone for your valuable input and pictures.

Thank you to Austin and Delsia Rogers for raising me to respect others, appreciate history, and to persevere. Thank you to my children and family for their love and support during the development of this book. Finally, I must acknowledge my editor, Katie McAlpin, for her knowledge and her patience, time, and dedication in seeing this project to fruition.

Unless otherwise noted, all images appear courtesy of Duane Hall's historical collection.

Introduction

Siler City began when Plikard Dedrick and Elizabeth Hartsoe Siler decided to journey from Germany to Philadelphia in 1741. They were married upon arriving in Philadelphia and decided to travel first to Virginia and then to North Carolina. Once they reached Chatham County, they decided it was time to put down roots and raise a family, settling four miles north of the Siler City downtown area in a spot called Lacy Creek. Once they established themselves, the couple had 10 children. According to the chronological historical documentations of Wade Hadley Jr., a geologist and author of *Siler City, North Carolina: 1887–1987,* two of those descendants were spirited in the development of a town called Siler City.

In February 1794, John Siler, son of Plikard, bought land where William Ditto had lived. At least three of the tracts of land purchased by John had previously been owned by David Smith and the Radcliff family. By 1805, John was living on a plantation of 615 acres in a house on the lot where the federal post office (116 East Raleigh Street) is now located. A useful spring of water was located about 350 feet east of the house. By 1815, John was operating a country store near his home. He and his wife are buried in the local Oakwood Cemetery.

On December 15, 1842, upon the death of John Siler, William W. "Captain Billy" Matthews bought Siler's house and 140 acres of land. Matthews and his wife, Margaret Cheek, provided food and lodging for stagecoach travelers at their house. The spot, located near the present-day intersection of North Chatham Avenue and Second Street, was soon called Matthews Crossroads. The north-south road passed in front of the Matthews house, which is where Scott Alley is today.

A gathering that can be seen today started on June 10, 1861, when a company of volunteers for the Confederate army, the "Chatham Boys," organized and drilled in the front yard of the William Matthews house. It was made up of men who volunteered from Matthews Crossroads and Albright Township. It later became Company G of the 26th North Carolina Regiment. Today, re-enactors portraying the company make appearances at the Veterans Day parade and other events in Siler City.

By 1870, Samuel Siler, a relative of Plikard Dedrick Siler, was operating a small water-powered gristmill about three blocks south of the Siler-Matthews house. The mill was located near where South Chatham Avenue crosses the creek that flows through downtown today. Samuel also owned a storehouse near the mill that was operated by his son Cincinnatus Siler. On July 13, 1880, the post office, named Energy, was opened in Samuel's storehouse, and Cincinnatus was appointed postmaster.

In 1882, Samuel Siler's storehouse was sold at auction. By 1884, the Siler-Matthews house was being operated as a hotel by A.C. Jordan. On April 16 of that year, the Cape Fear and Yadkin Valley Railway completed its rail line between Sanford and Greensboro. The depot was named Siler Station in recognition of Samuel Siler, who donated the land on which it was located. E.R. McLean was the railroad station's first agent. Later, on July 3, the post office was named Siler Station, and on December 10, J. George Hanner was appointed postmaster.

As for businesses, in 1884 E.R. McLean & Company was opened as a general merchandise store and was located along the east side of North Birch Avenue near the middle of the 100 block. Early in 1885, the post office was moved there. On November 11, 1885, a tobacco warehouse and market named the Chatham Warehouse Company opened at 138 and 144 North Chatham Avenue. The president/manager was O.A. Hanner, and the secretary/treasurer was E.R. McLean. Also in 1885, John F. Lambe and his brother A.A. Lambe opened the firm Teague & Lambe, a general merchandise and building-supply store. The store was located in what had formerly been the storehouse of Samuel Siler.

In 1885, the town government was starting to form as well. Prior to the town's incorporation, Dr. J.A. Turner was recognized as mayor of Siler City. His father and mother are buried at Oakwood Cemetery in town. On March 7, 1887, the North Carolina General Assembly incorporated the town of Siler City. The physical limits of the town were defined as being a half mile from the depot of the Cape Fear & Yadkin Valley Railroad and running with the four cardinal points of the compass. The following officers were named to serve until an election was held: Mayor J.B. Guthrie, Commissioner D.G. Fox, Commissioner A.A. Lambe, Commissioner E.B. McLean, Commissioner A.R. Siler, Commissioner R.C. Siler, and Marshal J.J. Crutchfield.

On July 28, 1886, the post office was named Siler City. On January 12, 1887, the Thompson School opened on the present-day site of city hall. The owner and superintendent was Prof. James Alexander Wilson Thompson. The bell from the Thompson School has been preserved and is mounted in W.F. Collins Park.

These are just a few of the many people who played vital roles in the town's development. The bibliography at the end of the book will direct readers to a more in-depth chronology, as well as the historical information at Siler City's website.

Most importantly—and what these pages document—is that Siler City has great people at its heart. Residents are rooted in the traditions that have helped the town survive and grow, but the community is also open and hospitable to new ideas and people. Citizens are very proud of the variety of cultures that make up the fabric of the town. A resolute community, residents are dedicated to the land, its businesses, its neighbors, and of course hard work, which is evident in the pledge to improve the town for future generations. These are the values that attracted "Aunt Bee," the favorite aunt of Mayberry, to choose Siler City as the town to spend her later years. The same pillars that made Mayberry the perfect rural small town can be seen everywhere in the community today.

One

Matthews Crossing

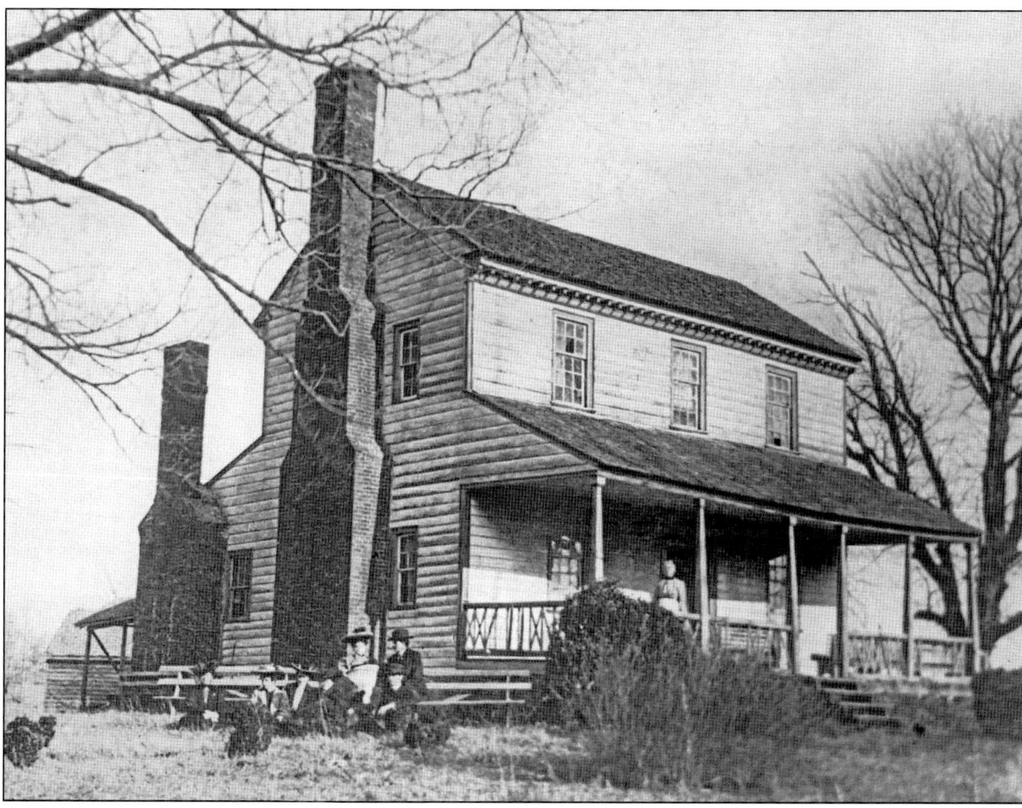

This is the Siler-Matthews house. It was built by John Siler in early 1800s, and William Matthews bought it in 1842. The site is now used by the federal post office at 116 East Raleigh Street. An old mill is in the background. This is the origin of Siler City.

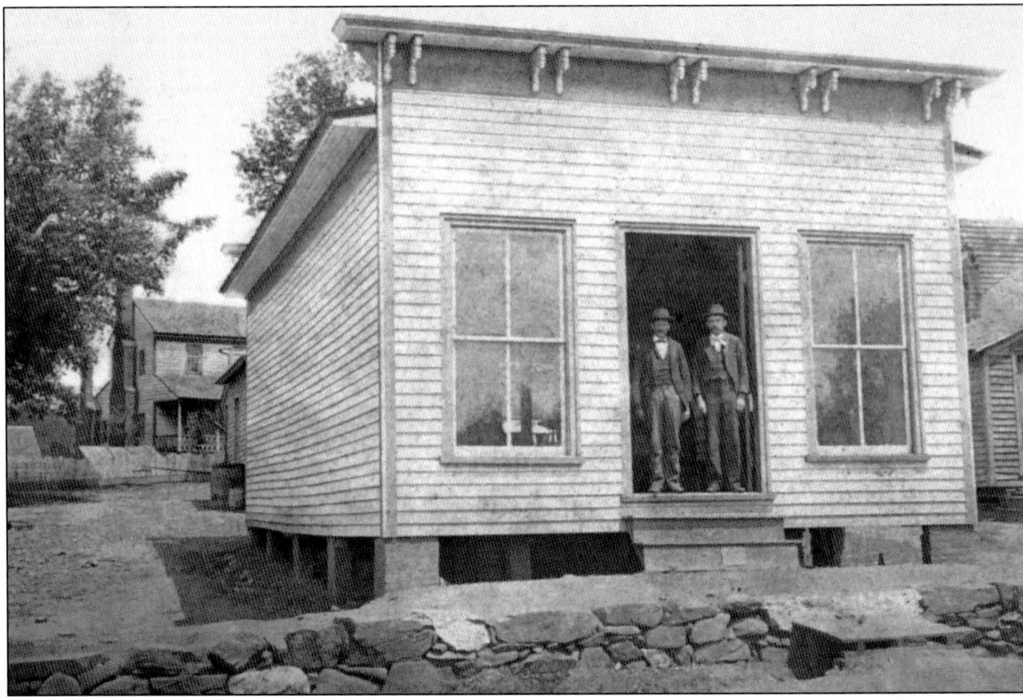

This 1890s image shows the D.G. Fox general merchandise and produce store in Siler City, located at what is now 115 South Chatham Avenue. The Siler-Matthews house is visible in the background. The owner, D.G. Fox, and his son M.M. Fox are standing in the doorway.

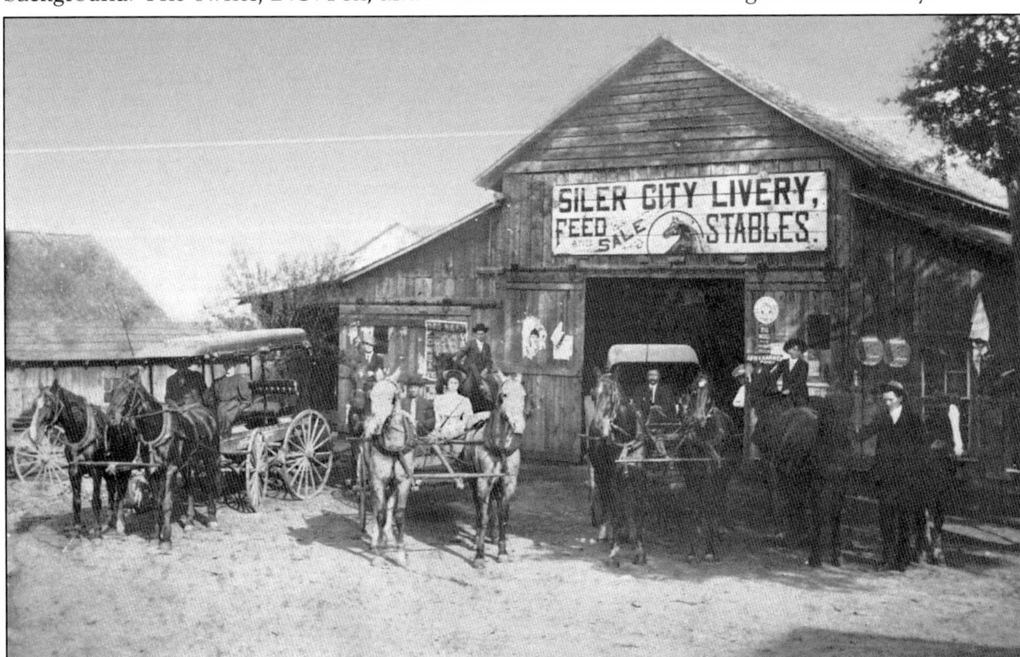

The Siler City Livery was built around 1890 on the northwest corner of North Chatham Avenue and West Second Street. The stables kept horses, buggies, and carriages for hire by traveling salesmen and also boarded horses and sold horses, feed, and buggies.

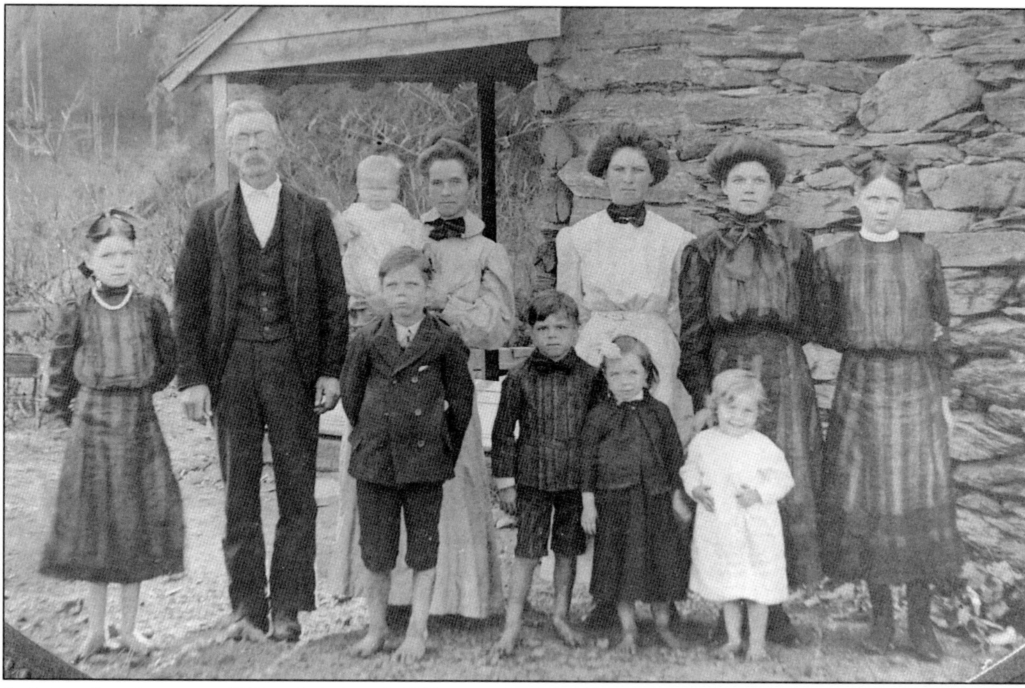

Judging by the age of Hazel Adcock White, who was born in 1905, this old cabin in the Siler City area is pictured around 1908. The individuals are, from left to right, (first row) Broadway Adcock, Plackard Adcock, Hazel Adcock White (who would later be Edwin White's mother), and Decie Adcock Smith; (second row) Fobie Adcock (buried in Loves Creek Cemetery), Joshua Joseph Adcock, baby Margaret Adcock Horner, Louise Siler Adcock, Samkie Adcock Thomas, Mildred Adcock Drum, and Arizona Adcock Johnson.

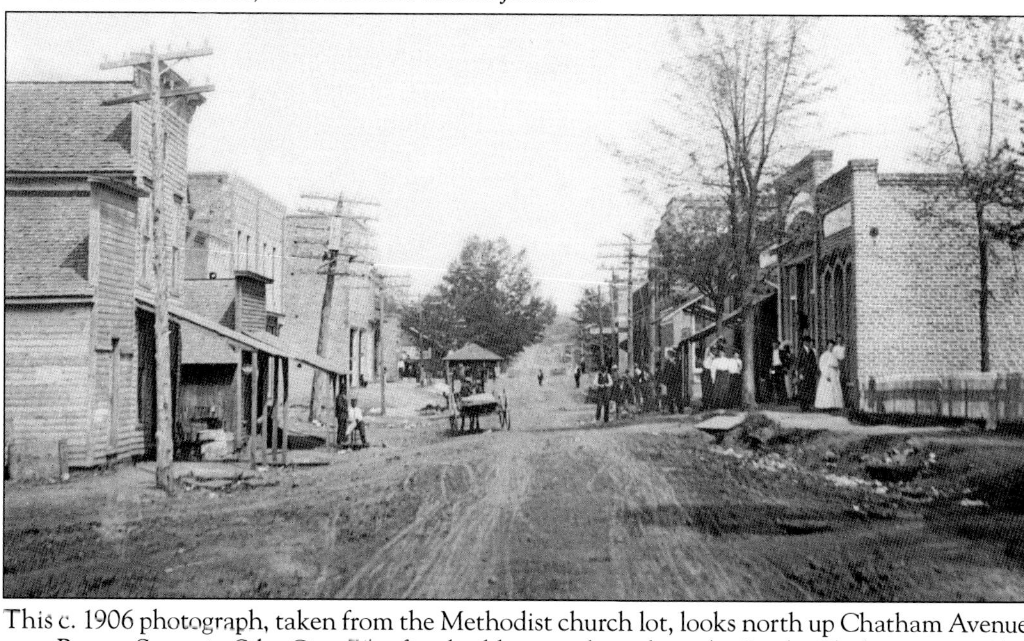

This c. 1906 photograph, taken from the Methodist church lot, looks north up Chatham Avenue near Beaver Street in Siler City. The first building on the right is the Banks Clothing store. Also visible is the roof over the town well, just north of Raleigh Street.

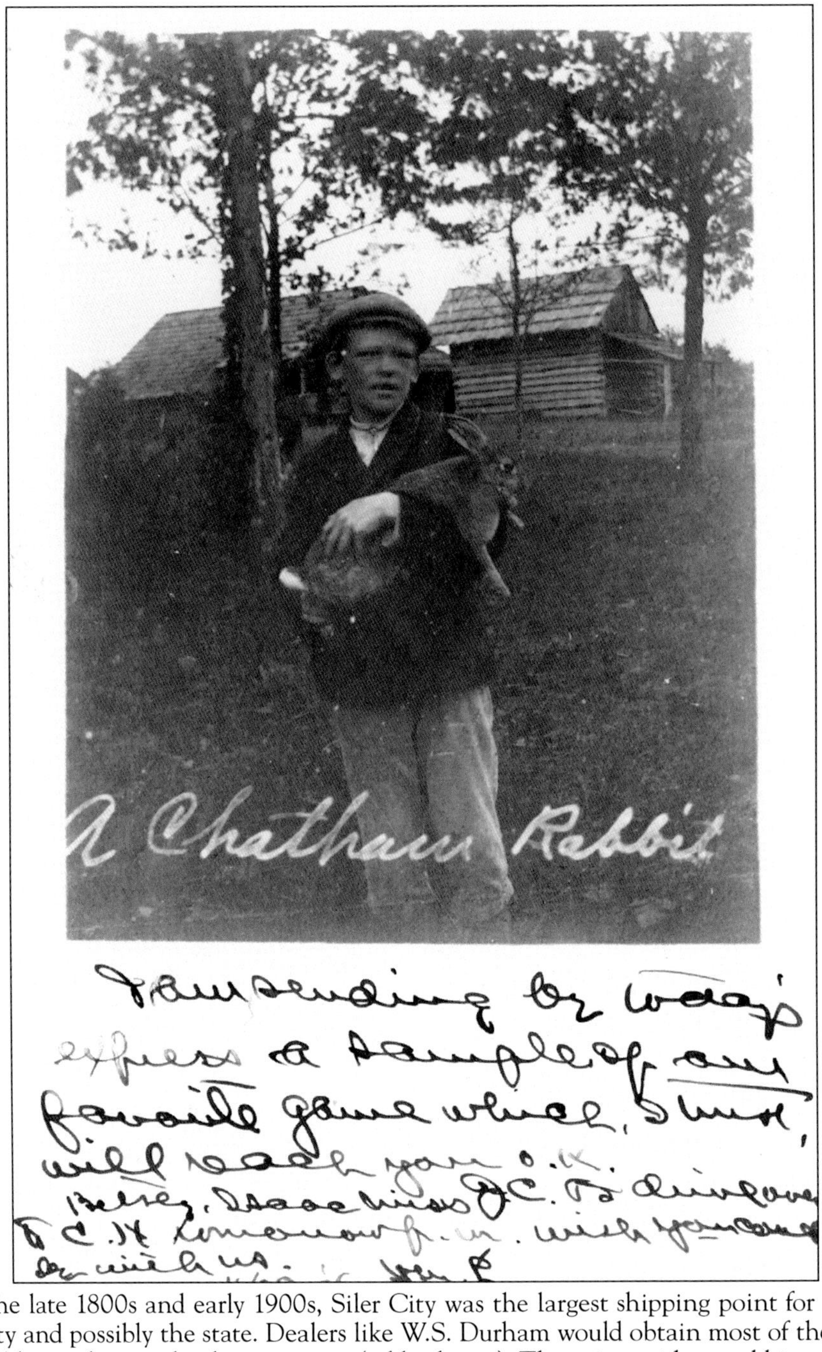

During the late 1800s and early 1900s, Siler City was the largest shipping point for rabbits in the county and possibly the state. Dealers like W.S. Durham would obtain most of their rabbits from rural boys who caught them in traps (rabbit boxes). The price paid per rabbit varied from 8¢ to 15¢. This postcard depicts a boy wearing a hat and holding a large rabbit, with a log cabin in the background. It was mailed out of Chatham County. The image is indicative of the size of the rabbits that actually populated Chatham County, particularly Siler City. Approximately 154,000 rabbits were taken from Chatham County between 1908 and 1916. (Courtesy of North Carolina Postcards Collection Photographic Archives, Wilson Library, University of North Carolina at Chapel Hill.)

The opening of a railroad through the area of Matthews Crossroads and/or Siler Station was the stimulus that caused a town to develop. The Cape Fear and Yadkin Valley Railway completed its line between Sanford and Greensboro in 1884. The announcement was made in 1888, encouraging people to take a rest and get some relaxation on the Cape Fear train. (Courtesy of Farmers' Alliance Store and Nancy Tysor.)

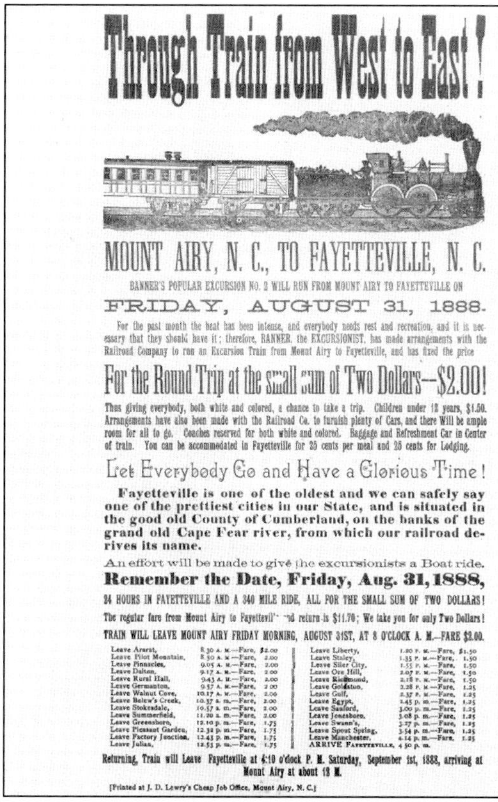

Through Train from West to East!

MOUNT AIRY, N. C., TO FAYETTEVILLE, N. C.

BANNER'S POPULAR EXCURSION NO. 2 WILL RUN FROM MOUNT AIRY TO FAYETTEVILLE ON

FRIDAY, AUGUST 31, 1888.

For the past month the heat has been intense, and everybody needs rest and recreation, and it is necessary that they should have it; therefore, BANNER, the EXCURSIONIST, has made arrangements with the Railroad Company to run an Excursion Train from Mount Airy to Fayetteville, and has fixed the price

For the Round Trip at the small sum of Two Dollars—$2.00!

Thus giving everybody, both white and colored, a chance to take a trip. Children under 12 years, $1.50. Arrangements have also been made with the Railroad Co. to furnish plenty of Cars, and there Will be ample room for all to go. Coaches reserved for both white and colored. Baggage and Refreshment Car in Center of train. You can be accommodated in Fayetteville for 25 cents per meal and 25 cents for Lodging.

Let Everybody Go and Have a Glorious Time!

Fayetteville is one of the oldest and we can safely say one of the prettiest cities in our State, and is situated in the good old County of Cumberland, on the banks of the grand old Cape Fear river, from which our railroad derives its name.

An effort will be made to give the excursionists a Boat ride.

Remember the Date, Friday, Aug. 31, 1888,

24 HOURS IN FAYETTEVILLE AND A 340 MILE RIDE, ALL FOR THE SMALL SUM OF TWO DOLLARS!

The regular fare from Mount Airy to Fayettevil[illegible] and return is $11.70; We take you for only Two Dollars!

TRAIN WILL LEAVE MOUNT AIRY FRIDAY MORNING, AUGUST 31ST, AT 8 O'CLOCK A. M.—FARE $2.00.

Leave Ararat,	8.30 A. M.—Fare,	$2.00	Leave Liberty,	1.20 P. M.—Fare,	$1.50
Leave Pilot Mountain,	8.50 A. M.—Fare,	2.00	Leave Staley,	1.35 P. M.—Fare,	1.50
Leave Pinnacles,	9.05 A. M.—Fare,	2.00	Leave Siler City,	1.55 P. M.—Fare,	1.50
Leave Dalton,	9.17 A. M.—Fare,	2.00	Leave Ore Hill,	2.07 P. M.—Fare,	1.50
Leave Rural Hall,	9.43 A. M.—Fare,	2.00	Leave Richmond,	2.18 P. M.—Fare,	1.50
Leave Germanton,	9.57 A. M.—Fare,	2.00	Leave Goldston,	2.28 P. M.—Fare,	1.25
Leave Walnut Cove,	10.17 A. M.—Fare,	2.00	Leave Gulf,	2.37 P. M.—Fare,	1.25
Leave Belew's Creek,	10.37 a. m.—Fare,	2.00	Leave Egypt,	2.45 p. m.—Fare,	1.25
Leave Stokesdale,	10.57 a. m.—Fare,	2.00	Leave Sanford,	3.00 p. m.—Fare,	1.25
Leave Summerfield,	11.20 a. m.—Fare,	2.00	Leave Jonesboro,	3.08 p. m.—Fare,	1.25
Leave Greensboro,	12.10 p. m.—Fare,	1.75	Leave Swann's,	3.27 p. m.—Fare,	1.25
Leave Pleasant Garden,	12.32 p. m.—Fare,	1.75	Leave Spout Spring,	3.54 p. m.—Fare,	1.25
Leave Factory Junction,	12.43 p. m.—Fare,	1.75	Leave Manchester,	4.14 p. m.—Fare,	1.25
Leave Julian,	12.53 p. m.—Fare,	1.75	ARRIVE FAYETTEVILLE,	4.50 p. m.	

Returning, Train will Leave Fayetteville at 4:10 o'clock P. M. Saturday, September 1st, 1888, arriving at Mount Airy at about 12 M.

[Printed at J. D. Lowry's Cheap Job Office, Mount Airy, N. C.]

This is Siler City's first sidewalk. The town's first paved sidewalks were put down in June 1909 and extended for one block in four directions from the intersection of Chatham Avenue and Raleigh Street. A granolithic method of pavement was used for the sidewalks.

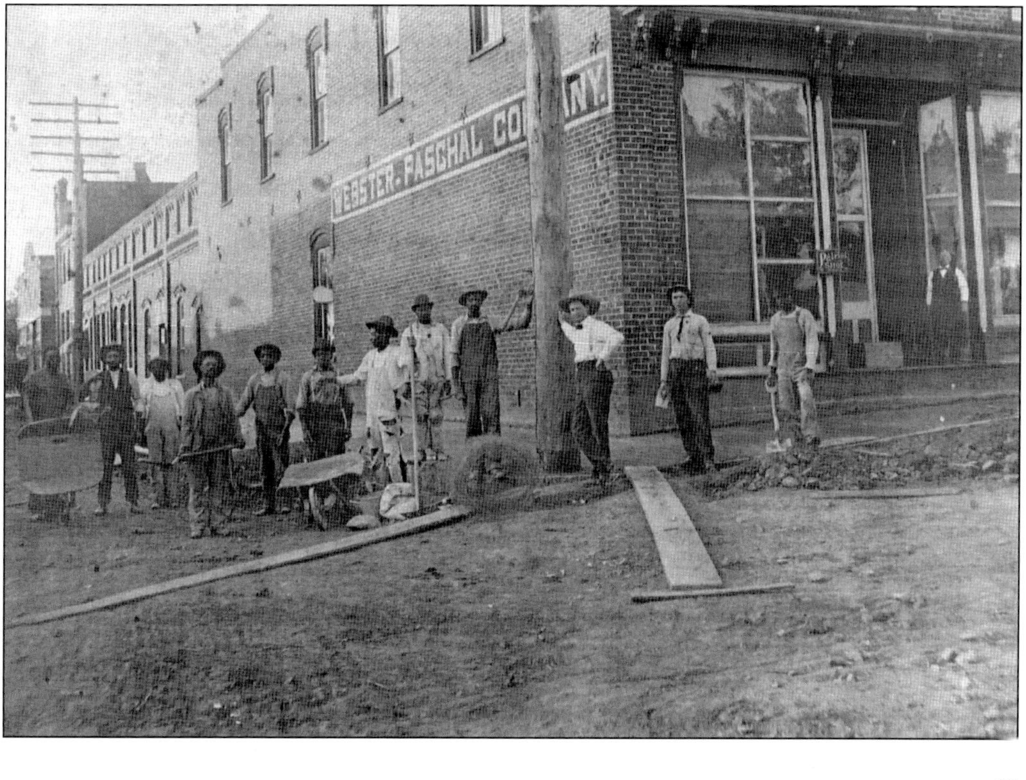

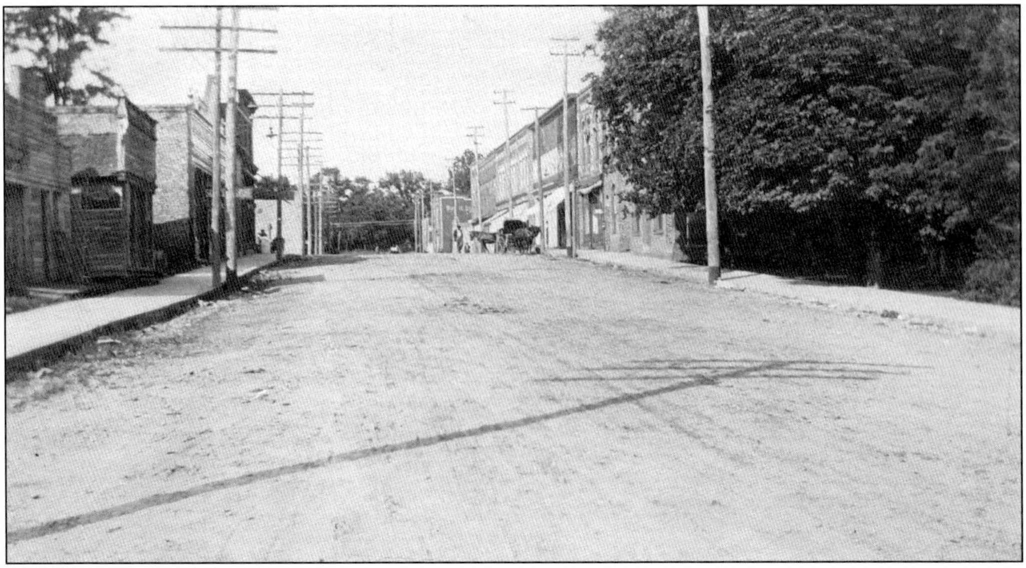

Around 1910, after the sidewalks had been installed, the dirt roads remained the same on Chatham Avenue. An ordinance passed prohibiting roller skates, wheelbarrows, handcarts, or other vehicles—except baby carriages—from being used on the town's sidewalks.

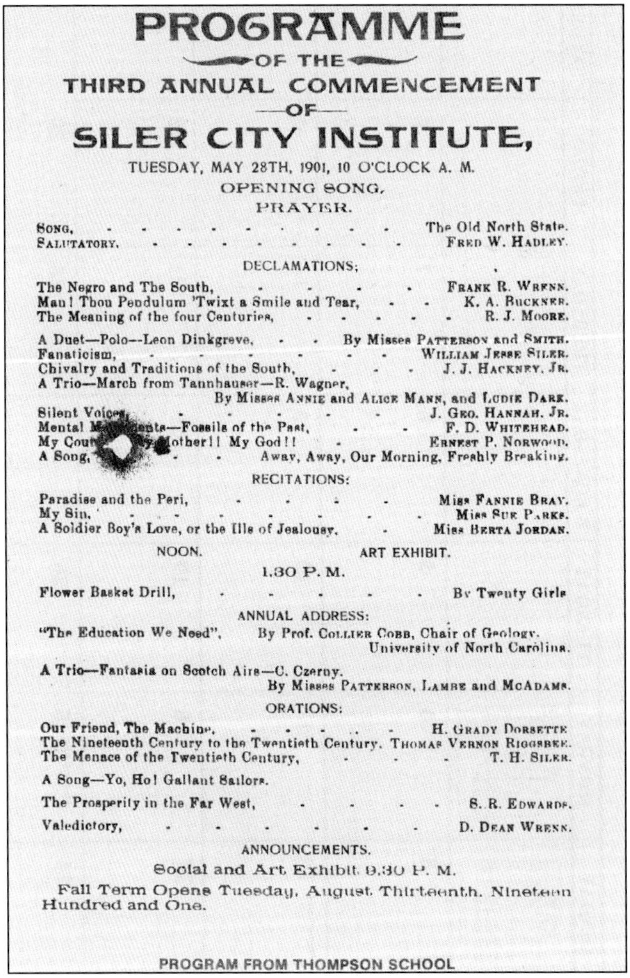

PROGRAMME

OF THE

THIRD ANNUAL COMMENCEMENT

OF

SILER CITY INSTITUTE,

TUESDAY, MAY 28TH, 1901, 10 O'CLOCK A. M.

OPENING SONG,

PRAYER.

Song, - - - - - - - - - - The Old North State.
Salutatory, - - - - - - - - - - Fred W. Hadley.

DECLAMATIONS;

The Negro and The South, - - - - - Frank R. Wrenn.
Man! Thou Pendulum 'Twixt a Smile and Tear, - - K. A. Buckner.
The Meaning of the four Centuries, - - - - - R. J. Moore.

A Duet—Polo—Leon Dinkgreve, - - By Misses Patterson and Smith.
Fanaticism, - - - - - - - William Jesse Siler.
Chivalry and Traditions of the South, - - - J. J. Hackney, Jr.
A Trio—March from Tannhauser—R. Wagner,
By Misses Annie and Alice Mann, and Ludie Dark.
Silent Voices[illegible] - - - - - J. Geo. Hannah, Jr.
Mental M[illegible]nts—Fossils of the Past, - - F. D. Whitehead.
My Cou[illegible]y Mother!! My God!! - Ernest P. Norwood.
A Song, - - Away, Away, Our Morning, Freshly Breaking.

RECITATIONS:

Paradise and the Peri, - - - - Miss Fannie Bray.
My Sin, - - - - - - - - Miss Sue Parks.
A Soldier Boy's Love, or the Ills of Jealousy, - Miss Berta Jordan.

NOON. ART EXHIBIT.

1.30 P. M.

Flower Basket Drill, - - - - - By Twenty Girls

ANNUAL ADDRESS:

"The Education We Need", By Prof. Collier Cobb, Chair of Geology, University of North Carolina.

A Trio—Fantasia on Scotch Airs—C. Czerny.
By Misses Patterson, Lambe and McAdams.

ORATIONS:

Our Friend, The Machine, - - - - - H. Grady Dorsette
The Nineteenth Century to the Twentieth Century. Thomas Vernon Riggsbee.
The Menace of the Twentieth Century, - - - T. H. Siler.

A Song—Yo, Ho! Gallant Sailors.

The Prosperity in the Far West, - - - - S. R. Edwards.

Valedictory, - - - - - - D. Dean Wrenn.

ANNOUNCEMENTS.

Social and Art Exhibit 8.30 P. M.

Fall Term Opens Tuesday, August Thirteenth, Nineteen Hundred and One.

PROGRAM FROM THOMPSON SCHOOL

This program is from the Siler City Institute in 1901. The institute was operational from 1897 to 1903. The Thompson School first occupied the building, from January 12, 1887, to 1897, when the name changed. The city hall of Siler City currently stands at the site. (Courtesy of Farmers' Alliance Store and Nancy Tysor.)

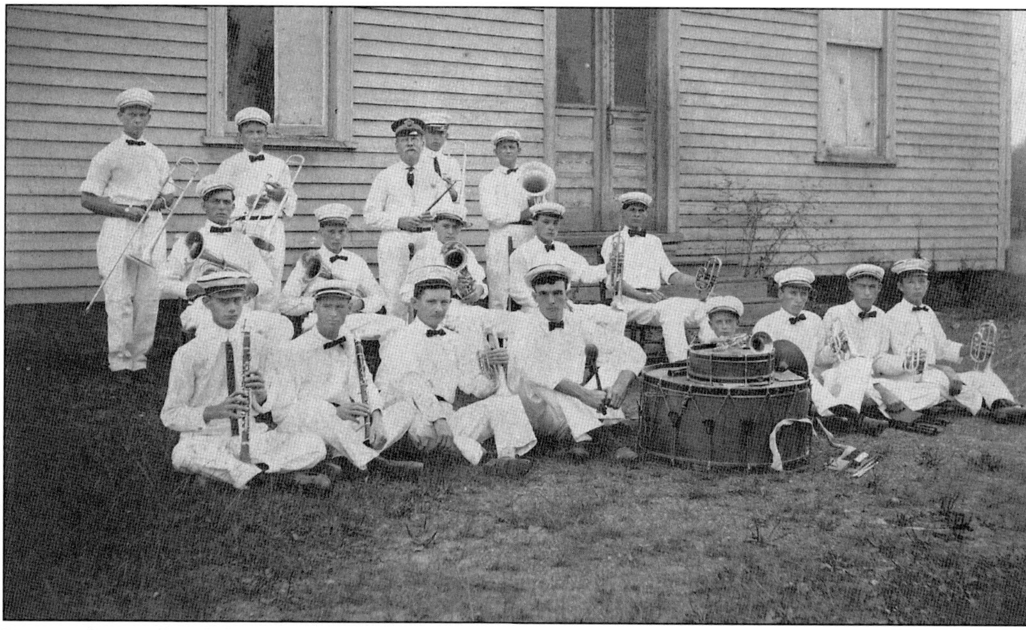

Pictured outside of the Thompson School is a band that was organized in 1912. The members are, from left to right, (first row) unidentified, John McLaughlin, unidentified, Allie Johnson, Clayton Snyder, Cletus Lowe, Ed Marsh, and George Roberts; (second row) Rufus Campbell, Stedman McMasters, Henry Light, Joe Light, and Laughter Smith; (third row) Allie Smith, Will Signer, Prof. D.S. Warburton, unidentified, and Will Snyder.

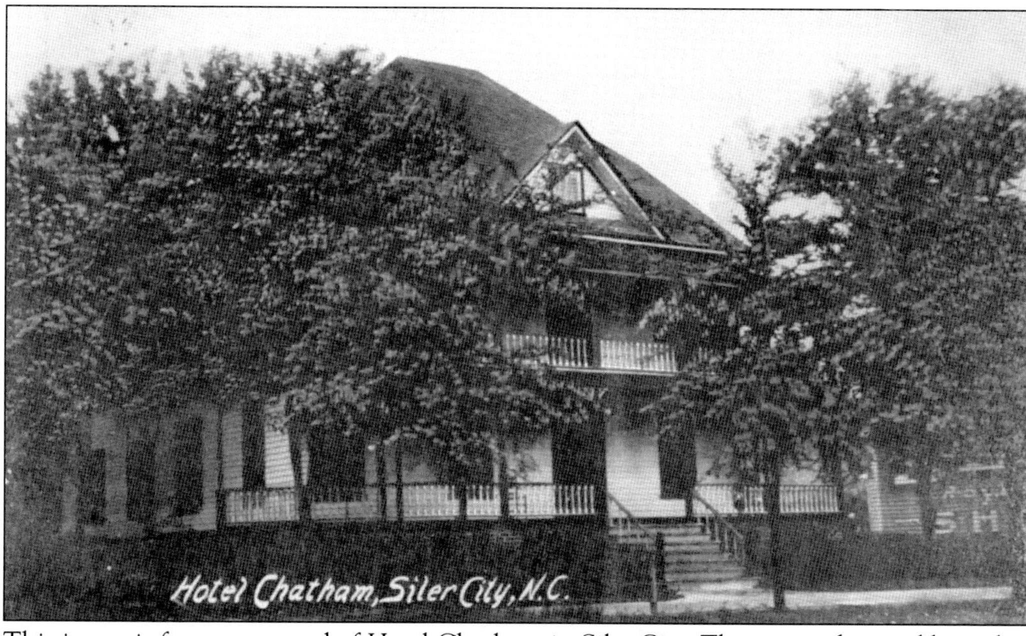

This image is from a postcard of Hotel Chatham in Siler City. The postcard was addressed to "Miss Mabel White, Siler City, Route 2, North Carolina" and was postmarked July 1914. The view is of a two-story wooden hotel, largely obscured by trees. (Courtesy of North Carolina Postcards Collection Photographic Archives, Wilson Library, University of North Carolina at Chapel Hill.)

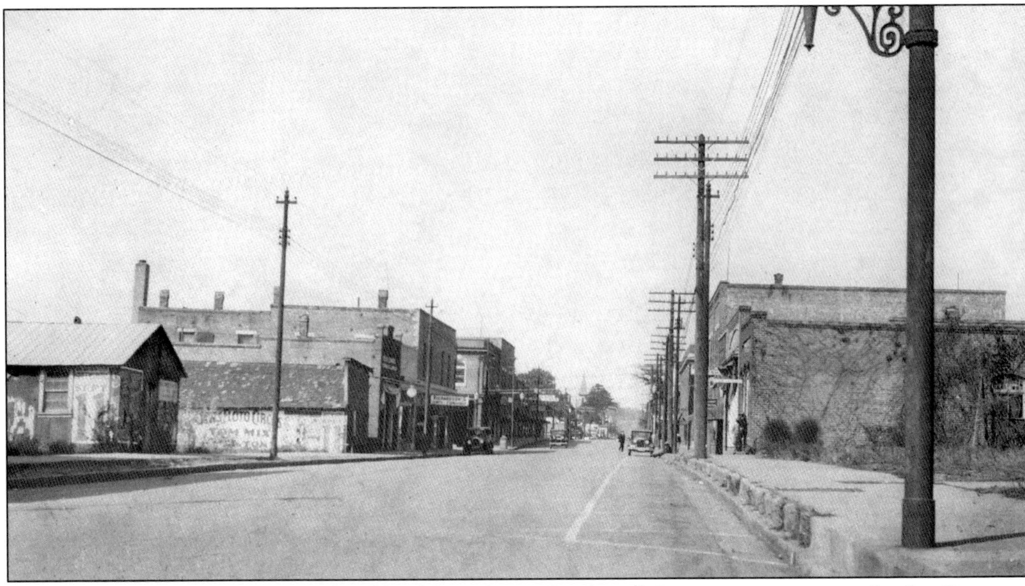

Tod R. Edwards (on the left, third building from the front) for many years was the leading and largest jewelry store in Siler City and Chatham County. The business was unusual for its time in that it was owned and operated by an African American family. The store occupied this building from 1905 to 1961.

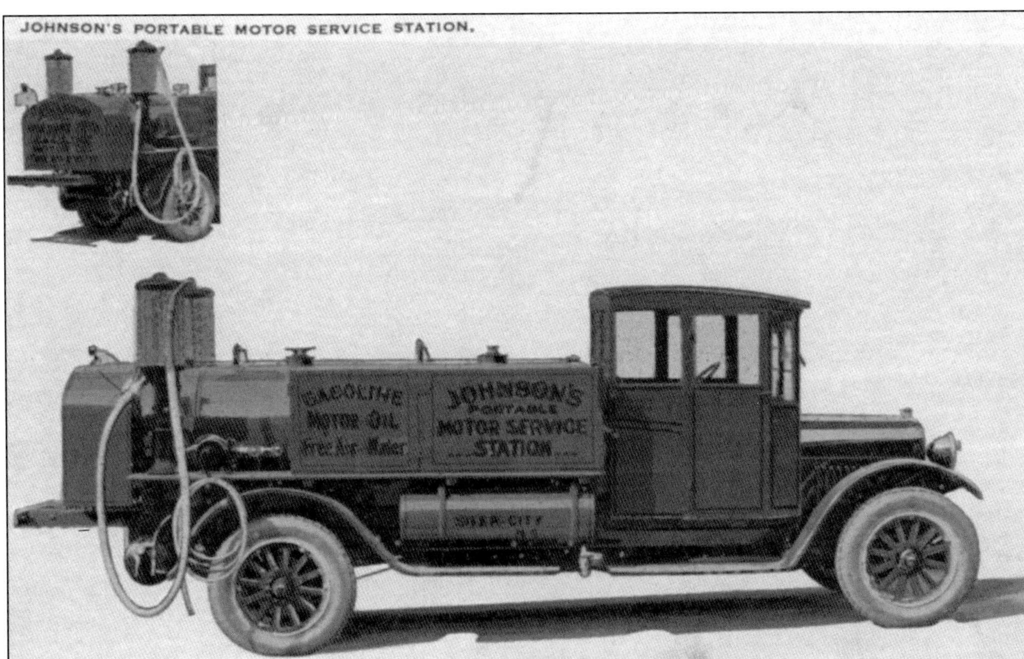

This is a photograph of the first portable motor-service station in Siler City. The truck, called Johnson's Motor Service Station, carried gasoline, motor oil, free air, and water.

Two

BUSINESSES

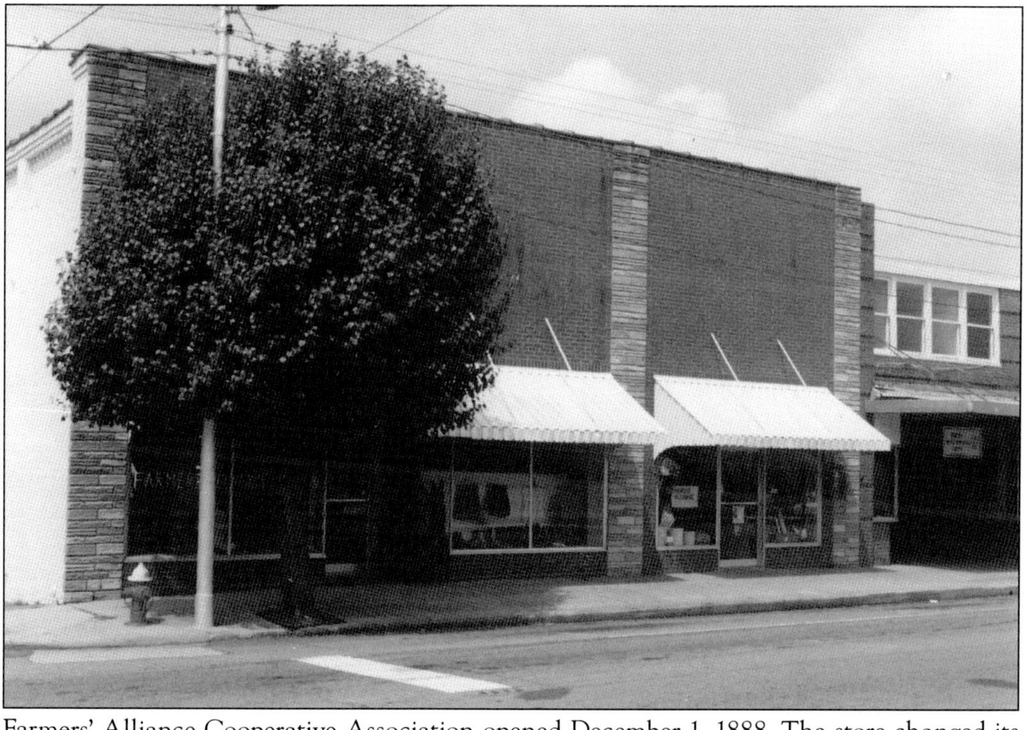

Farmers' Alliance Cooperative Association opened December 1, 1888. The store changed its name to Farmers' Alliance and Farmers Union Store Company in 1910. The original wooden building of 1888 was torn down in October 1939. The Farmers' Alliance Store was the first general merchandise store to open in downtown Siler City, and it is the last one remaining today. (Courtesy of Farmers' Alliance Store and Nancy Tysor.)

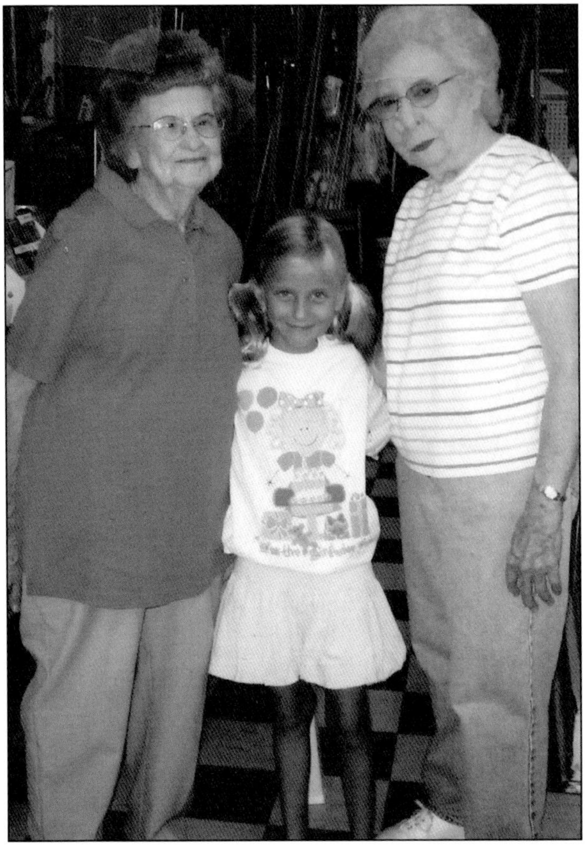

From left to right are Mildred Fields, Katya ? , and Nancy Brown Tysor. Nancy has been employed with Farmers' Alliance for 50 years and has been manager since 1975. Farmers' Alliance required all members to be farmers and belong to an alliance lodge, usually named after local churches, schools, and communities. (Courtesy of Farmers' Alliance Store and Nancy Tysor.)

Farmers' Alliance Store Inc., viewed here from the front of the store with Billy Holt stopping for the camera on December 26, 1977, started as an agriculture-based store with equipment, groceries, apparel, and items for the farm and home. Farmers' Alliance is only a year younger than the town, making it the oldest business still in operation in Siler City. (Courtesy of Farmers' Alliance Store and Nancy Tysor.)

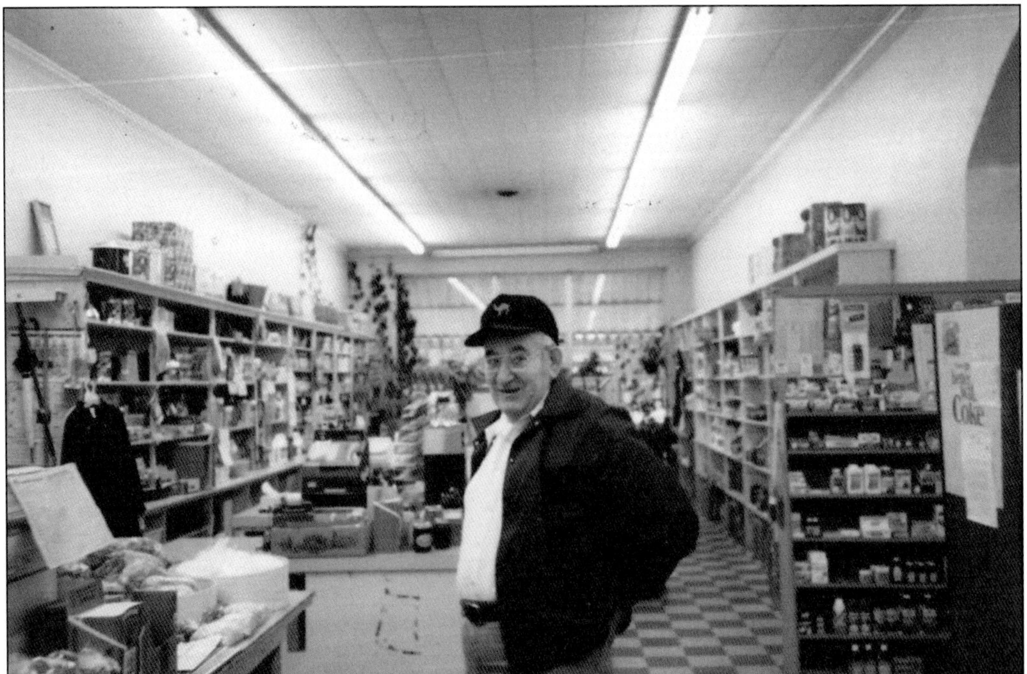

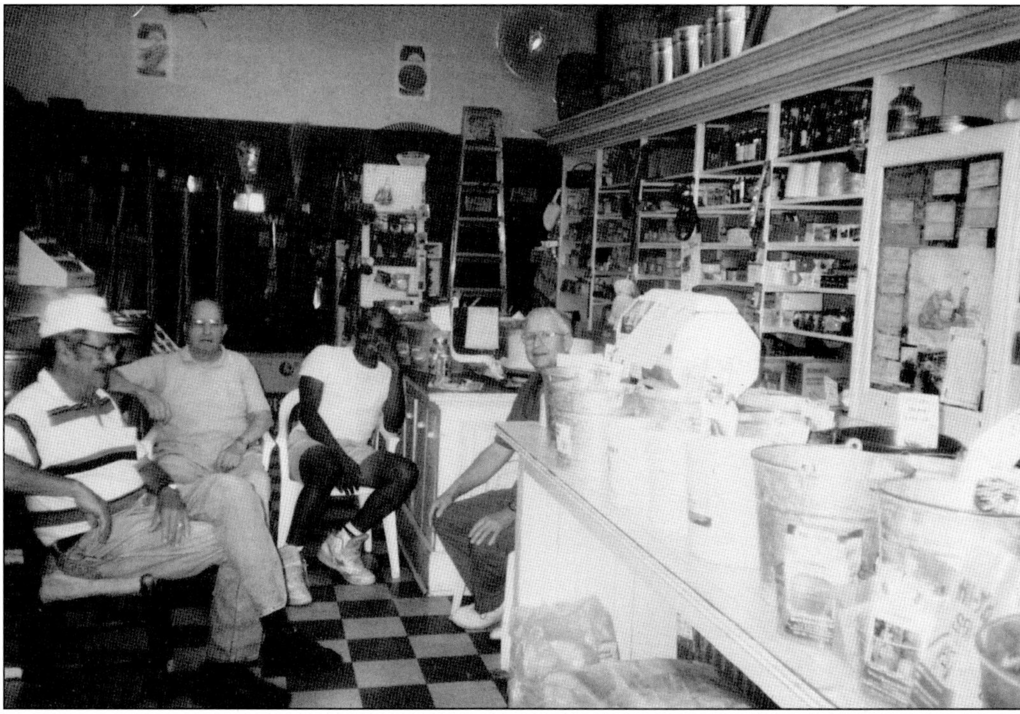

Pictured from left to right are Homer Horney, Dean Sizemore, unidentified, and June Tillman. In the store, customers can find lawn and garden supplies, ladies' and men's apparel, Western wear, shoes, cowboy boots, galoshes, hats, jeans, bib overalls, food items, stick candy, oil lamps, and the famous old Rawleigh products. (Courtesy of Farmers' Alliance Store and Nancy Tysor.)

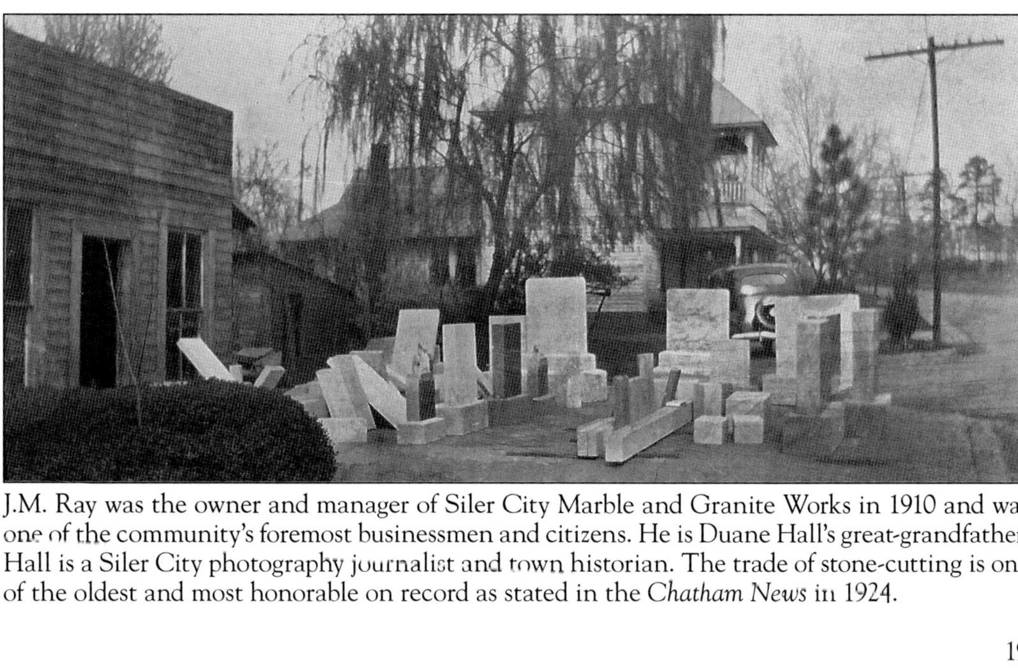

J.M. Ray was the owner and manager of Siler City Marble and Granite Works in 1910 and was one of the community's foremost businessmen and citizens. He is Duane Hall's great-grandfather. Hall is a Siler City photography journalist and town historian. The trade of stone-cutting is one of the oldest and most honorable on record as stated in the *Chatham News* in 1924.

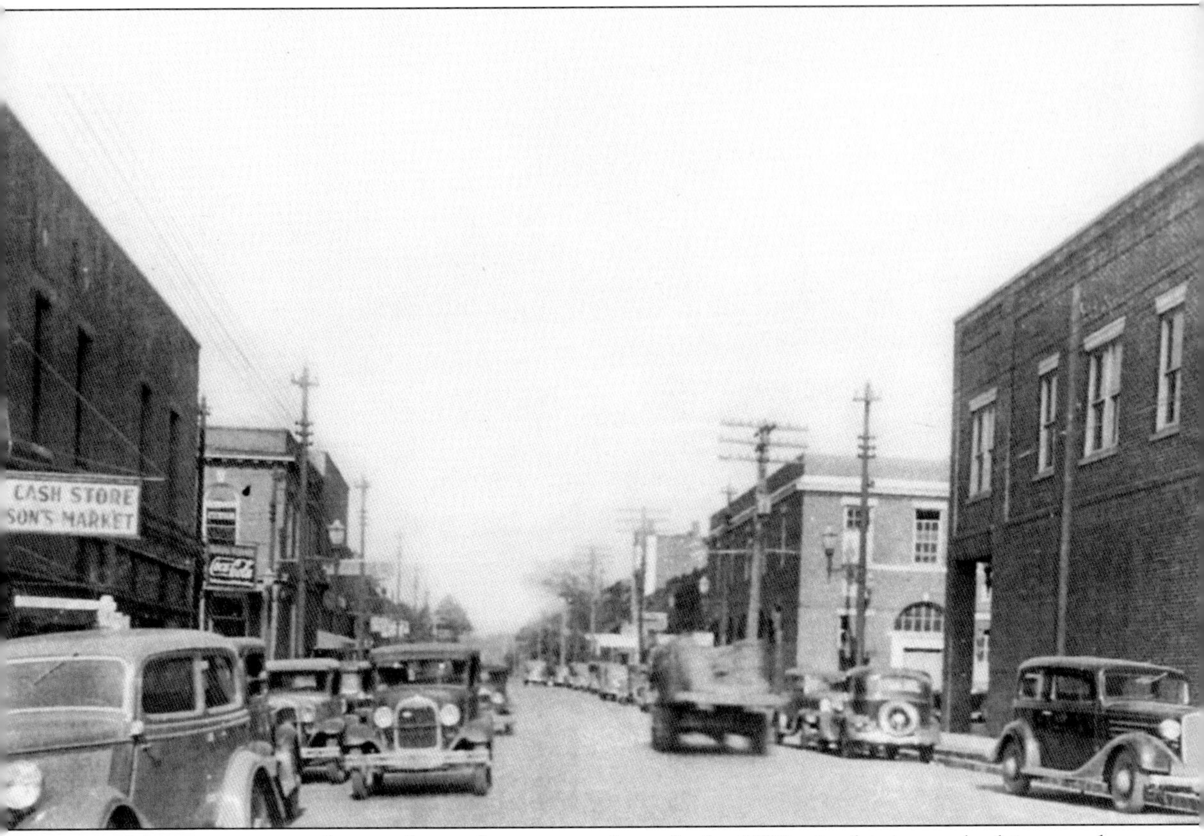

Siler City remained a popular trading center through the 1920s. In this image looking north on Chatham Avenue, the old Chatham Bank is the second building on the right; it later changed to First Union National Bank.

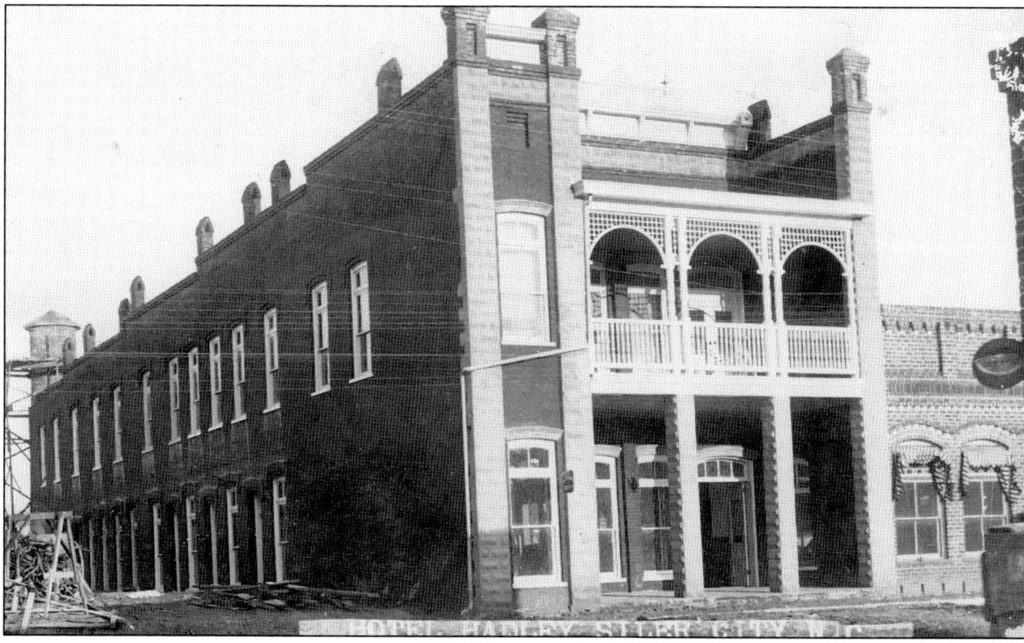

Hotel Hadley opened in the spring of 1908 with about 30 guest rooms. It featured what at that time was termed "water works," or piped-in running water for the basins in the rooms and water closets (toilets and washbowls). A central steam-heating system was installed in October 1914. It was originally lighted by acetylene gas. The hotel is located at 130 North Chatham Avenue. (Courtesy of Jonus Nobles.)

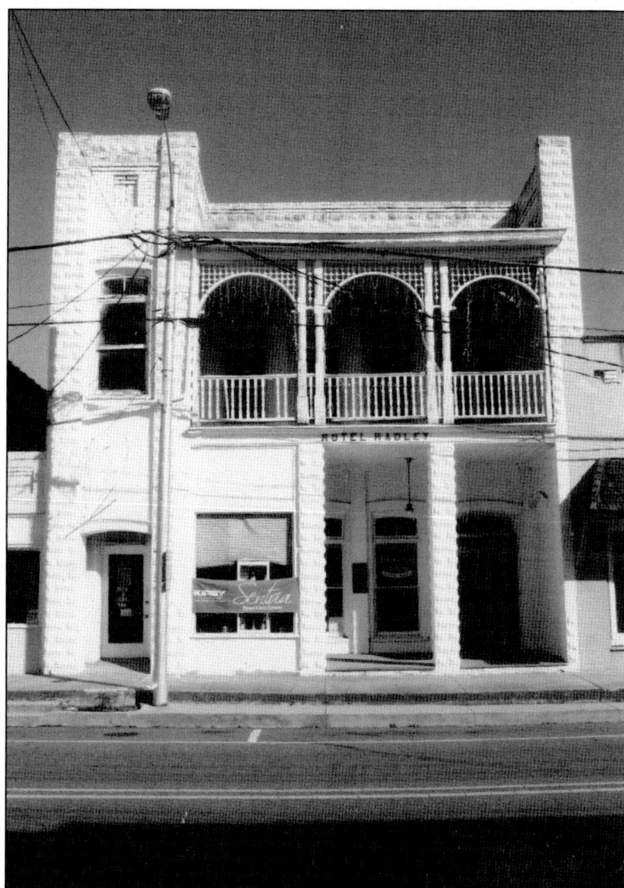

W.C. and Perry Craft Marley Thaxton of Greensboro, North Carolina, were managers of Hotel Hadley during its first year of operation. It was built and owned by Franklin Minter Hadley, who lived there until his death in 1940. (Courtesy of Dennis Sawyer.)

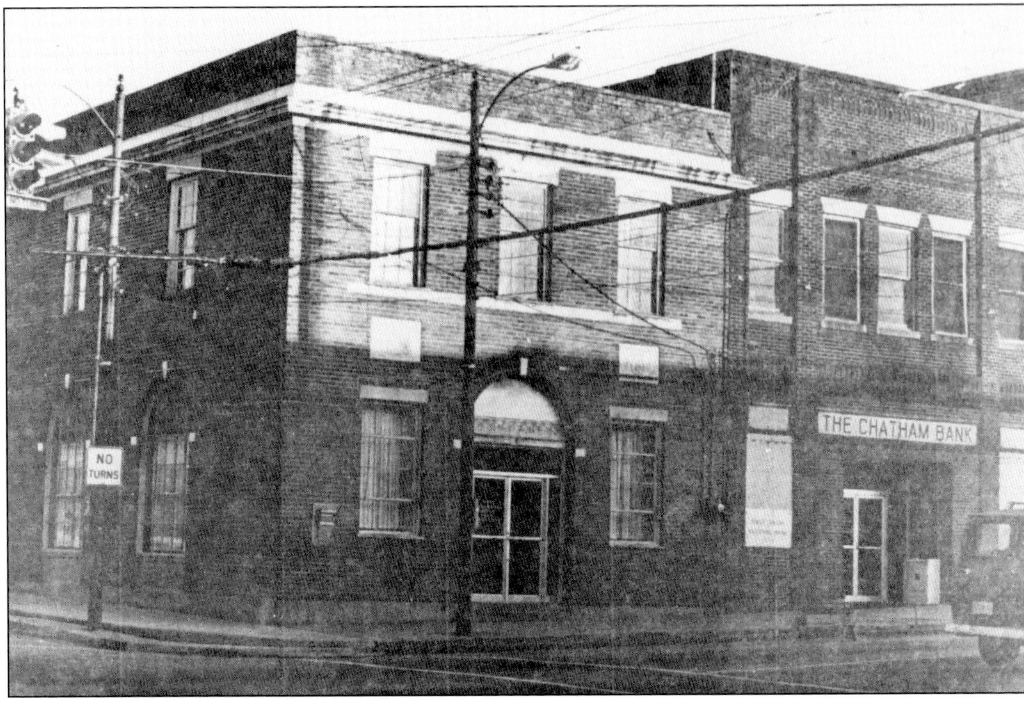

The first financial institution in Siler City was Chatham Bank. It opened for business in January 1902. The original officers were president F.M. Hadley, vice president Lossing L. Wren, and cashier J.J. Jenkins. Chatham Bank merged with First Union National Bank of North Carolina on November 10, 1961. (Courtesy of Farmers' Alliance Store and Nancy Tysor.)

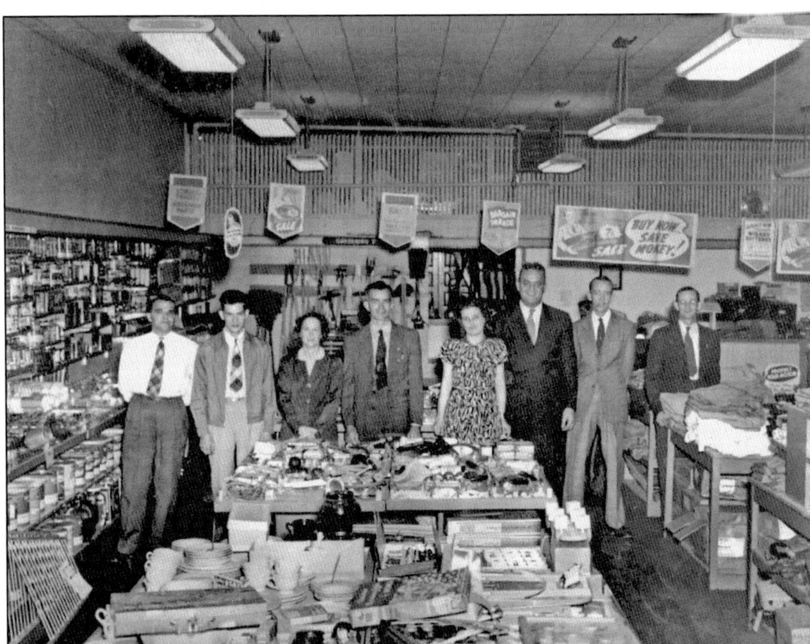

Pictured from left to right in Western Auto are Lawrence Moore, Horace Stinson, Frances Boren (Nellie Wheeler's sister), Ben Boren, Rep's wife, "Rep," Charles White, and John Truelove. The store was located on the corner across from the new coffee shop.

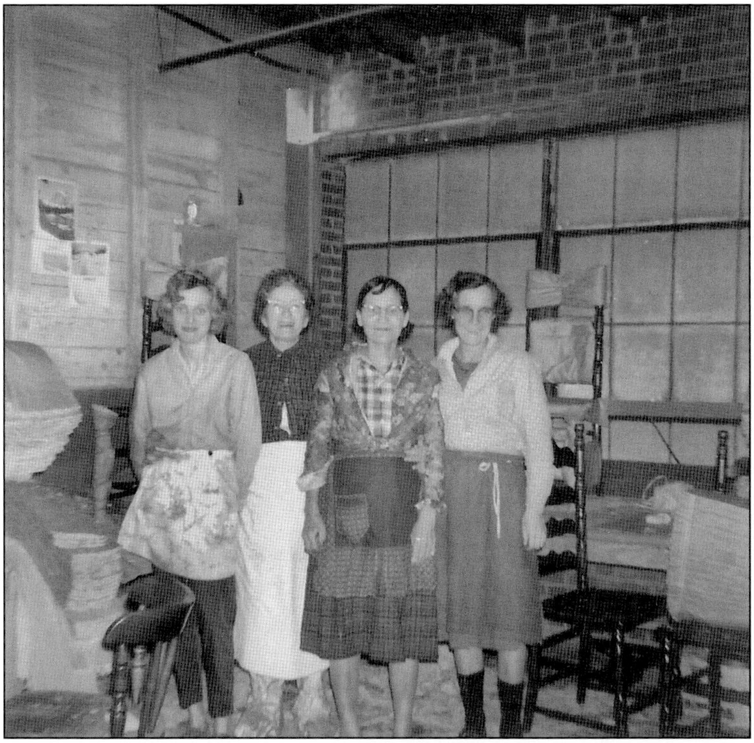

From left to right, Christine Ritter, Blanche Swanie Brown, Effie Rose, and unidentified pose for the camera at the Boling Company. In 1956, the name was changed to Boling Chair Company. It built desks, tables, and bookcases out of its Mount Olive, North Carolina, plant, which went into production in 1968. The founder was Malvola Jackson Boling.

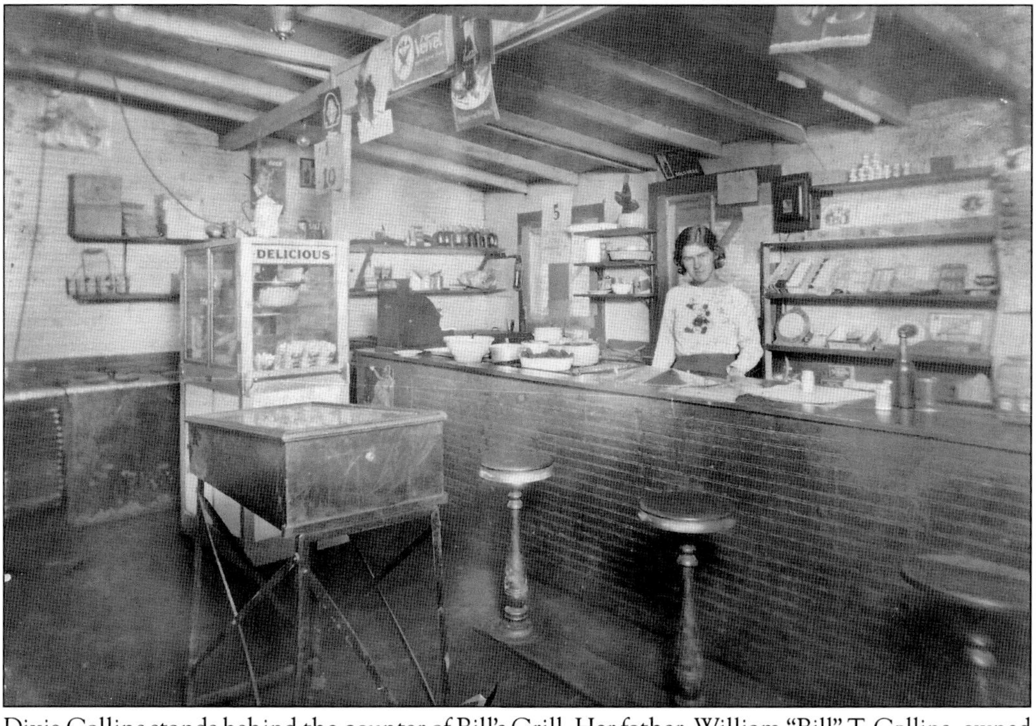

Dixie Collins stands behind the counter of Bill's Grill. Her father, William "Bill" T. Collins, owned the establishment. William's two boys, Bill and Payne, both opened separate restaurants in town, and each was a success. Dixie married Johnny Bowers, and they ran Bill's Grill together.

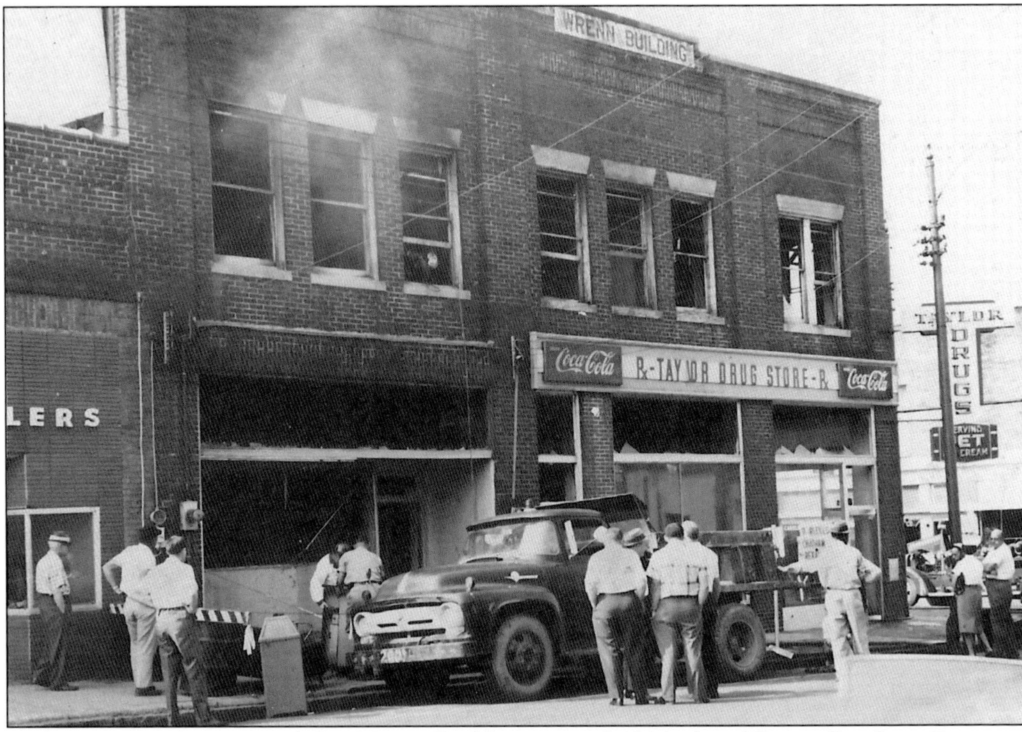

Taylor Drug Store occupied the Wrenn Building around 1924 when Wrenn Brothers Company converted it to a two-story brick structure. On December 18, 1924, the *Chatham News* reported that Wrenn Brothers Company was adding 1,500 square feet to its floor space.

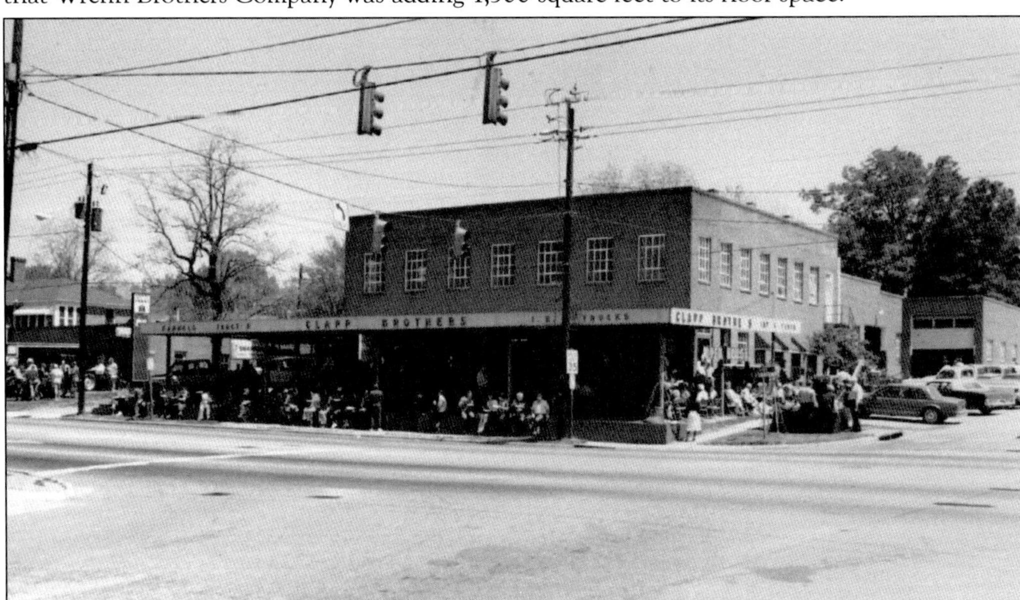

Clapp Brothers Implement and Tractor Company was started in 1937 by two brothers, Sam and Ben Clapp. When Sam died in 1978, his cousin Ed Clapp took over the business. Ed died in 2005, and his son Al runs the business today after purchasing it from John Winslow, who bought it from Ed in 1994 with handshake. (Courtesy of Clapp Brothers.)

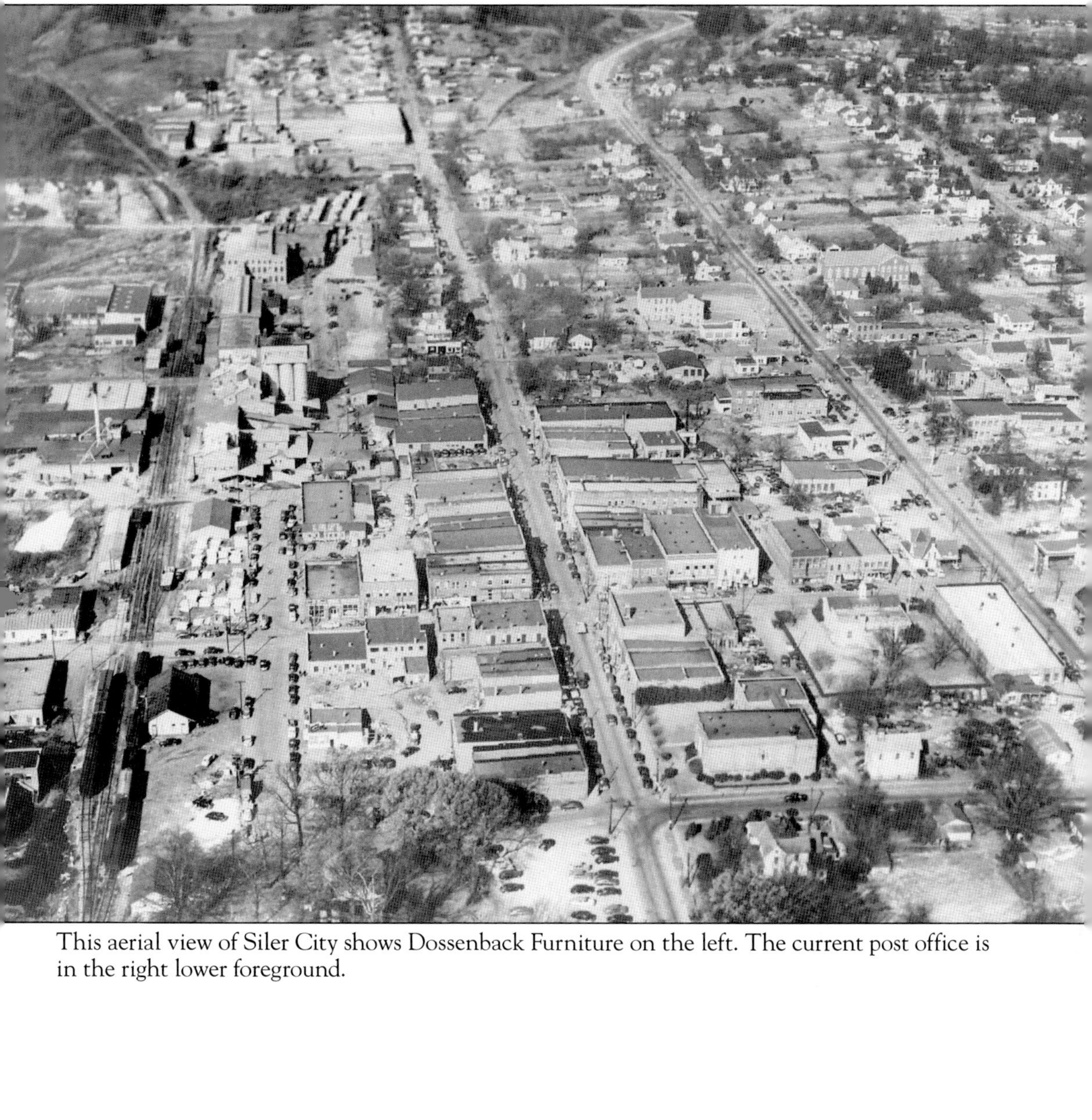

This aerial view of Siler City shows Dossenback Furniture on the left. The current post office is in the right lower foreground.

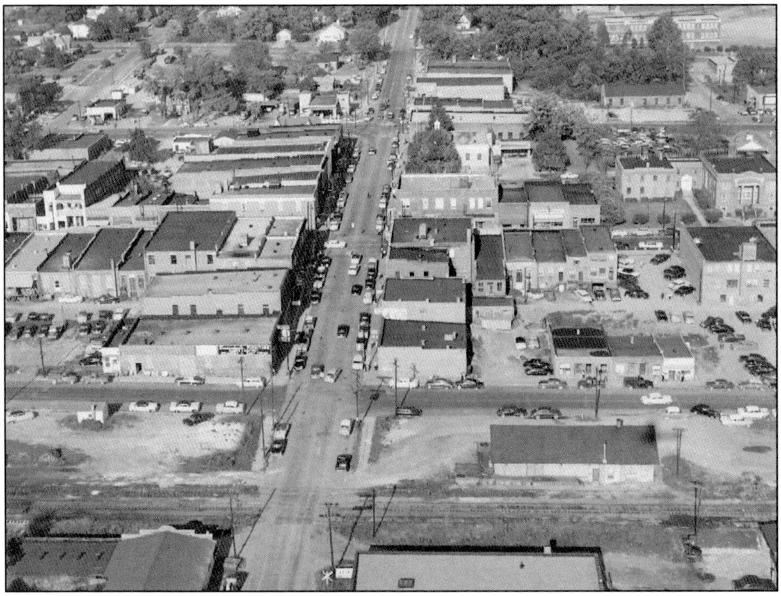

Another aerial view of downtown Siler City, taken in the 1940s, shows the train tracks on the left. In the center is Chatham Avenue, and the second building is Farmers' Alliance Store, Inc.

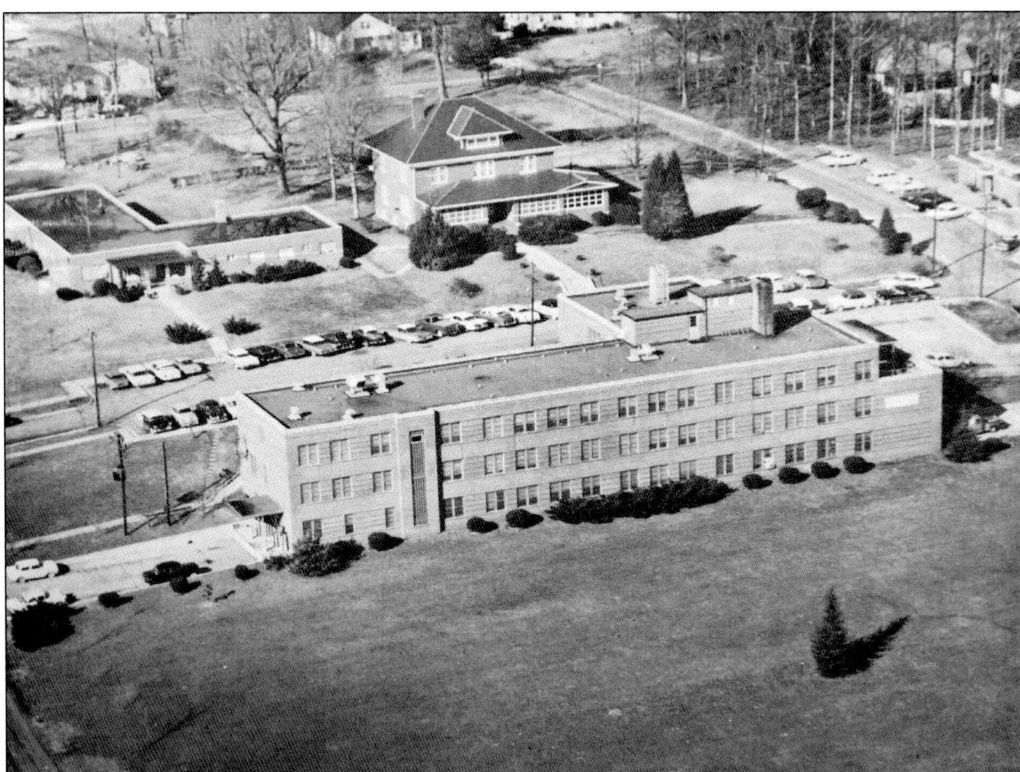

Construction started on the Chatham Hospital in Siler City on September 23, 1948, after a bid to construct a 50-bed hospital for $525,549.47 was accepted. This new facility was dedicated on June 11, 1950. The old hospital is in the back left, and on the right is a home built for nurses.

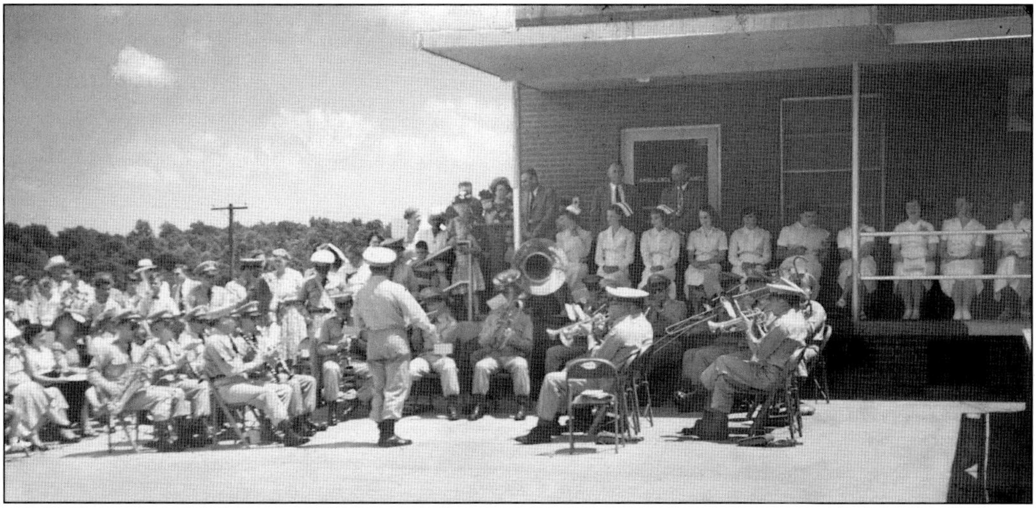

The dedication ceremony for the new Chatham Hospital on June 11, 1950, was celebrated with a band. The hospital was enlarged in 1969 with the addition of a wing to the original building. It provided room for 30 additional beds and space for several hospital facilities.

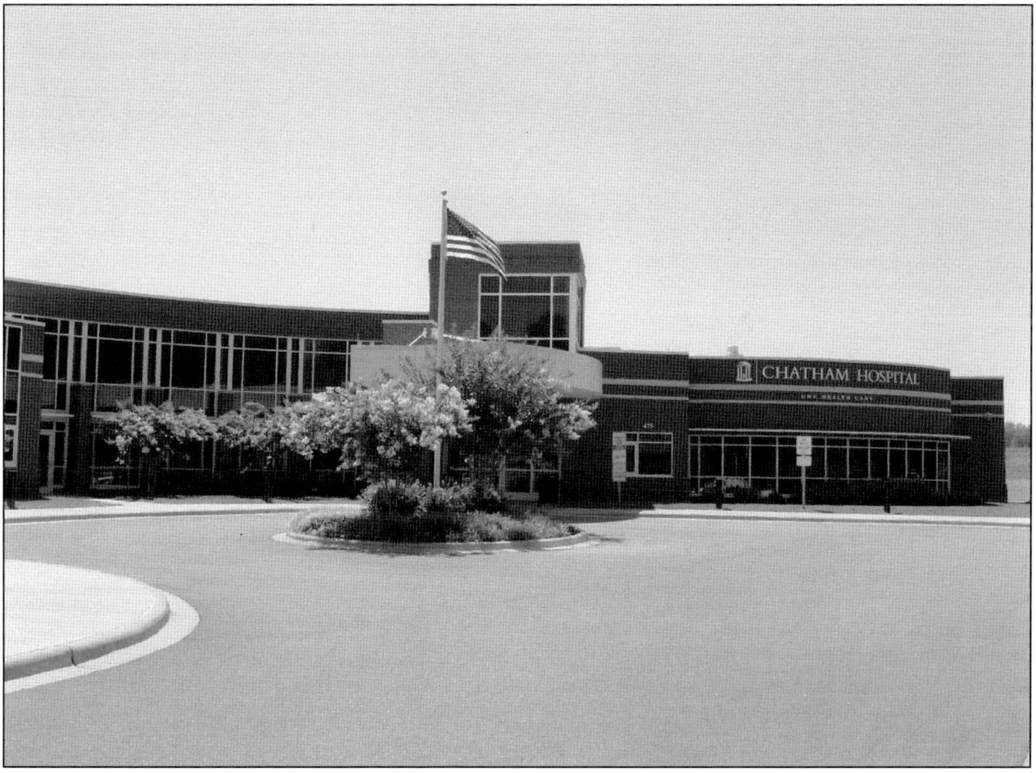

The new Chatham Hospital was built around May 2007 near the intersection of US Highways 64 and 421 and opened in July 2008. In February 2011, Chatham Medical Park opened, housing the Chatham Hospital business office, a wellness program, physician offices, and a conference center. (Photograph by Jeff Davis, courtesy of the Town of Siler City.)

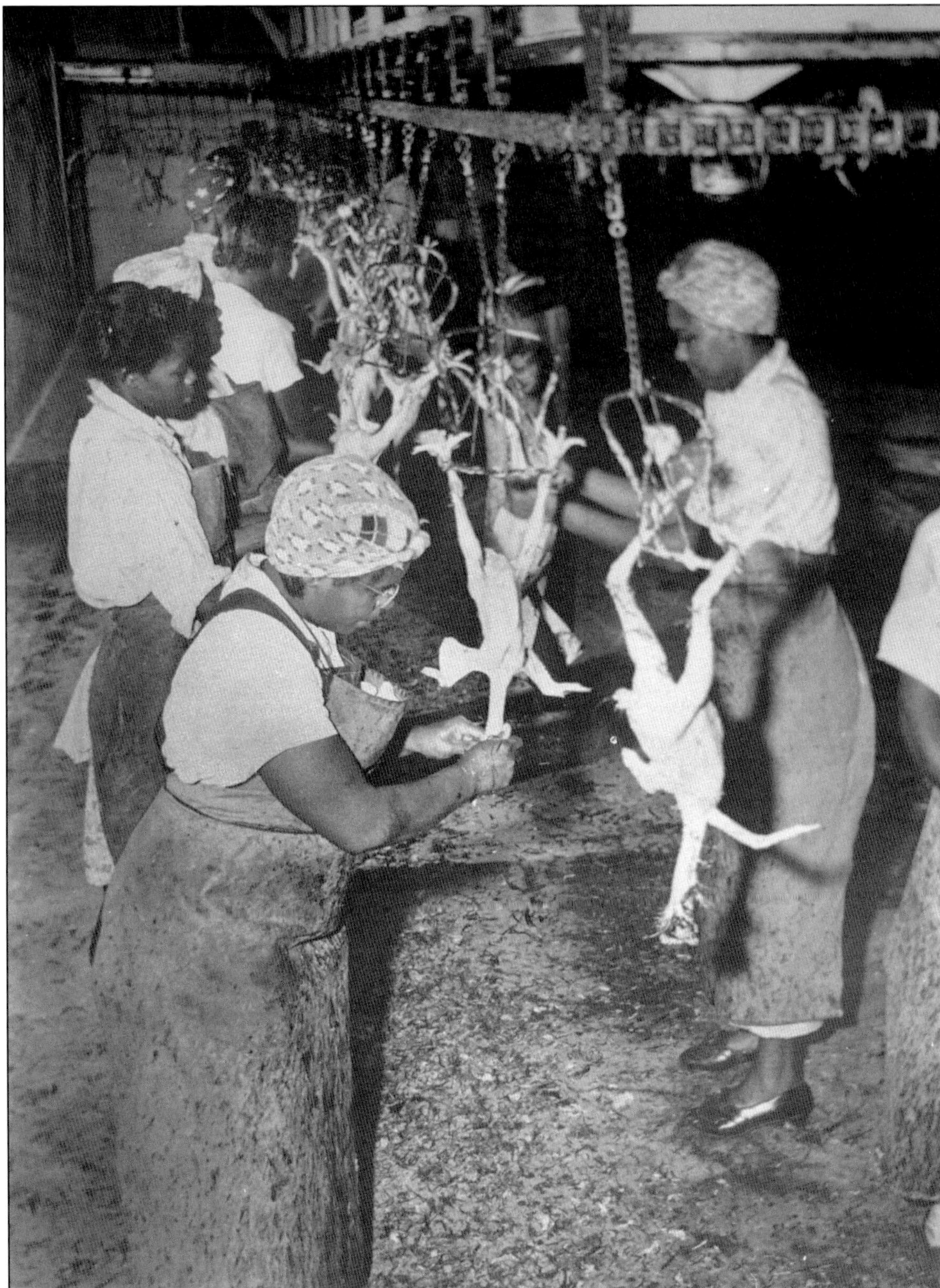

During the summer of 1915, local poultry dealers exported 2,000 pounds of dressed chickens per week. Large-scale Siler City poultry plants came to fruition when Mid-States Farms Company started operating in 1965, which was a continuation of the Siler City Poultry Exchange that opened in 1939. The *Siler City Grit* newspaper on July 24, 1912, referenced Siler City poultry dealers shipping most of their hens and chickens alive to the seashore, but after some rebuttal from hotels, the dealers started killing and dressing the fowl and then shipping them daily in barrels packed with ice.

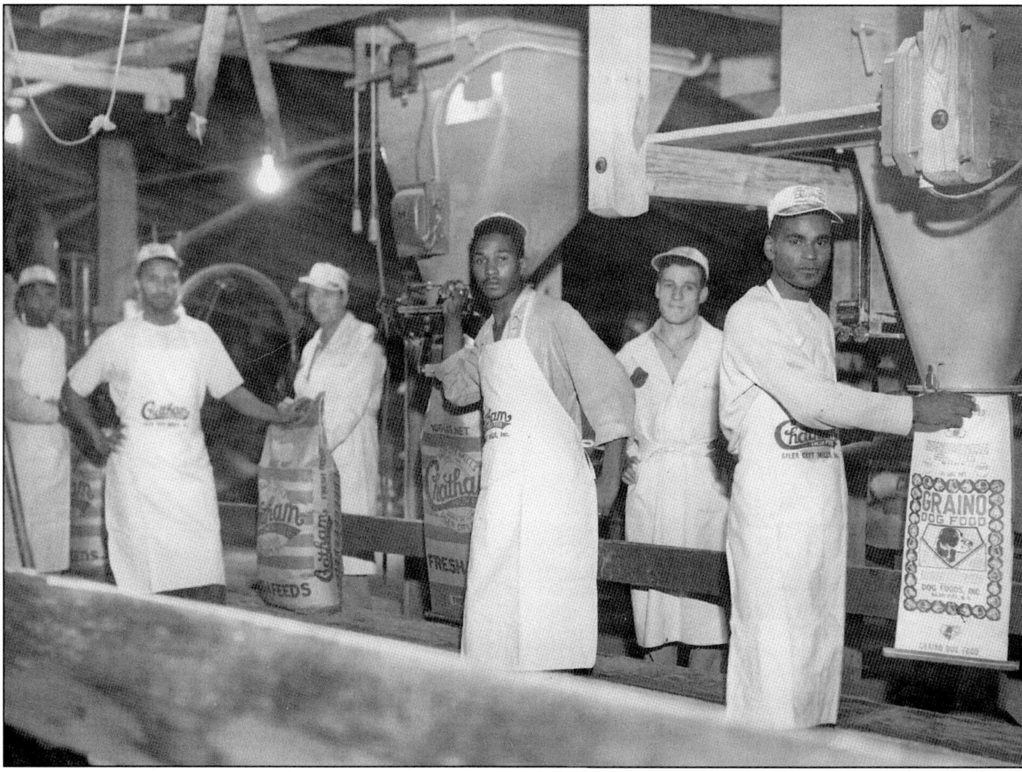

Siler City Mills was organized in 1910. The original partners were Peter Beane, J.W. McAdams, J.M. Stout, and Lossing Lafayette Wren. The company produced flour and cornmeal for human consumption. In 1954, the company began producing commercial livestock feed and pet food, all under its proprietary trademarks and private labels.

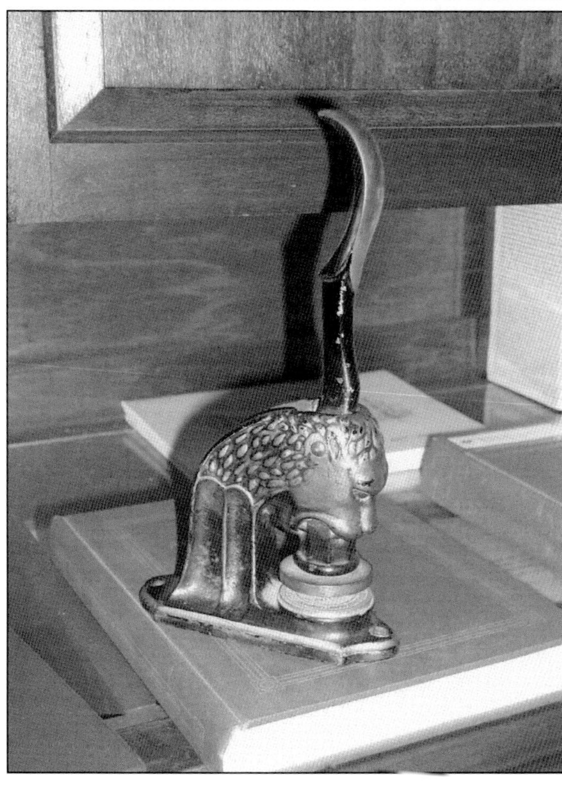

The 1910s corporate seal of the Hadley Company is pictured here. The Hadley Company was an old Siler City enterprise. Initially, the Hadleys worked in agriculture and had a mill; they later branched out into a grocery and general mercantile business. (Courtesy of Chatham County Historical Association, North Carolina ECHO Project.)

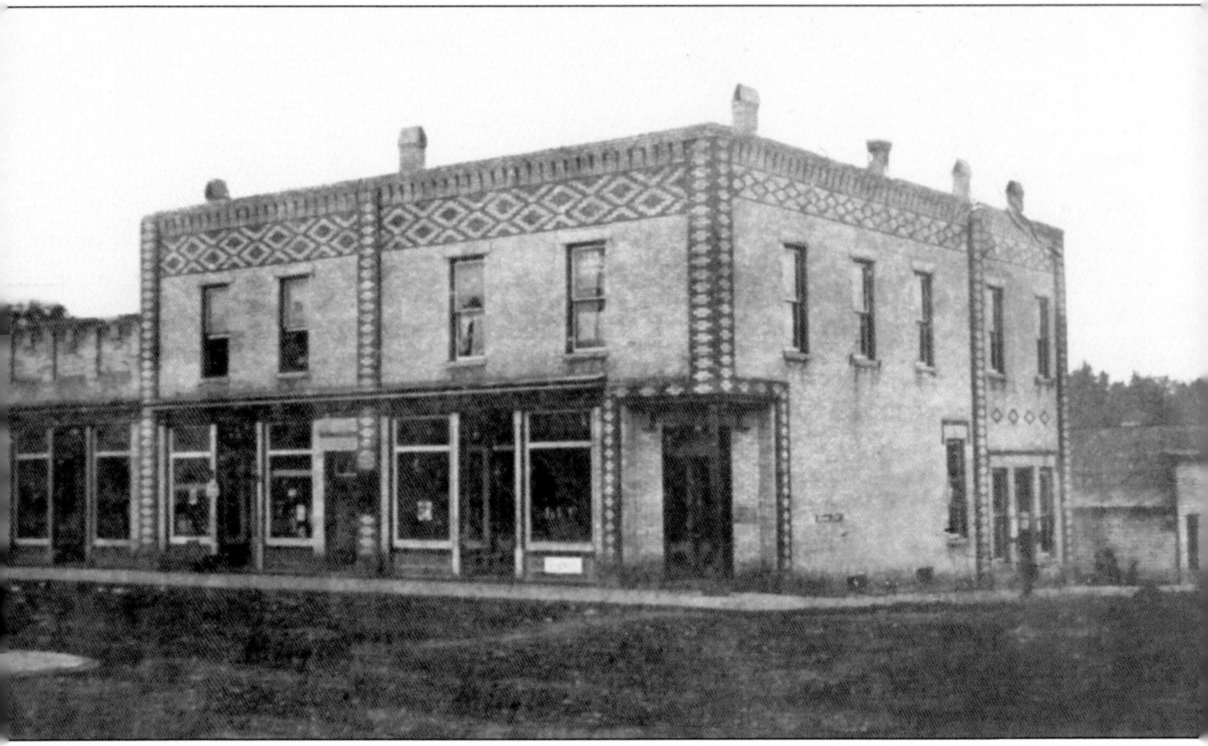

The Edwards-Wren Building was constructed in 1906 by Dr. J.D. Edwards and Lossing Lafayette Wren. The structure was the town's largest and finest when it was completed. Over the course of 61 years, it was occupied by L.L. Wren Pharmacy (1906–1907), Dr. G.E. Matthews Drug Store (1907–1916), Dr. Van B. Elkins Pharmacy (1916–1921), and Siler City Drug Company (1922–1967).

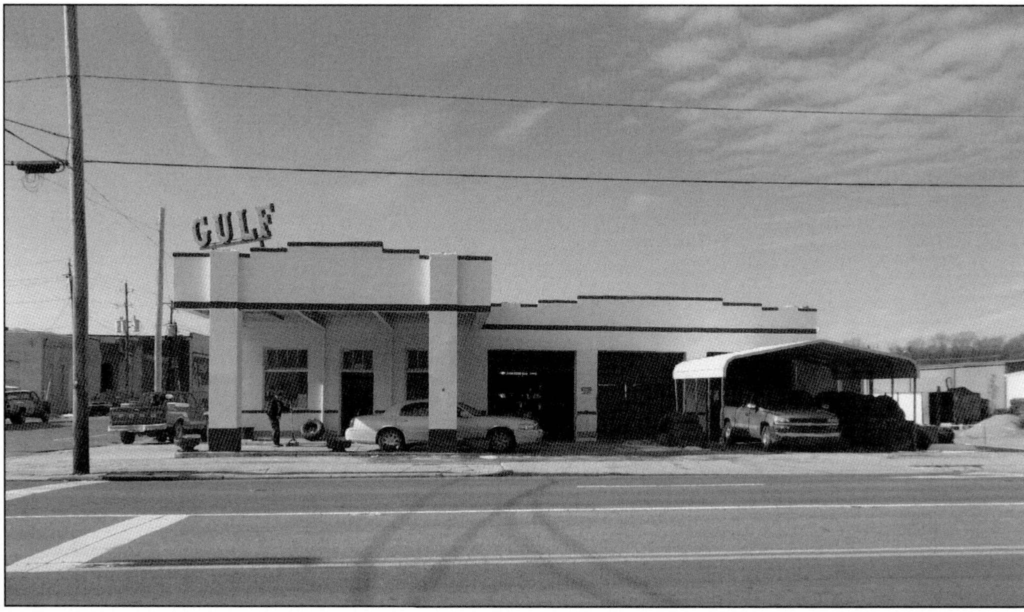

Bill & Bill Gulf Service Station opened in September 1936 at 201 North Second Avenue. Operators of the service station included Guy Williams, W.R. Fitts Sr., Lewis Hinshaw, Roland Hinshaw, Wayne Richardson, and Wilbert Degraffenreidt.

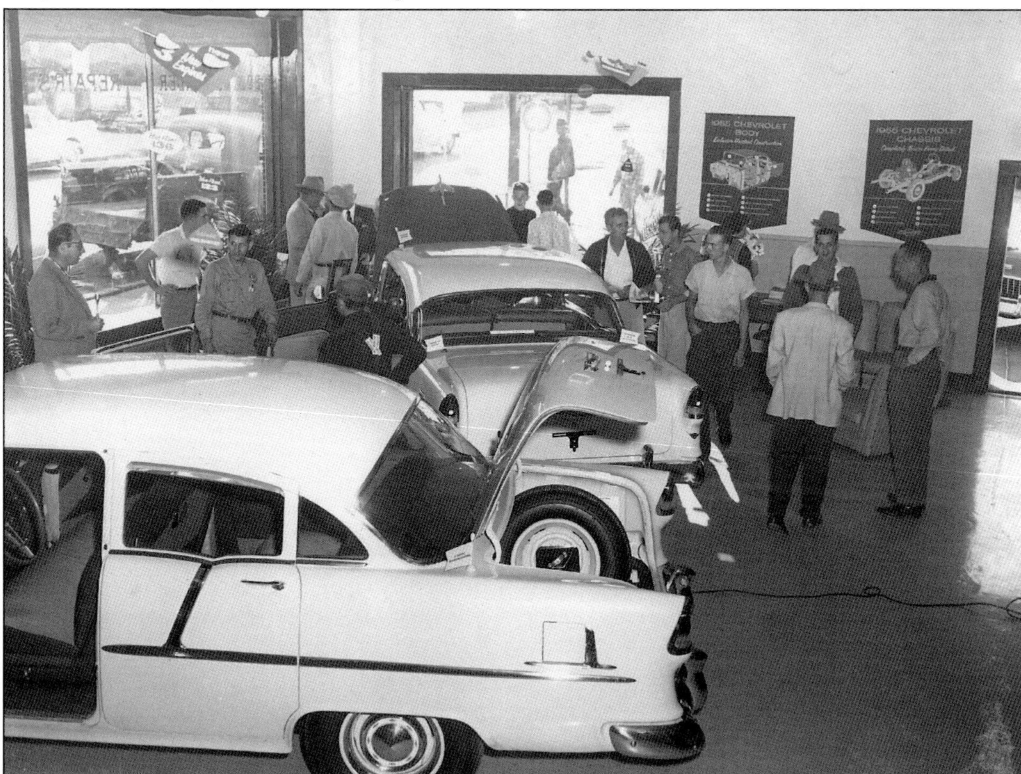

This is the first 1956 Chevrolet showroom in Siler City, North Carolina. At one time, the whole building was a dealership and repair shop. It is now the location of a coffee shop.

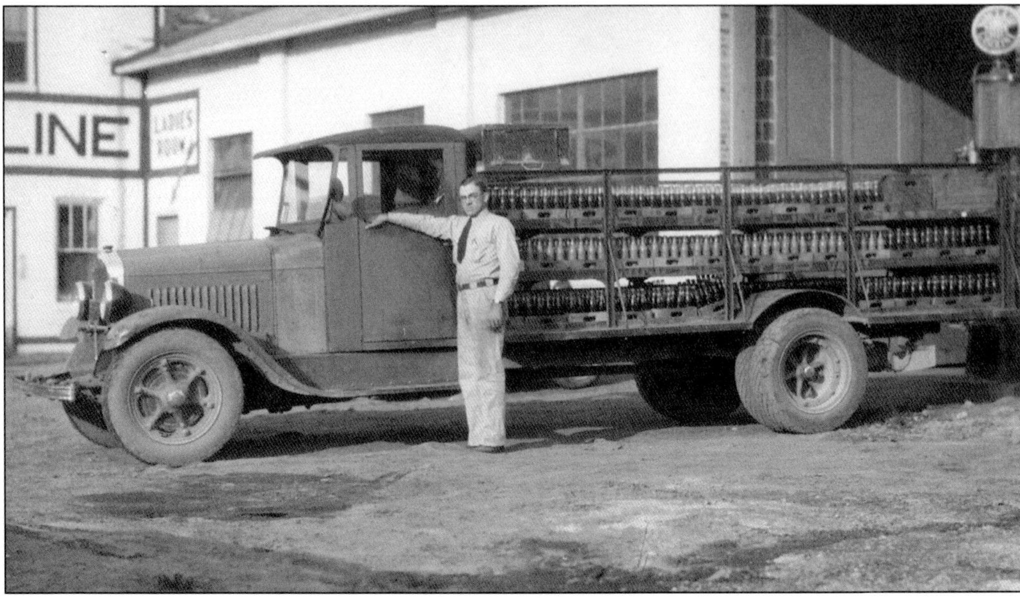

Nehi Bottling Company truck is pictured here in Siler City. The Nehi facility was based out of Virginia. Harold Dorsett Hackney of Siler City stands beside the truck filled with soft drinks.

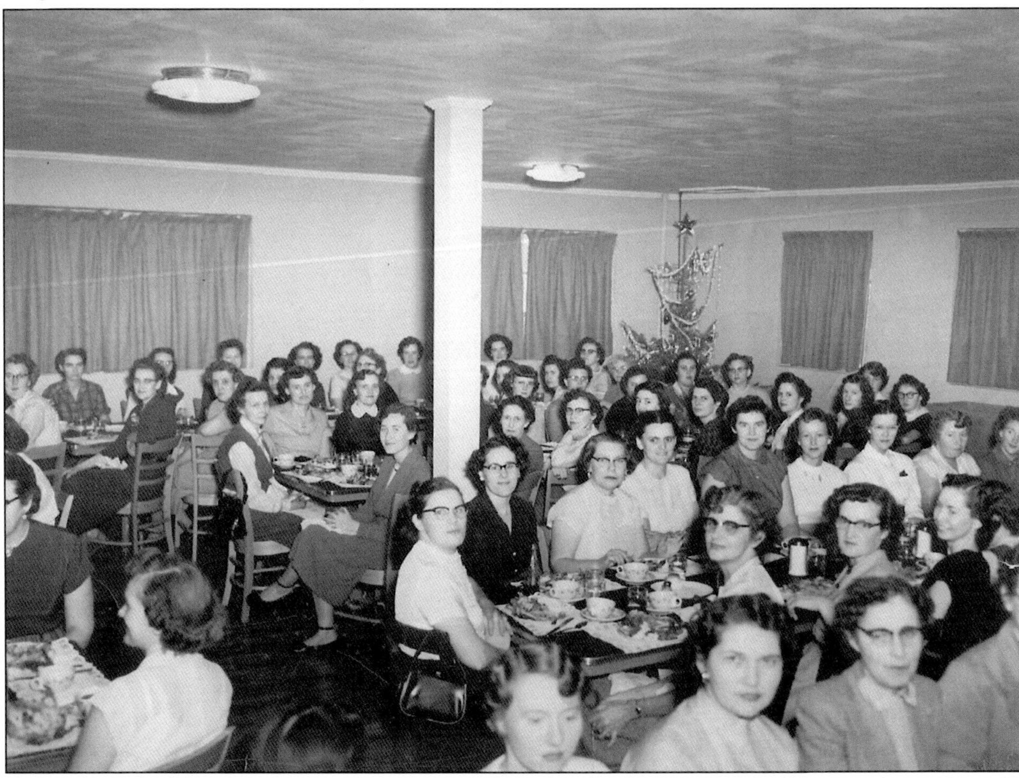

In this image, the A.J. Schnierson & Son factory is having a Christmas party in the early 1950s at Club Diane's. The club was located above what was the Sidewalk Café. The factory made women's slips, half coats, and gowns for companies like J.C. Penney. It was located where Hart's Furniture Company warehouse is now.

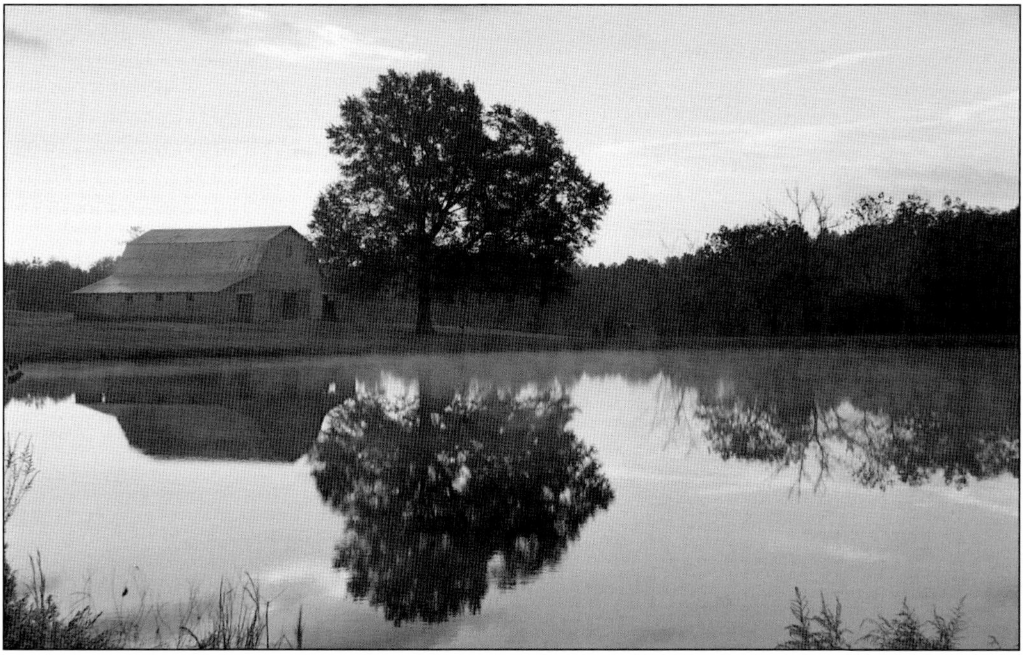

The Wood family has served up authentic, pit-cooked barbeque since the 1970s. Jerry "Bubba" Wood founded Brookwood Farms in 1978, and his sons Craig and Twig joined shortly after. Bubba soon found that real Southern-style barbeque is made from roasting the meat low and slow over hickory charcoal. The first stainless-steel pits were built in 1982 and are still used today. (Courtesy of Town of Siler City.)

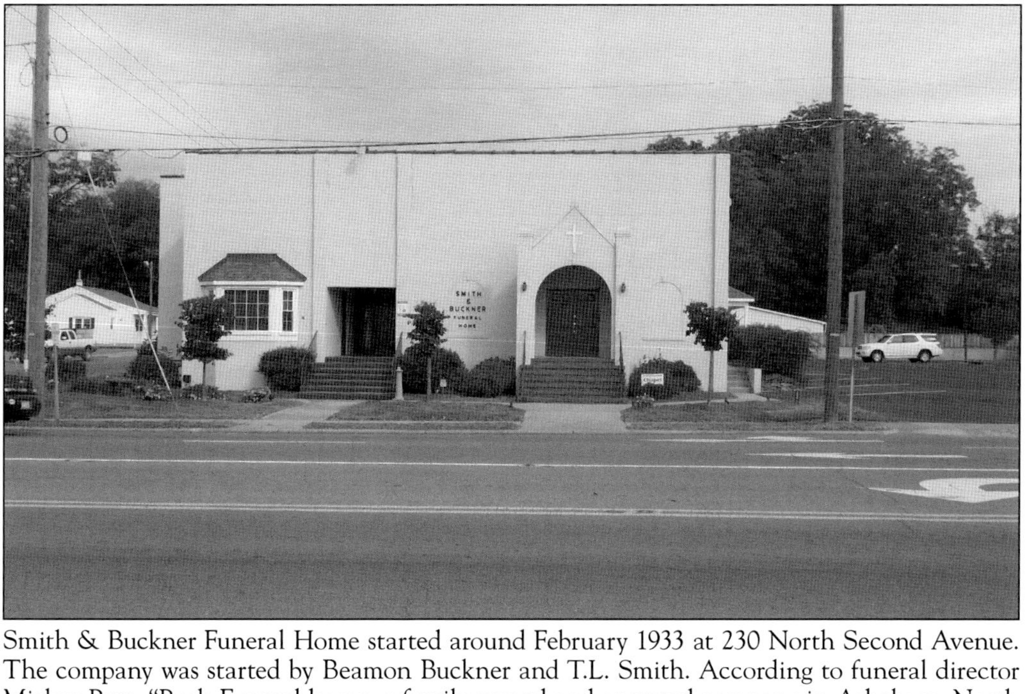

Smith & Buckner Funeral Home started around February 1933 at 230 North Second Avenue. The company was started by Beamon Buckner and T.L. Smith. According to funeral director Mickey Pore, "Pugh Funeral home, a family owned and operated company in Asheboro, North Carolina, now owns Smith & Buckner." (Photograph by author.)

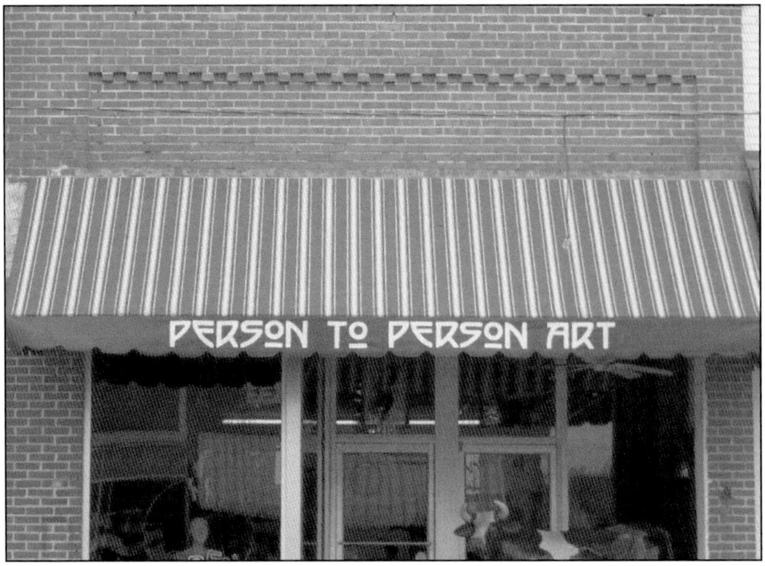

Artist Roger Person offers mixed-media assemblages, paintings, and sculptures. His art is profoundly inspiring, unique in design, and often blatantly humorous. His is listed as one of the top art galleries in Siler City. Person to Person is located at 210 North Chatham Avenue. (Photograph by author.)

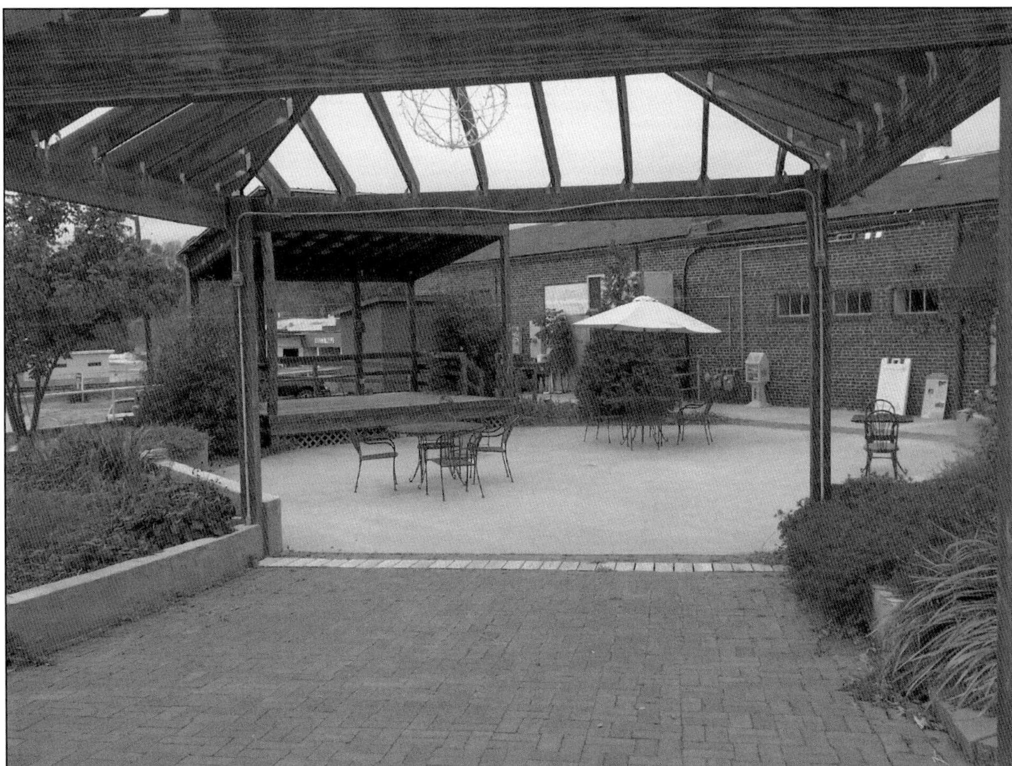

Mitch Woodward from the North Carolina Cooperative Extension worked with Andrew Wright to install a new rain garden, including a well-designed catchment and dispersal system, at the Courtyard Café located at 223 North Chatham Avenue. The system helps water the trees and shrubs that give color to the courtyard. The location also houses the North Carolina Arts Incubator. The area is used for entertainment and National Night Out. (Photograph by author.)

Laurel Ridge Bed and Breakfast was the first of its kind to open in Siler City. Dave Simmons and his wife launched the business on November 22, 1992. Simmons retired on November 10, 2010, and closed the bed-and-breakfast. Upon entering, the long driveway opened up to a beautiful mountain laurel bush area. Laurel Ridge hosted weddings on the deck, gazebo, and in the gardens. (Courtesy of Dave Simmons.)

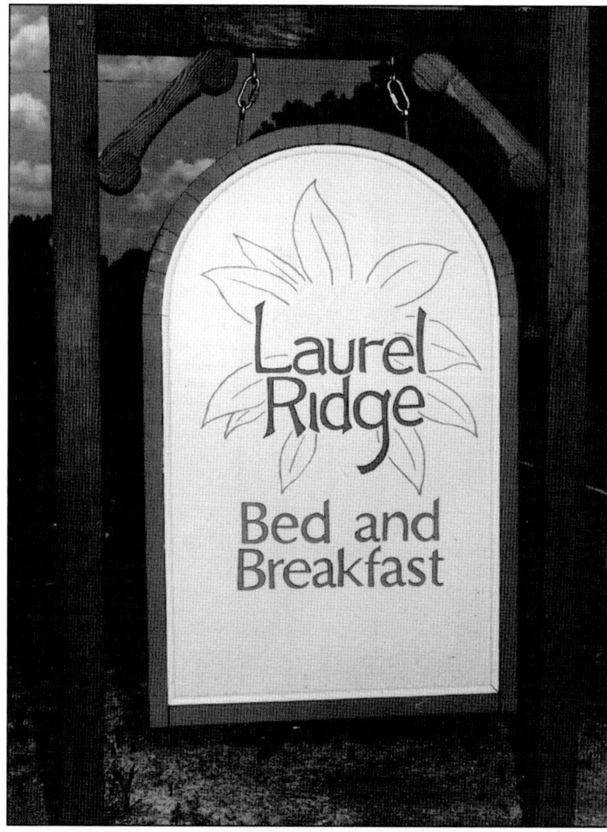

Like its name suggests, Laurel Ridge sat on a ridge. From the gazebo at the bed-and-breakfast, one could look down a 30-foot drop. Visitors stayed in the main house; adjacent to that was a cottage with what appeared to be stained-glass windows but were actually mirrors with paint on them. Among its many guests, Laurel Ridge hosted visitors from Poland, Spain, France, and Africa. (Courtesy of Dave Simmons.)

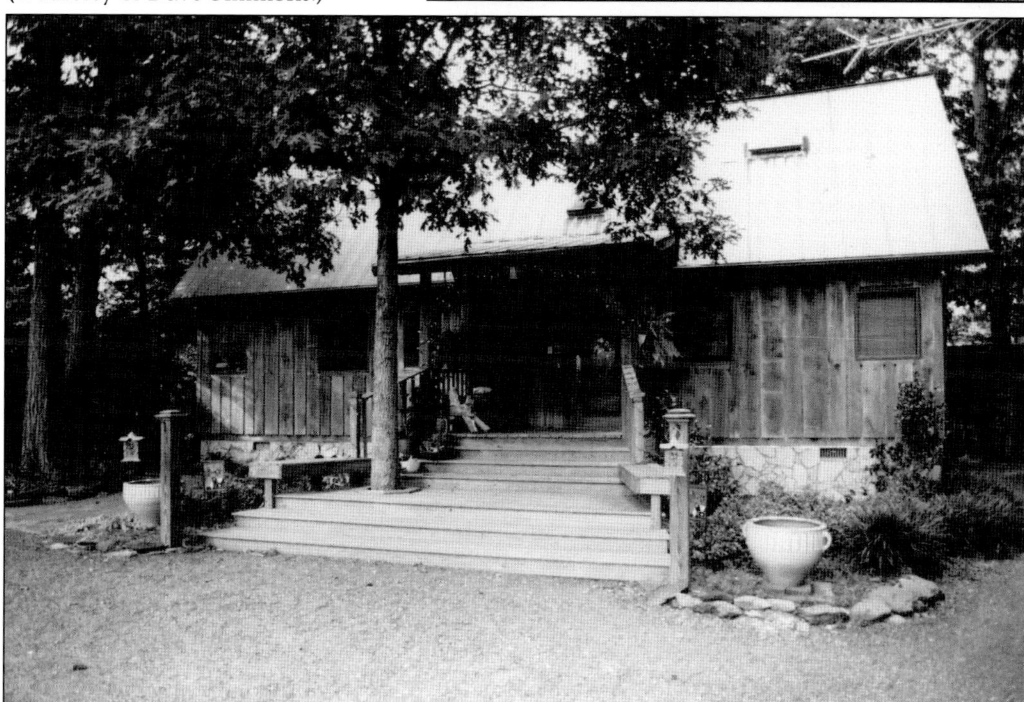

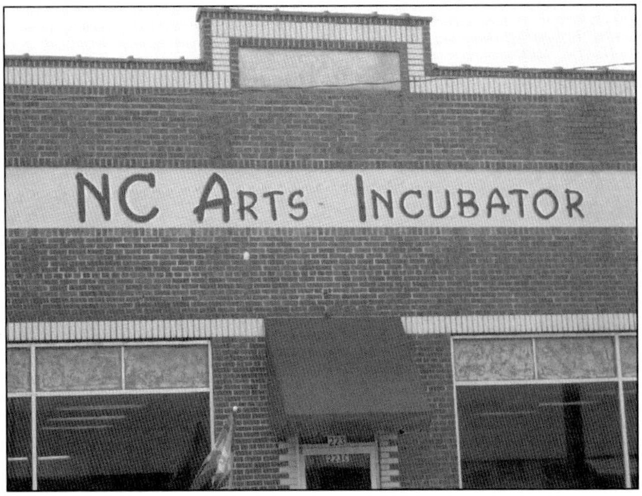

The North Carolina Arts Incubator's mission is to create a self-sustaining arts community dedicated to providing new and emerging artists with rental spaces to create art, to have access to shared resources, and to be exposed to ongoing support and training opportunities. It is an effort in partnership with Central Carolina Community College to promote economic development in historic downtown Siler City. (Photograph by author, courtesy of Town of Siler City.)

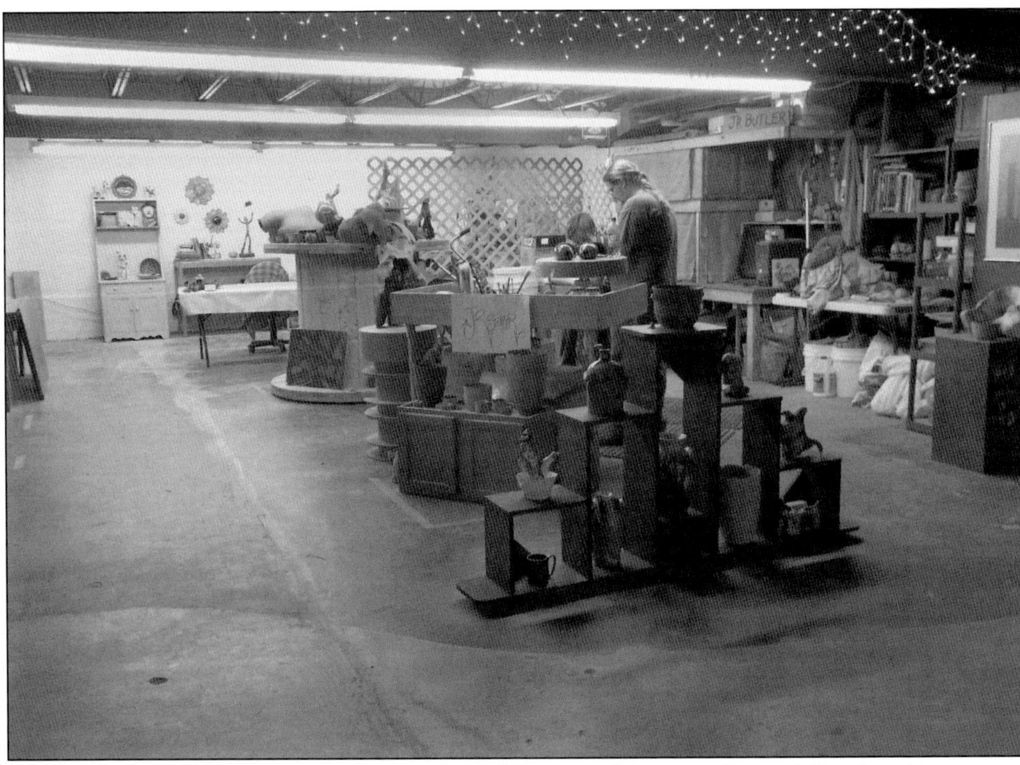

In the late 1990s, Leon Tongret, the former small-business director at Central Carolina Community College, saw an opportunity to harness the energy of local artisans toward the revitalization of downtown Siler City. After securing the finances, Tongret renovated three buildings in downtown Siler City, giving birth to the North Carolina Arts Incubator. (Photograph by author, courtesy of the Town of Siler City.)

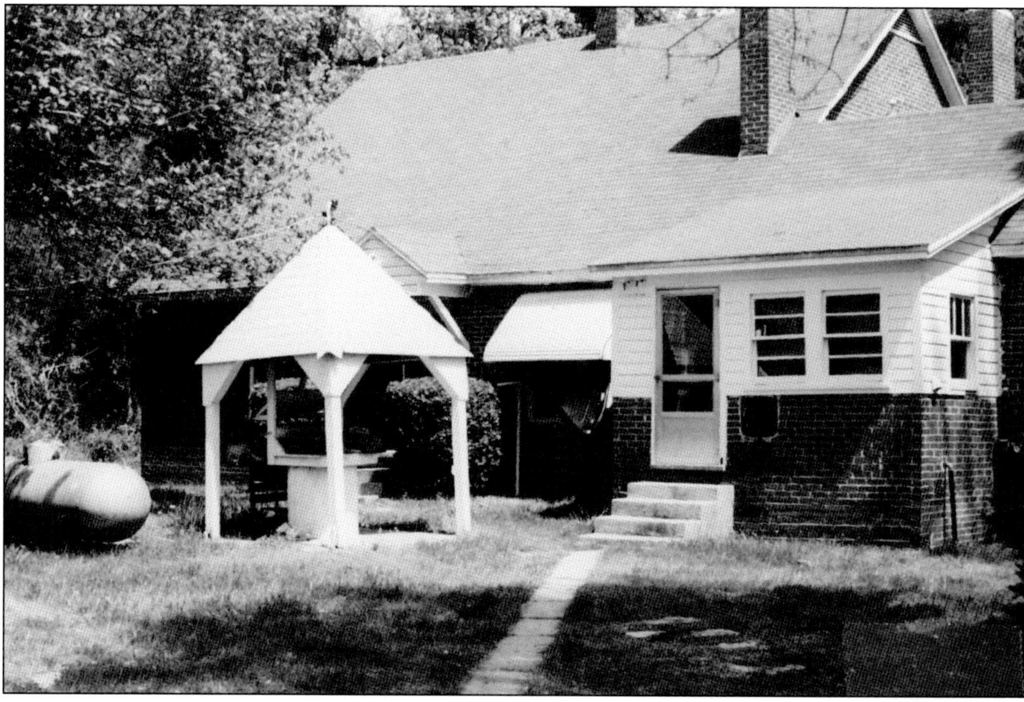

Heartfriends Inn was built in 1940 by Colonel Engles. Yvonne C. Stegenga and Paula F. Arnold bought the house in 1994 from Burton Jessup. At the time of purchase, the house was one-and-a-half-stories tall with low ceilings. (Courtesy of Yvonne Stegenga.)

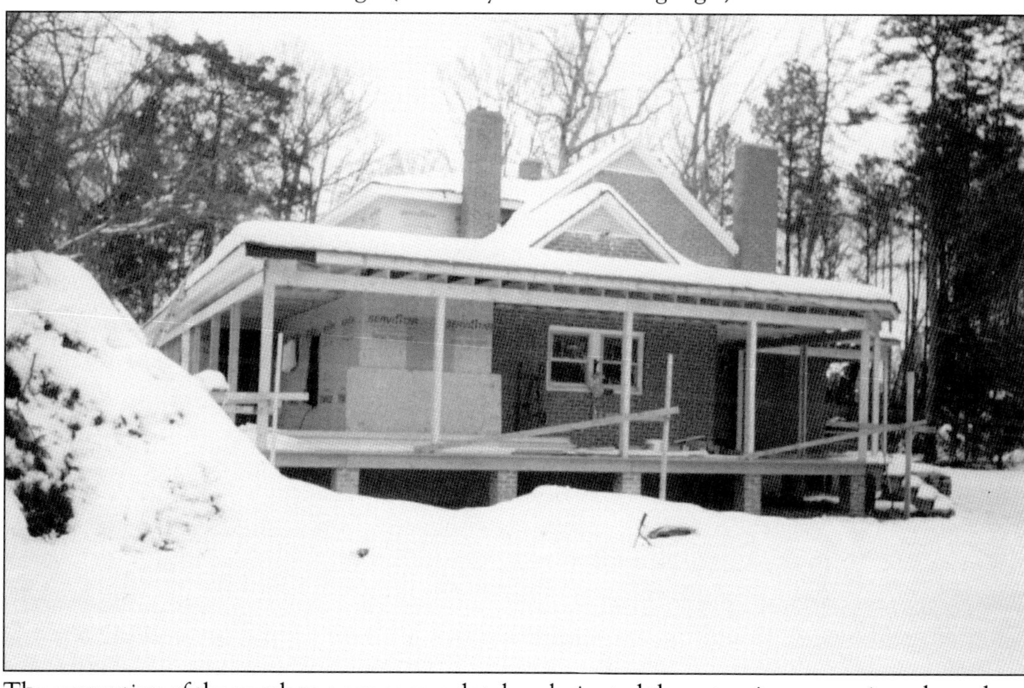

The renovation of the porch to a wraparound style culminated the extensive renovations throughout the house. "Everything was so run down and falling in," recalls Yvonne Stegenga, who labored so long and hard on the house that she feels like she gave birth to it. (Courtesy of Yvonne Stegenga.)

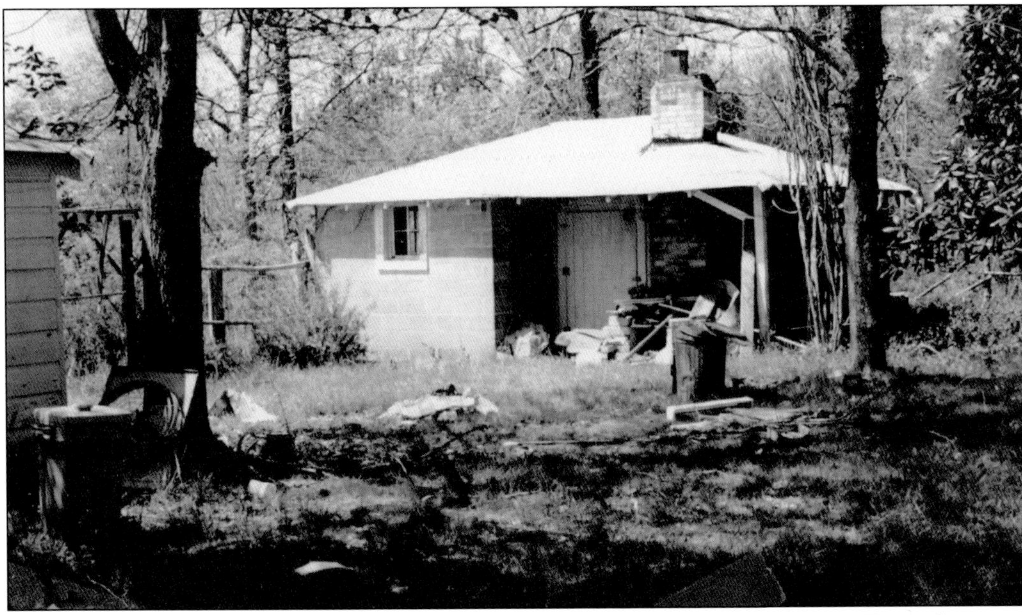

The cottage of Heartfriends Inn also went through some major renovations. Everything was torn down except the fireplace. The cottage is located across the courtyard from the main house and is called the Periwinkle Cottage because of the periwinkle surrounding it. (Courtesy of Yvonne Stegenga.)

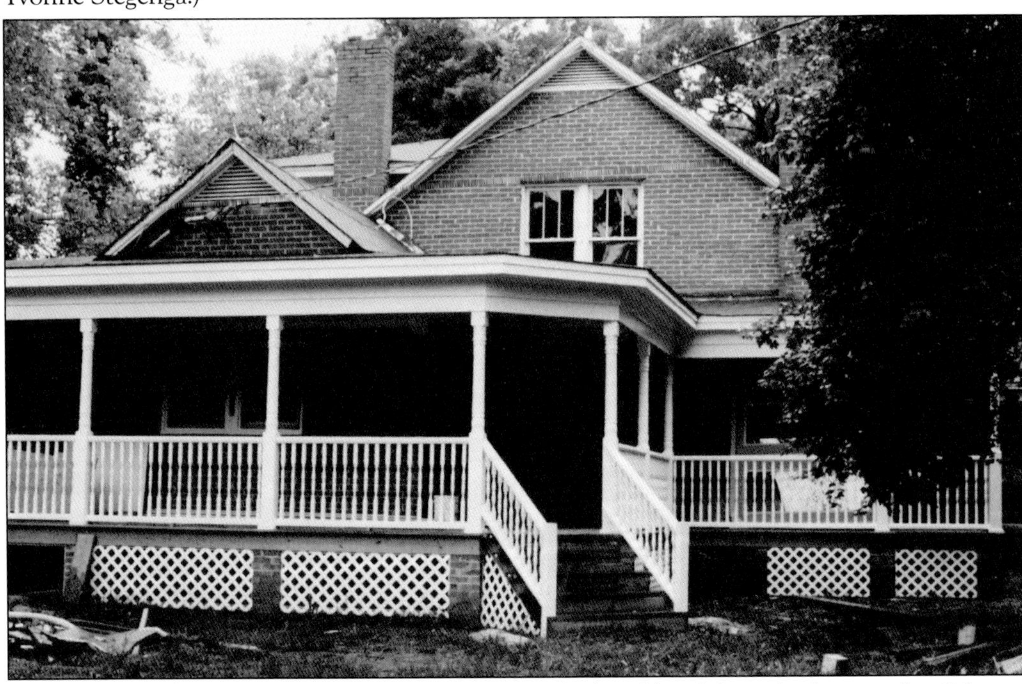

The house was specifically bought to be turned into a bed-and-breakfast, which opened in February 2010. Paula F. Arnold found out she had brain cancer in December 2010 and subsequently died in August 2011. During Christmas, the house is decorated with a Christmas tree train from Germany. Yvonne C. Stegenga still operates the bed-and-breakfast, and more information is available at www.heartfriendsinn.com. (Courtesy of Yvonne Stegenga.)

Three

Churches

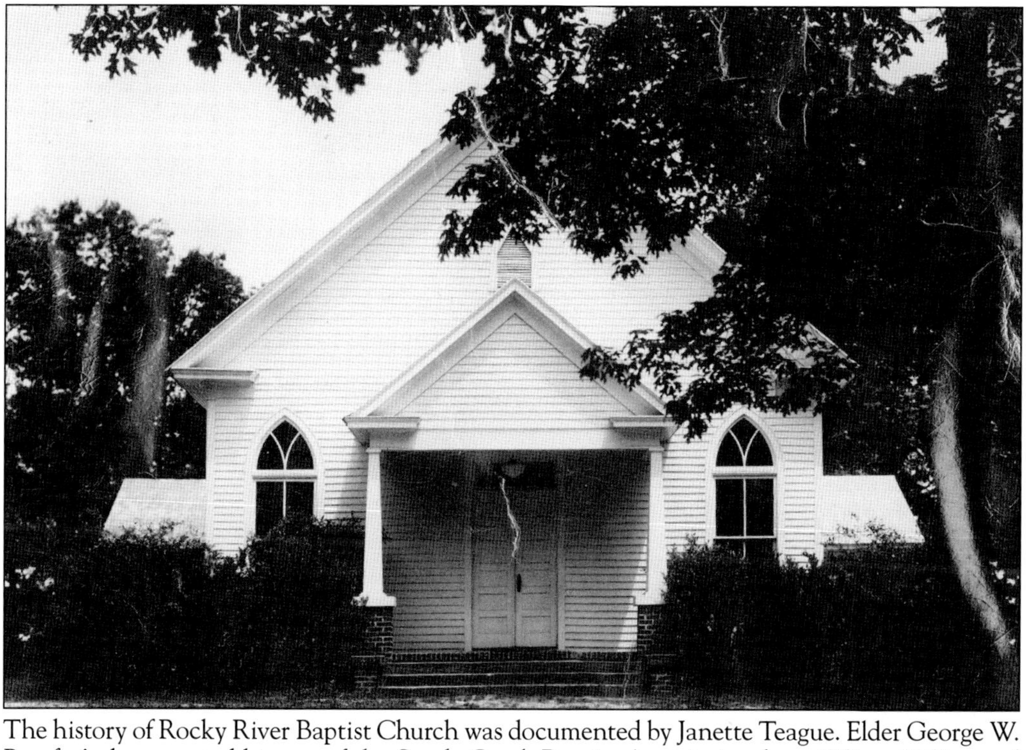

The history of Rocky River Baptist Church was documented by Janette Teague. Elder George W. Purefoy's documented history of the Sandy Creek Baptist Association from 1758 to 1858 stated that Rocky River Baptist Church was constituted in 1757 as an arm of the Sandy Creek Baptist Church, which Elder Shubal Stearns constituted in 1755. But, according to information handed down to Teague from forefathers of some present members, Rocky River Baptist Church was constituted in 1756. Both beliefs are in agreement that it was started through the fervent revival spirit of Elder Stearns. (Courtesy of Rocky River Baptist Church.)

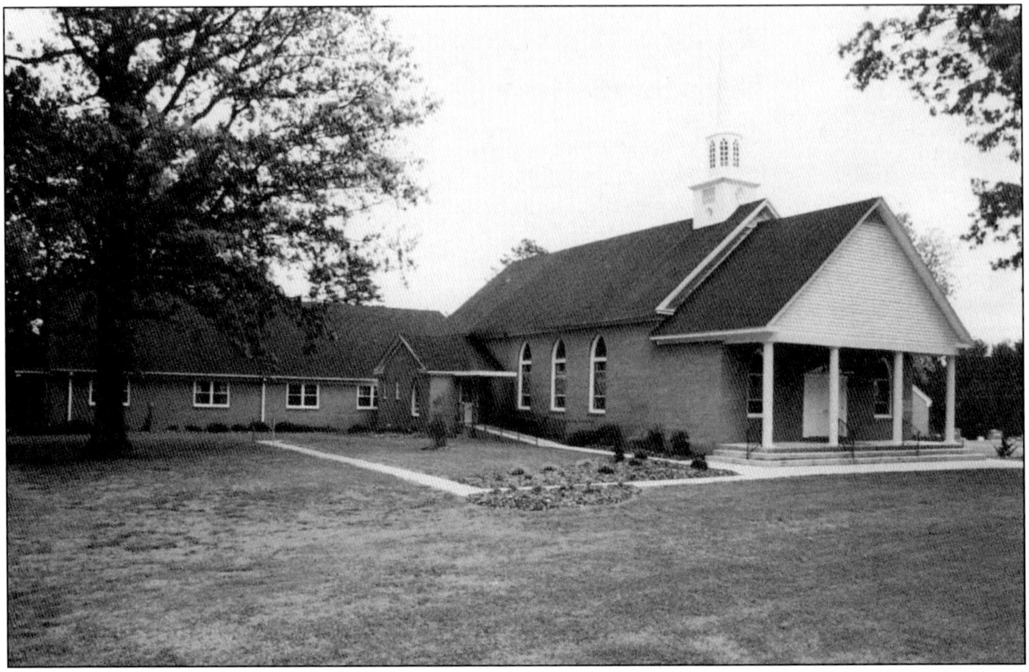

Elder Stearns helped organize and build the log-cabin church for the Scotch-Irish settlers who lived along the banks of the Rocky River (for which the church is named). It first classified itself as part of the Separate Baptist movement that originated in New England during the Great Awakening. In 1872, the log-cabin church building burned, and a new one had to be built. In 1917 and 1918, the third church structure, a wooden frame building, was erected. The church sanctuary standing today began with that structure. In the 1930s, renovation to the building included the addition of eight small Sunday school rooms. Further renovations and additions to Rocky River Baptist Church led to the current, beautifully designed structures. The children's wing and four additional classrooms behind the fellowship hall were built in 1968. The Reverend Greg Burriss was called as pastor of the church in June 1996 and has inspired the fellowship with his spirit-filled messages and his loving, caring, personal touch. (Courtesy of Rocky River Baptist Church.)

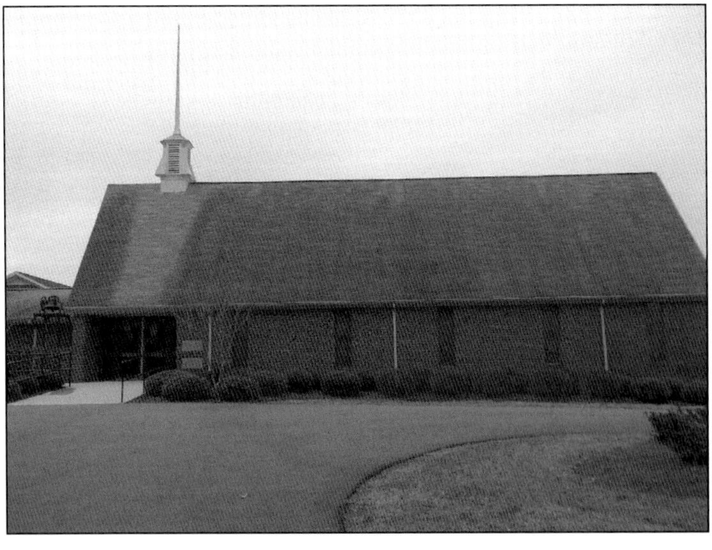

Piney Grove originated in 1836 as a "preaching appointment" in the minutes of the Methodist Protestant Church. Piney Grove was organized as a church in May 1850 and was named for the many pine trees that surrounded it. The first worship service in the present building was held on December 23, 1973. (Courtesy of Piney Grove United Methodist Church.)

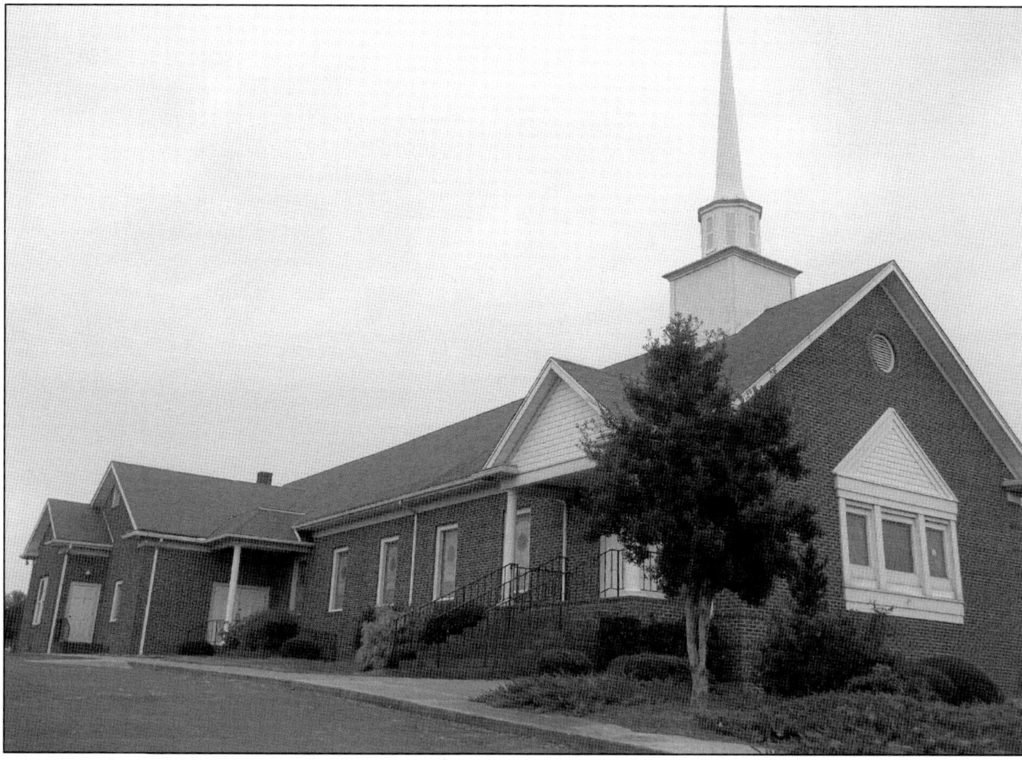

During a business meeting of Rocky River Baptist Church in June 1825, the church canvassed its members to determine if there were enough people to keep up two churches. Those who so desired formed a new church known as Loves Creek Baptist Church. On a Sunday in August 1825, Loves Creek Church was constituted under a brush arbor. (Photograph by author, courtesy of Loves Creek Baptist Church.)

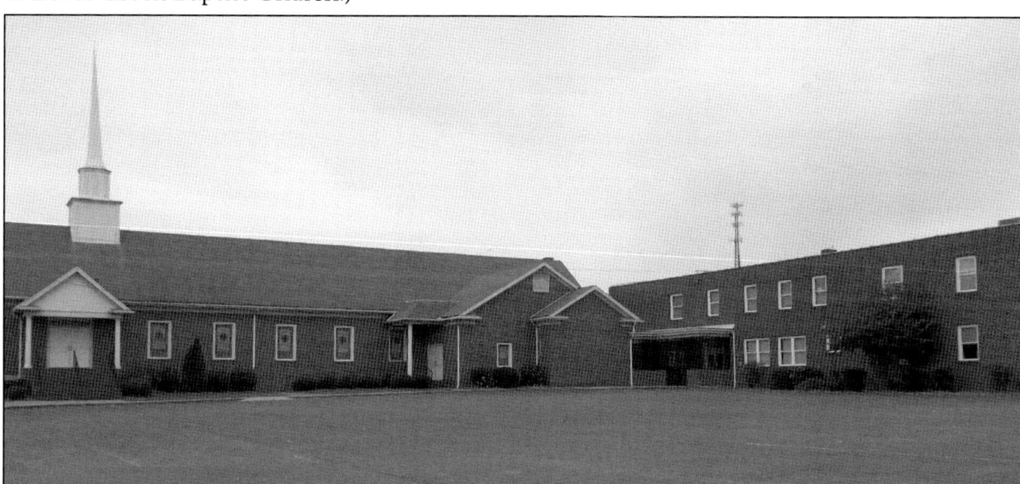

Soon, the church was in need of more space, and from 1943 to 1944 seven Sunday school rooms and the choir loft were built while Rev. Alfred Gibson was pastor. In 1955, Loves Creek called its first full-time pastor, Rev. Edward C. Elliott. The church has been served by 29 pastors from 1825 until the present and is currently served by Pastor Bob Boyd. (Photograph by author, courtesy of Loves Creek Baptist Church.)

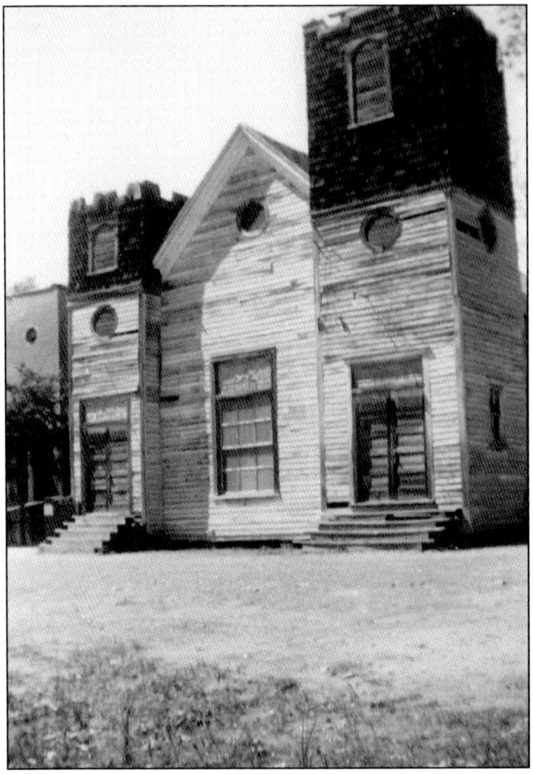

Corinth African Methodist Episcopal Zion Church began in 1884 and is located at 491 Martin Luther King Boulevard. The Sunday school first met under a brush arbor before moving to a small, white, wood-frame building. Corinth A.M.E. Zion is the first church organized to serve the black population in Siler City. (Courtesy of Corinth African Methodist Episcopal Zion Church and Norma Boone.)

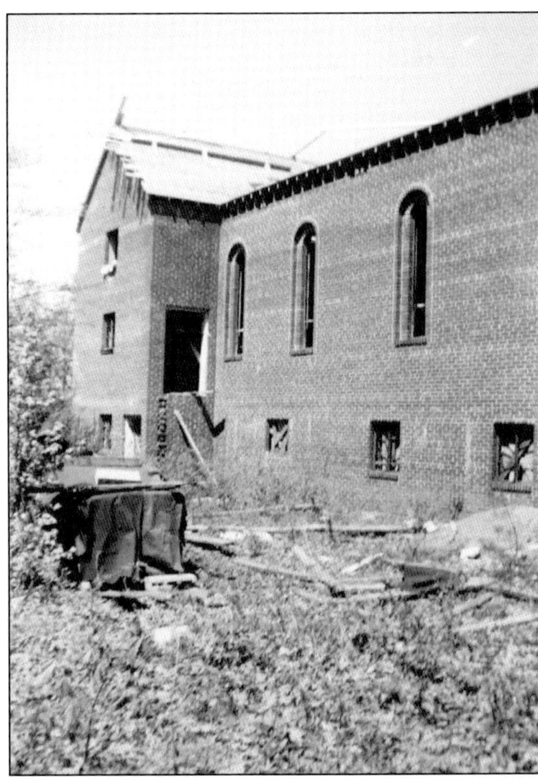

Around 1900, Jordan Dorset donated land to build a new church. This large facility had two front entrances and a wooden-frame construction and was painted white. In 1929, the second church was remodeled with double steeples that served the congregation for 56 years. In 1944 and 1945, under Rev. S.P. Cook's leadership, a massive building program began. (Courtesy of Corinth African Methodist Episcopal Zion Church and Norma Boone.)

The members raised money for a new brick building, and Thomas Brooks matched the amount raised. With Rev. Lee Roy Williams as pastor, on Easter Monday, April 1952, the task of building the new edifice began. There were several brick masons amongst the members, and in the time-honored tradition of self-reliance, the men decided to construct the new facility. (Courtesy of Corinth African Methodist Episcopal Zion Church and Norma Boone.)

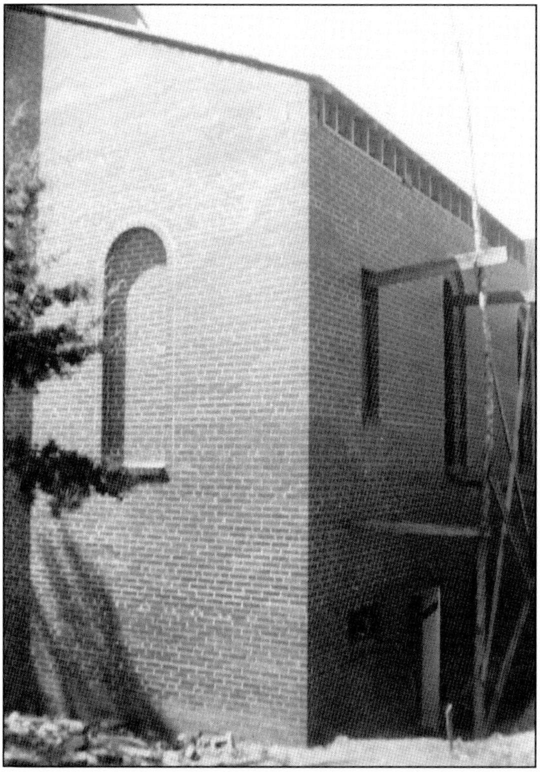

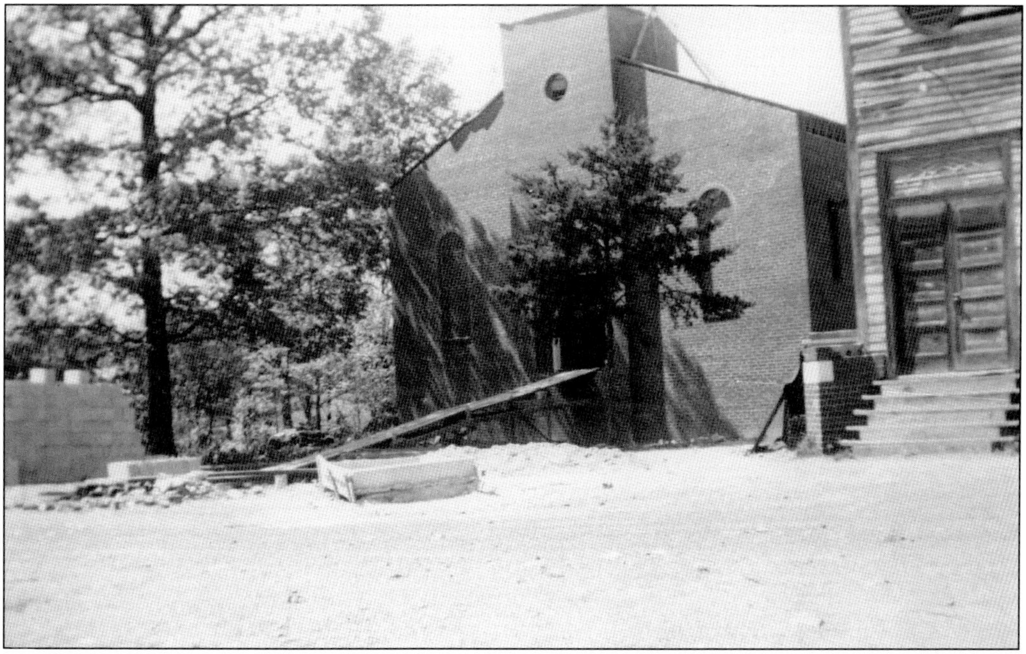

Men busied themselves with brick, mortar, and carpentry work after their regular jobs in the evenings and on Saturdays, donating their time and labor. On June 30, 1957, the first service was held in the new house of worship. (Courtesy of Corinth African Methodist Episcopal Zion Church and Norma Boone.)

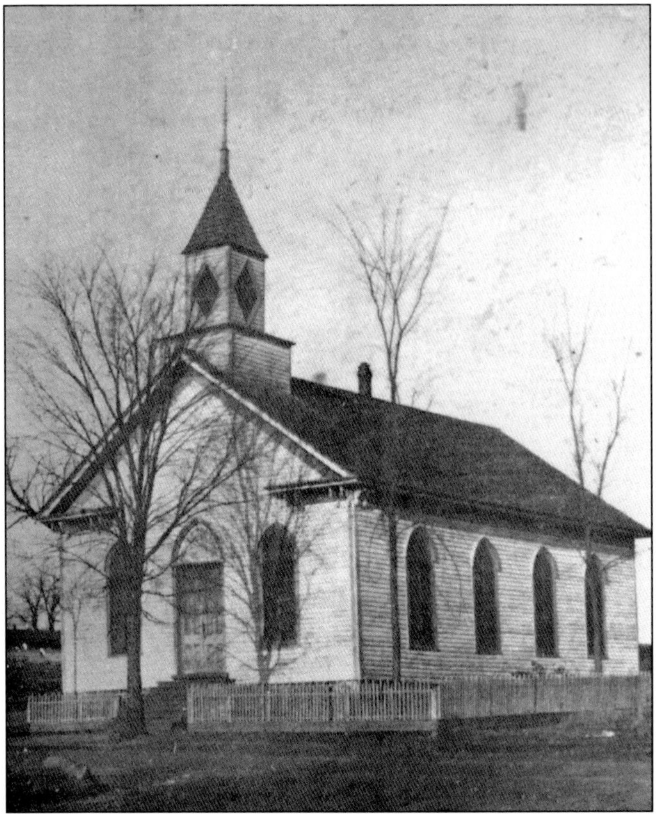

The town's first church building was dedicated in April 1887. First Methodist Episcopal Church, South was organized on November 1, 1886. That December, the walls were raised, the roof put on, and rough slab seats installed. The church was located on the corner at 121 South Chatham Avenue and East Beaver Street. The wooden building was used until July 1920. (Courtesy of Farmers' Alliance and Nancy Tysor.)

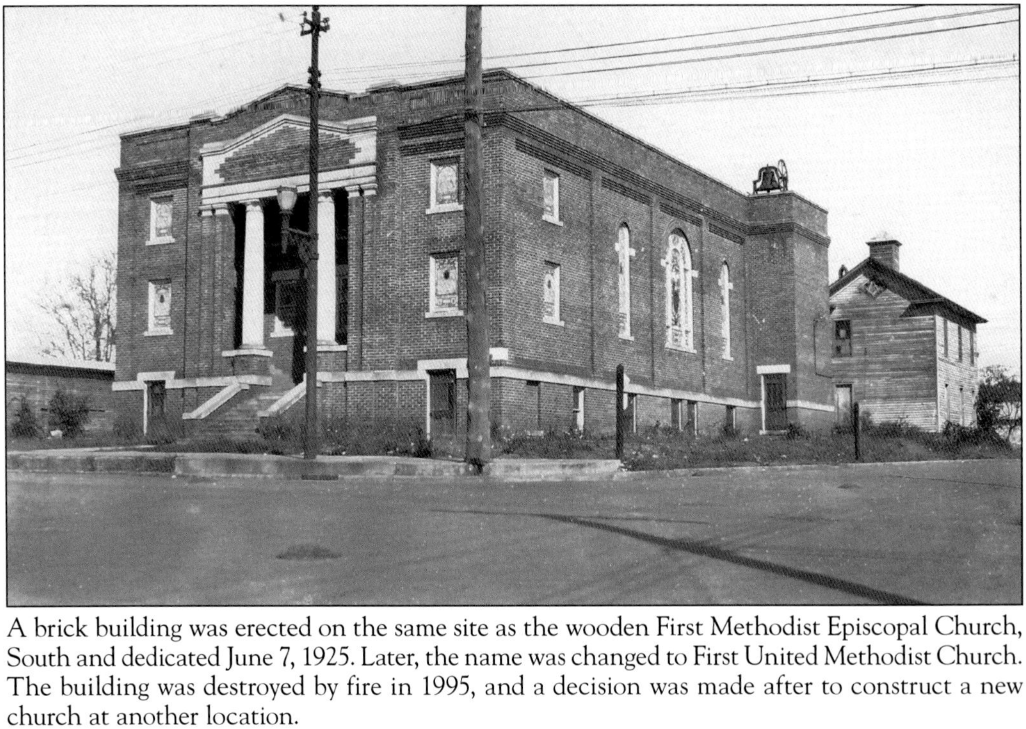

A brick building was erected on the same site as the wooden First Methodist Episcopal Church, South and dedicated June 7, 1925. Later, the name was changed to First United Methodist Church. The building was destroyed by fire in 1995, and a decision was made after to construct a new church at another location.

Construction started on the church in the spring of 1921, and the new church was dedicated on June 7, 1925. Adjoining educational units were built in 1939 and 1959. A large Sunday school program was an integral part of the church.

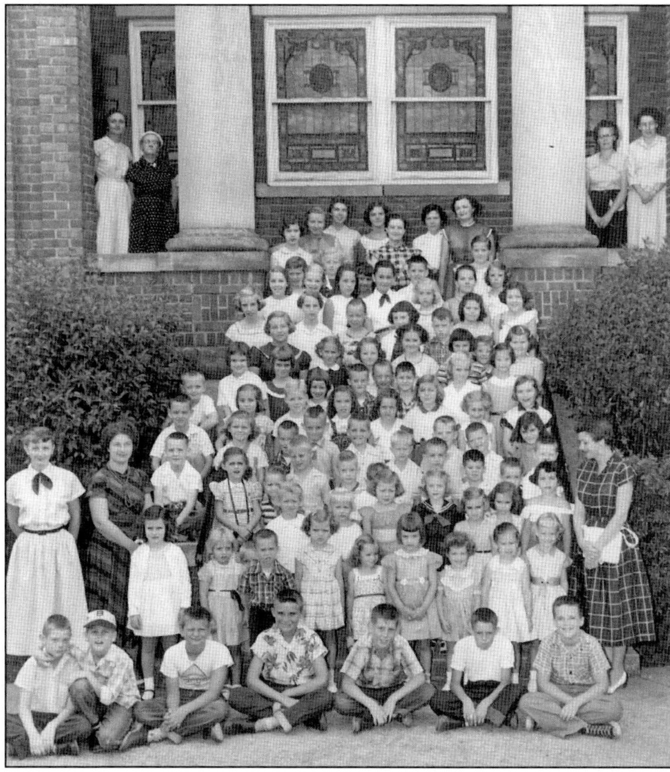

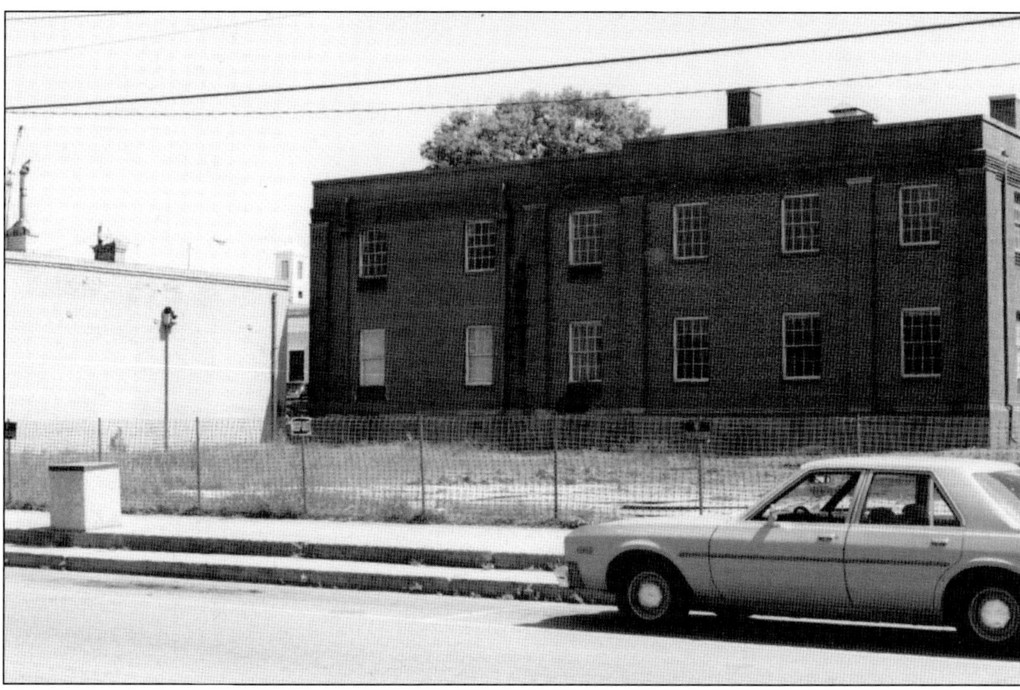

After the fire at First Methodist Episcopal Church in 1995, the educational units built in 1939 and 1959 were still standing. In this image, Rufus Johnson's car is sitting on the street. (Courtesy of Farmers' Alliance Store and Nancy Tysor.)

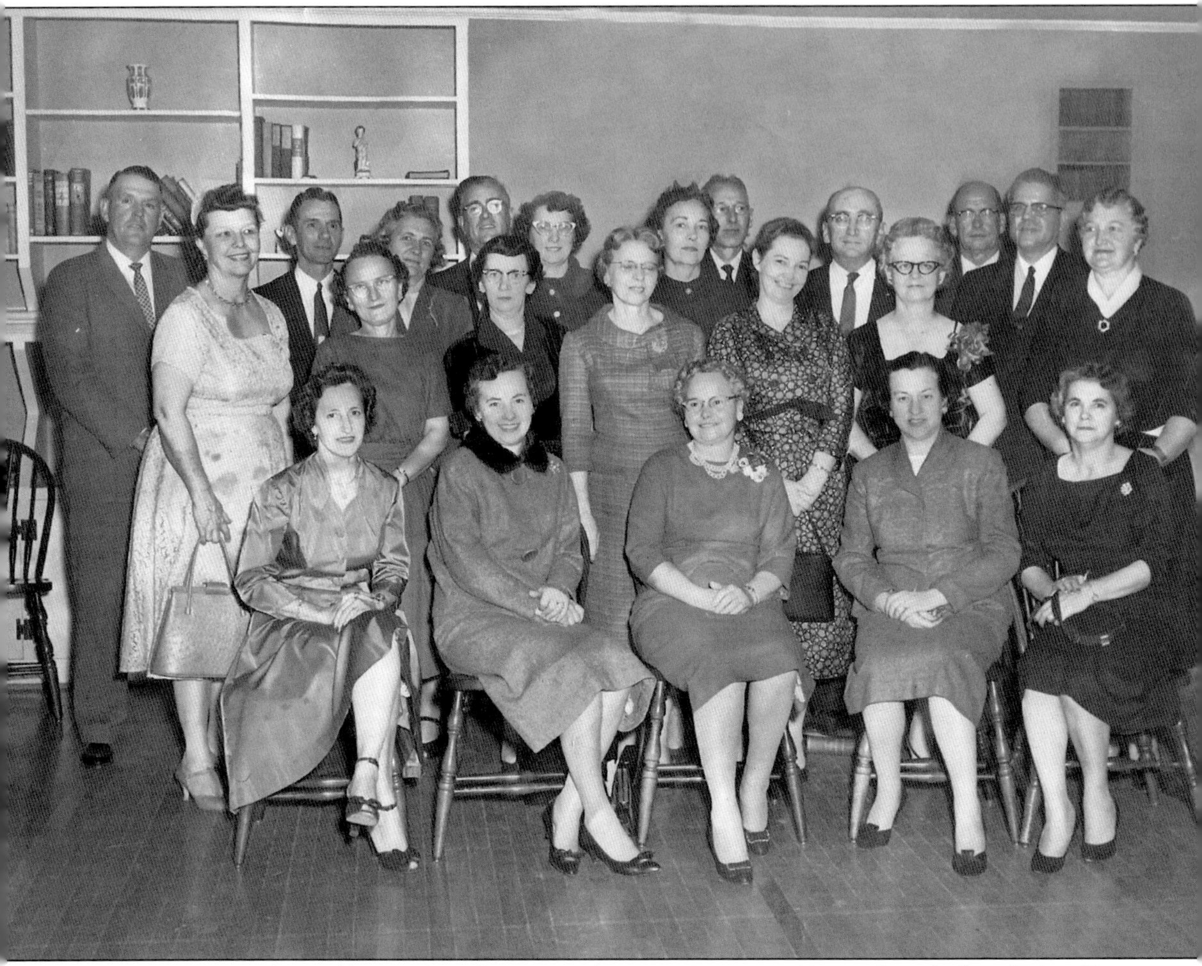

From left to right are (first row) Pauline Straughn, Vera D., Marcie D., unidentified, and Mary Decci Teague; (second row) Estle Jones, Eloise Straughn, unidentified, Berta Bray, Maxine McLaughlin, Mildred Pendergress, and Mary Joyce Edwards; (third row) Mark Lindley, Robert Dark, Helen Andrew, Sam Siler, unidentified, Margaret Harris, Wade McMaster, Stacy Budd, Paul Braxton, and Rev. Parks Hackney. The group is seen during a Farmers' Alliance stockholders meeting at the First United Methodist Church. It met regularly until the church burned down in 1994.

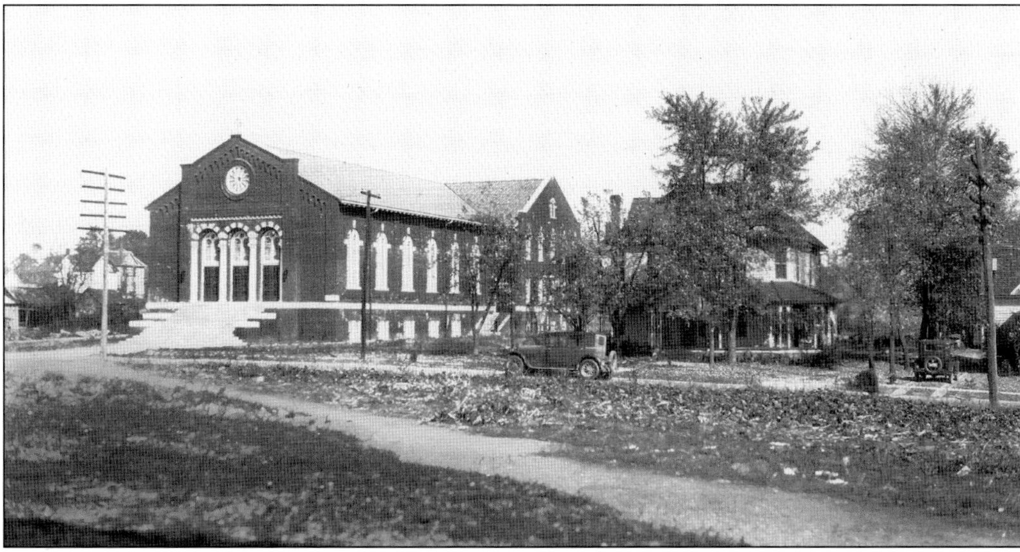

On May 17, 1889, a presbytery consisting of 10 elders met in the Thompson School Academy to consider organizing a Missionary Baptist church. This was the beginning of the ministry of the First Baptist Church of Siler City. On August 19, 1889, a house of worship was planned, and four years later the first church was completed.

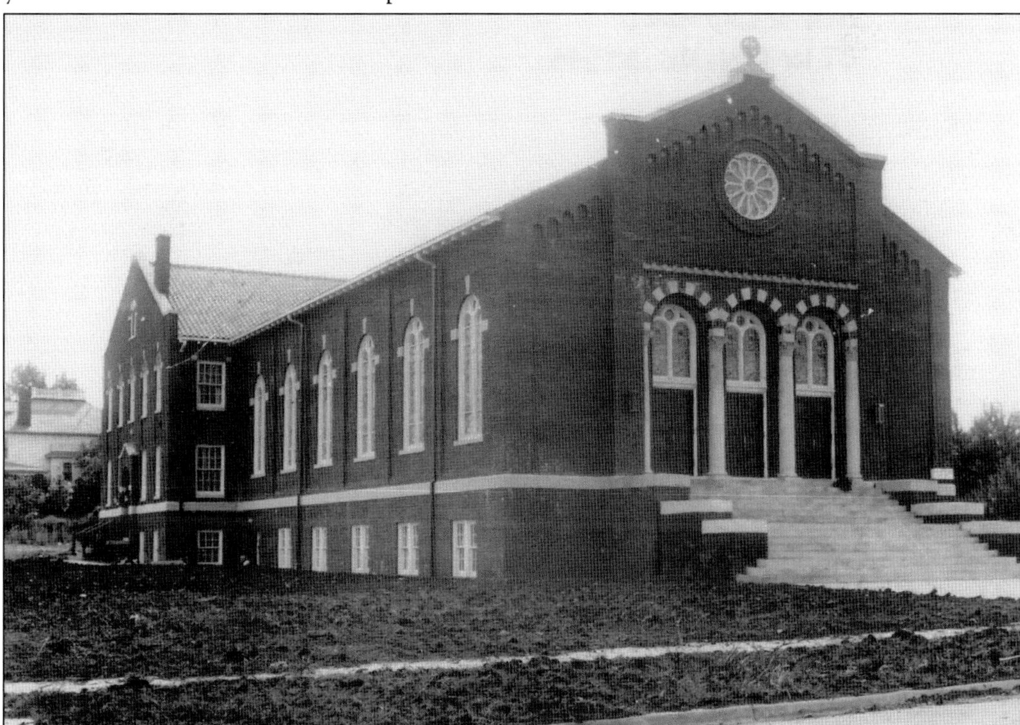

In October 1927, the church launched plans for a more adequate facility. Construction of the new church began on April 20, 1928, and was completed two years later. On July 13, 1930, the congregation met at the old church and marched to the new church for its first service. This historic procession was led by the Reverend J.C. Canipe. (Courtesy of First Baptist Church.)

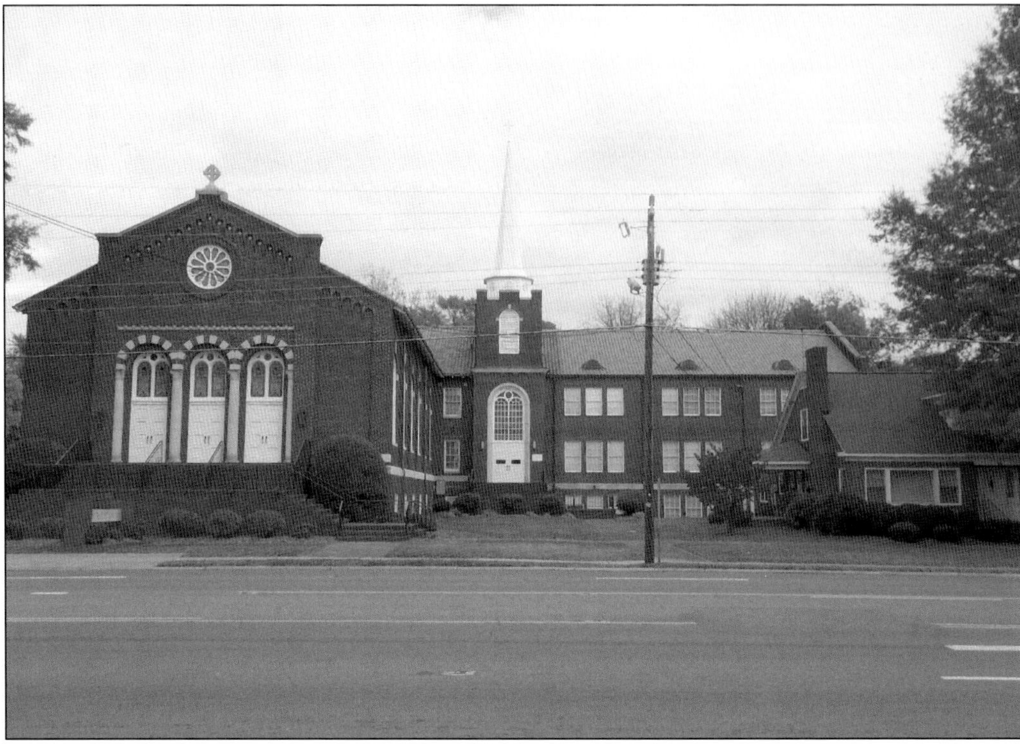

A new parsonage was built in 1952. On June 2, 1963, a third major building project that involved expansion and remodeling of the church began; it was completed February 1965. The congregation renovated the fellowship hall in 1975, built a covered driveway entrance in 1981, and renovated the church administrative offices in 1985. (Photograph by author, courtesy of First Baptist Church.)

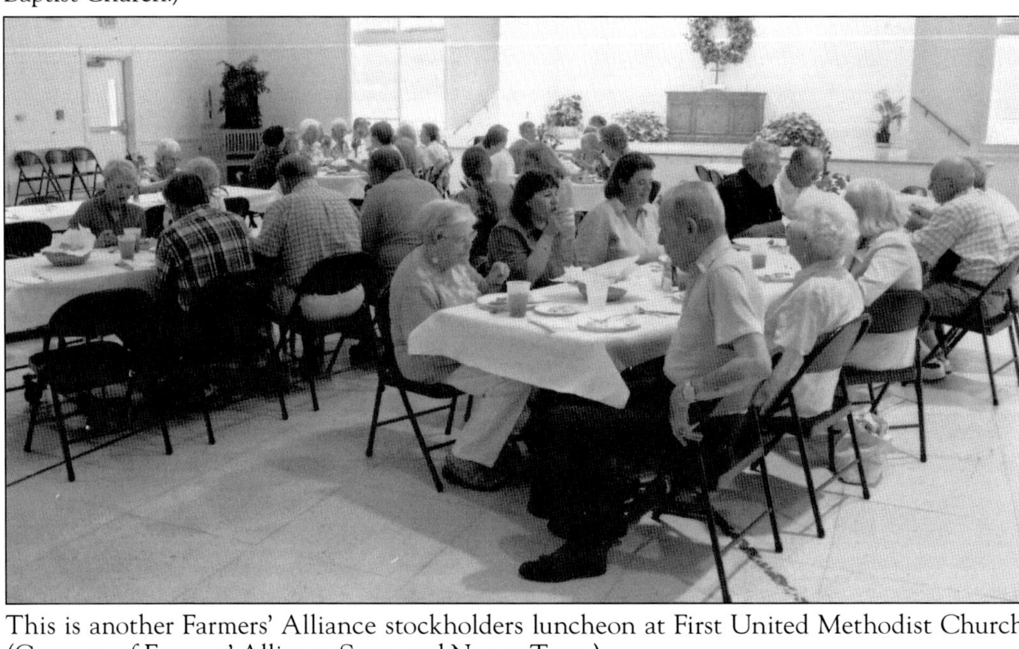

This is another Farmers' Alliance stockholders luncheon at First United Methodist Church. (Courtesy of Farmers' Alliance Store and Nancy Tysor.)

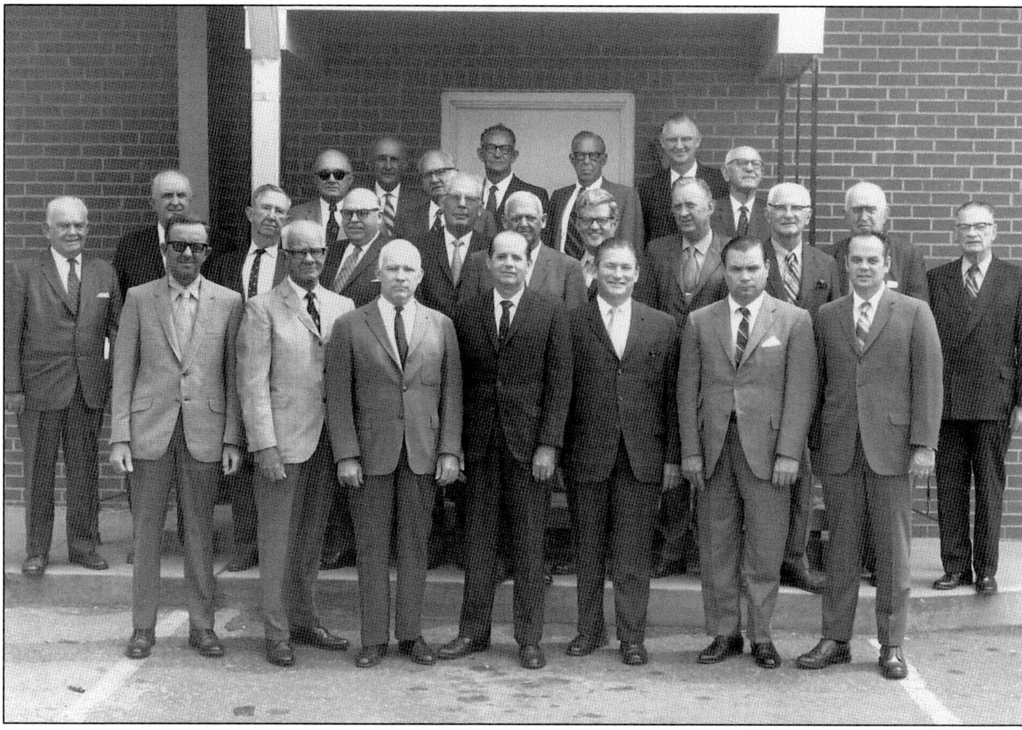

During a rotary meeting, a large group of men stands in front of the First United Methodist Church. Among them are Tam de St. Aubin (first row, second from right) and Dr. Edwards (first row, third from the left). St. Aubin and his son own the North Carolina Travel Agency in Siler City.

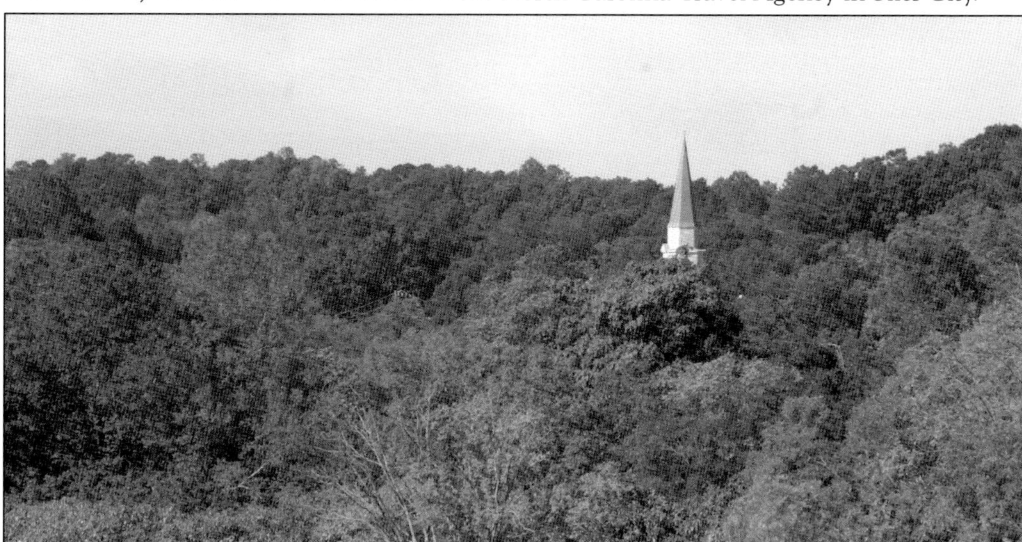

Other churches in the area have included Methodist Protestant Church (1894), Holy Trinity Church (1906), West End Methodist Church (1909), North Sixth Avenue First Baptist Church (1919), First Wesleyan Church (1925), Pentecostal Holiness Church (1932), Siler City Chapel (1945), Presbyterian Church (1951), and Saint Mark's Episcopal Church (around 1951), now located in Raleigh. The steeple of the Presbyterian Church is seen here. (Photograph by Arnette Muldrow, courtesy of the Town of Siler City.)

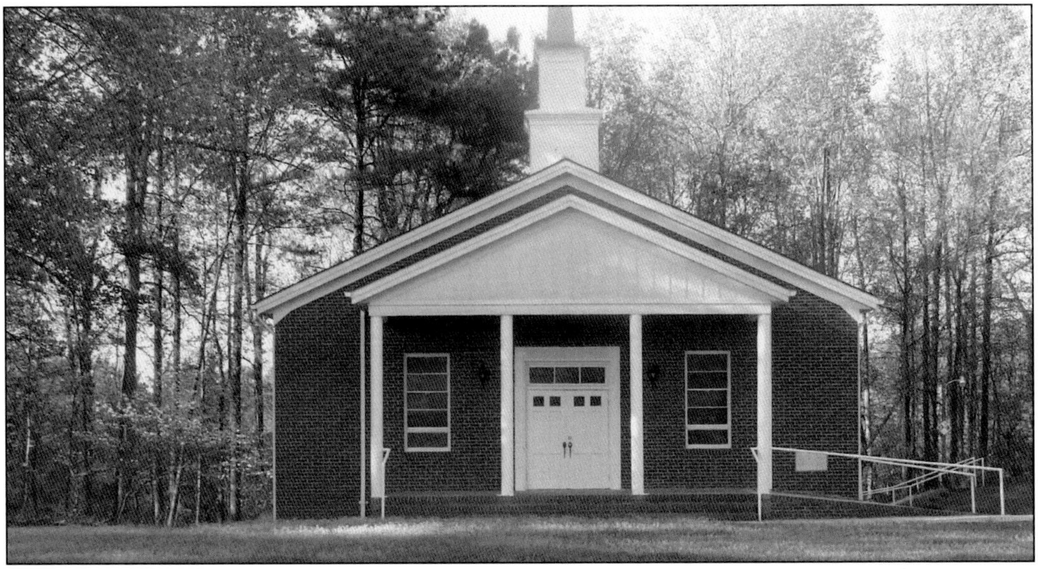

This is Evans Chapel African Methodist Episcopal Zion Church, located at 241 Evans Chapel Road. Evans began in a brush arbor around September 11, 1890, in Hickory Mountain Township, Chatham County, North Carolina. The first church was built of logs, the second had a wood frame, and in 1955 this third and present edifice began under the leadership of Rev. R.S. Smitherman. (Courtesy of Evans Chapel African Methodist Episcopal Zion Church.)

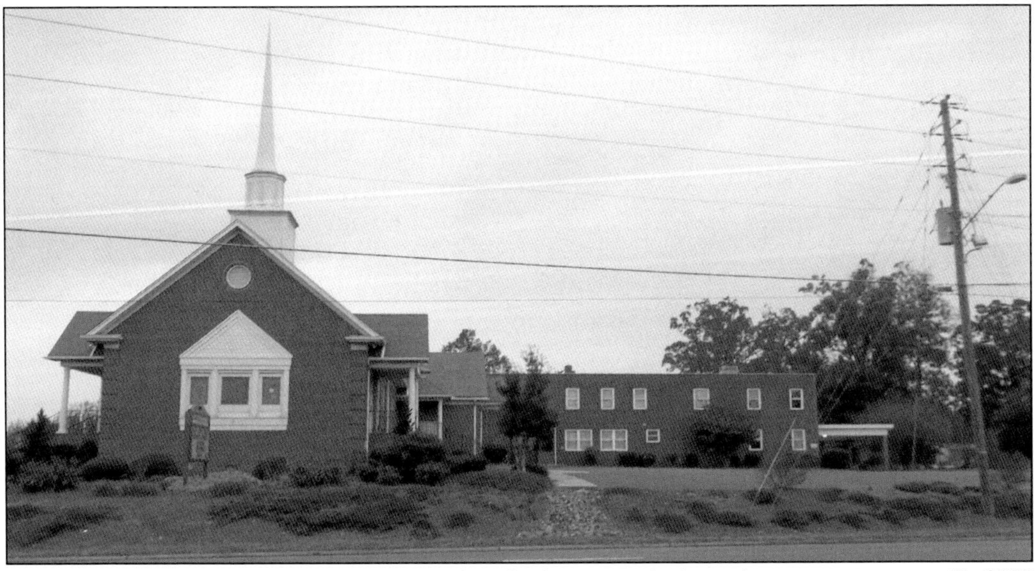

This is the view of Loves Creek Baptist Church the way it looks today as one comes off of US Highway 421 and Highway 64. O.T. Edwards was elected pastor in January 1883 when he first started preaching. He served in the position for the remainder of his life. Church minutes show his salary for a year's service as $40, $60, $75, and then $80; the highest salary Edwards ever received per year was $100. One day, Pastor Edwards called on Brother "Z" to pray, who stated, "Dear God, Bless our church, have mercy on our pastor. We do not treat him with the respect of a decent dog. The dog receives his food daily at our hands, but our pastor, depending upon us for his daily bread, is more than four months hungry." It worked, and Pastor Edwards's salary was raised. (Photograph by author.)

Four

Schools

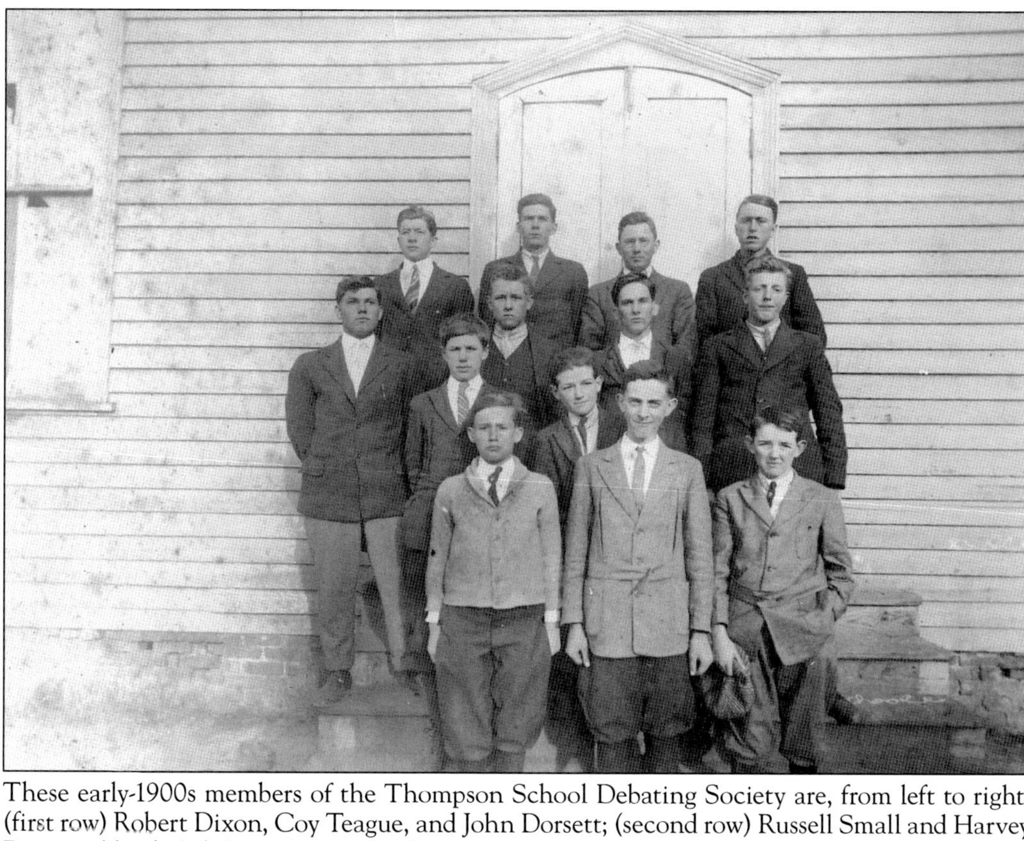

These early-1900s members of the Thompson School Debating Society are, from left to right, (first row) Robert Dixon, Coy Teague, and John Dorsett; (second row) Russell Small and Harvey Dorsett; (third row) Artie Harper, Diffie Dorsett, Stedman McMasters, and Ralph Blair; (fourth row) Pauly Dorsett, Arthur Lineberry, Clyde Beavers, and Henry Clapp.

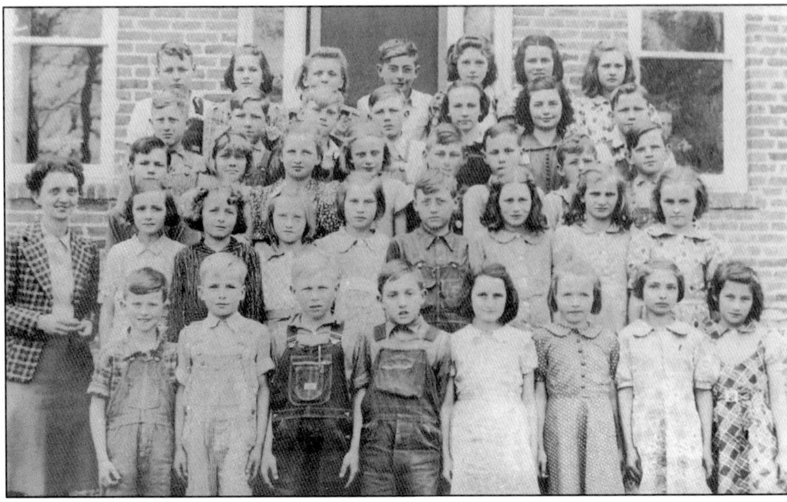

Henry Siler School, located at 502 West Third Street, went into service in early 1931. The school eventually closed in 1977 when the new Siler City Elementary School was built. These children pose for the camera around 1936.

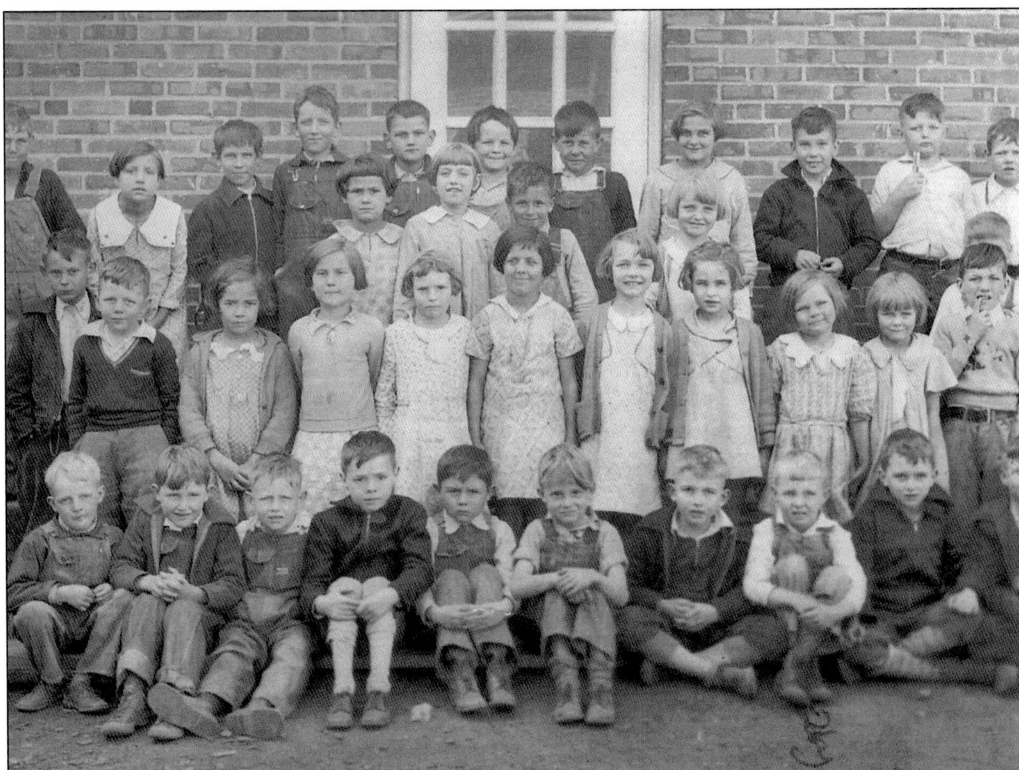

Pictured from left to right around 1936, these students of the Henry Siler School are (first row) Jesse Stanley, two unidentified boys, Benton Clark, unidentified, Jack Stone, Hoyle Dixon, Gene McLaughlin, Joe Green, and unidentified; (second row) Norman Jordan, Mary Frances Johnson (Davis), two unidentified girls, Jaunita Lopossay, Laurel Ellen Dixon, Virginia Dixon, Dorothy Lowe, Elizabeth "Tookie" Light, Bobby Langley, and Ray Teague Jr. (behind Langley); (third row) Calvin Brower, Alene Gilliland, Polly Poe, Bill Snyder, Minney and Myrle Scott; (fourth row) Marvin Lopossay, Louise Martin, Junior Harris, Curtis Burns, Ray Gilliland, J.W. Moody, unidentified, Ruth Page, Billy Carter, Charlie Buckner, and Bobby Allred.

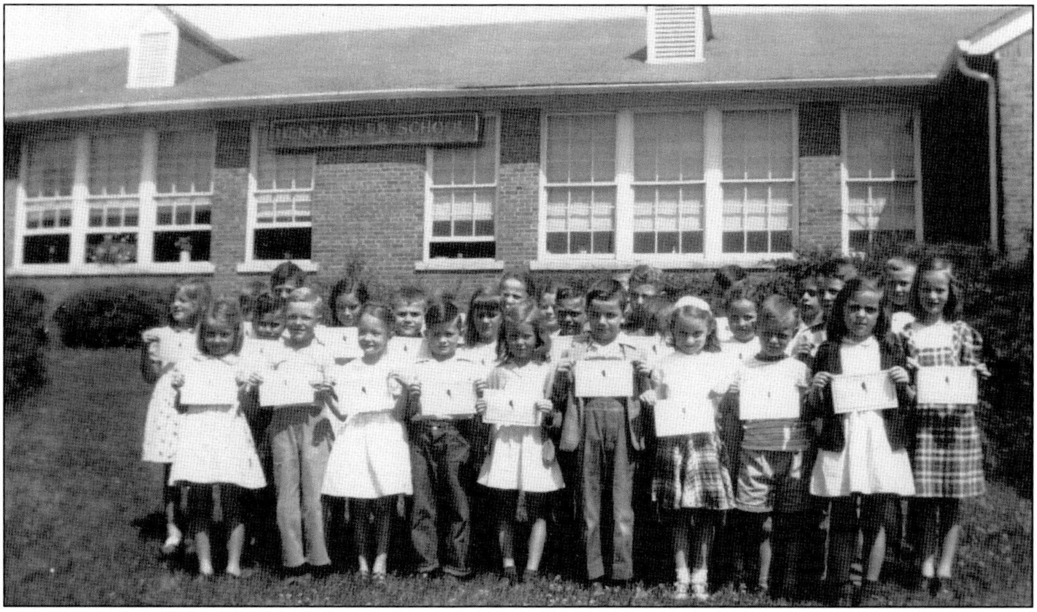

This image of a second-grade class was taken on the front schoolyard of Henry Siler School when Clyde Dorsett was the school principal. (Courtesy of Farmers' Alliance Store and Nancy Tysor.)

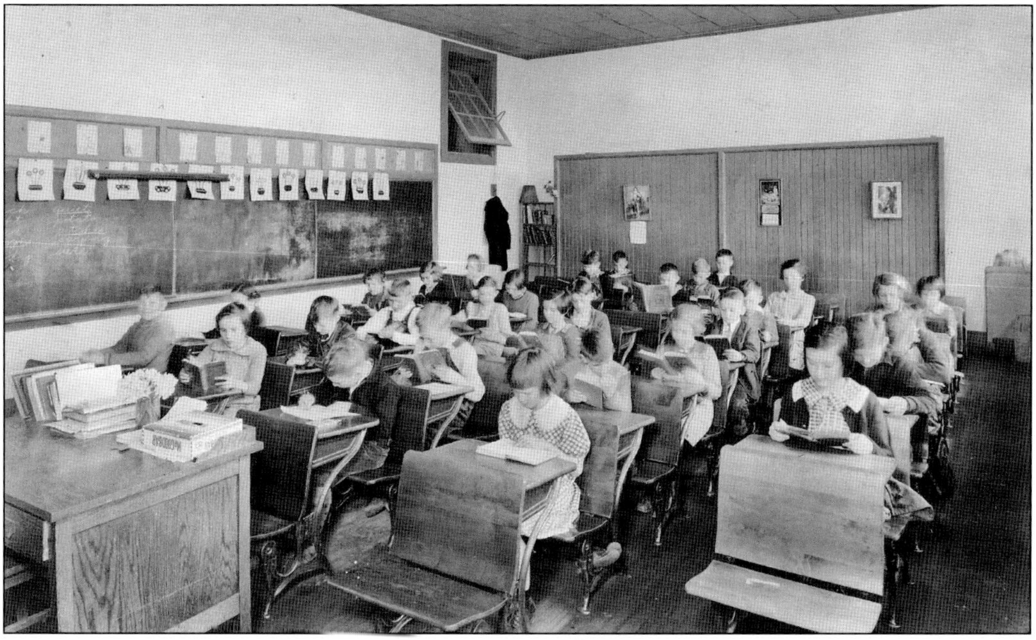

This is an interior shot of Henry Siler Elementary School around 1931.

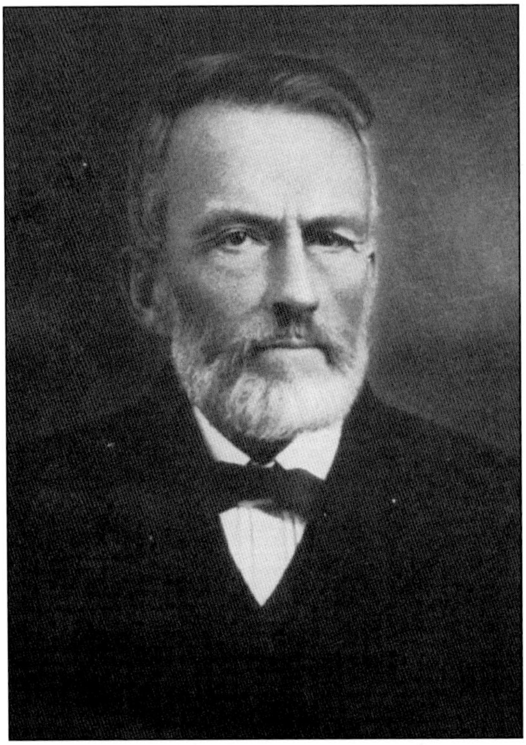

Henry H. Siler was a teacher from 1842 to 1918. This photograph was taken on March 28, 1932, for his years of service to education. He taught at Loves Creek and Siler City Institute while also being an active land surveyor. (Courtesy of Farmers' Alliance Store and Nancy Tysor.)

These students of Siler City High School are, from left to right, (first row) unidentified, Maxine McLaughlin, and Mary D. Teague; (second row) Mary J. Edwards, Magdaline Johnson, Mildred Pendergrass, Bertha Bray, and unidentified; (third row) five unidentified (fourth row) Mark Lindley, Sam Siler, and Sam Phillips; (fifth row) Howard Elkins, Jack Brooke, and Max Bray.

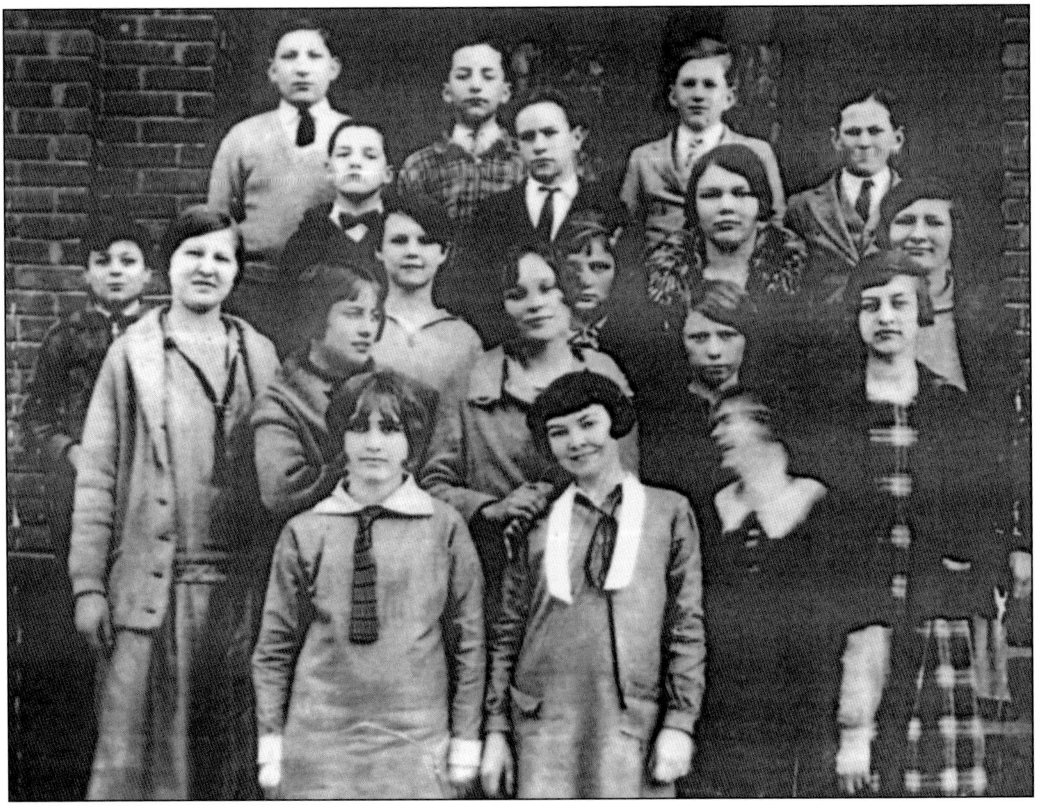

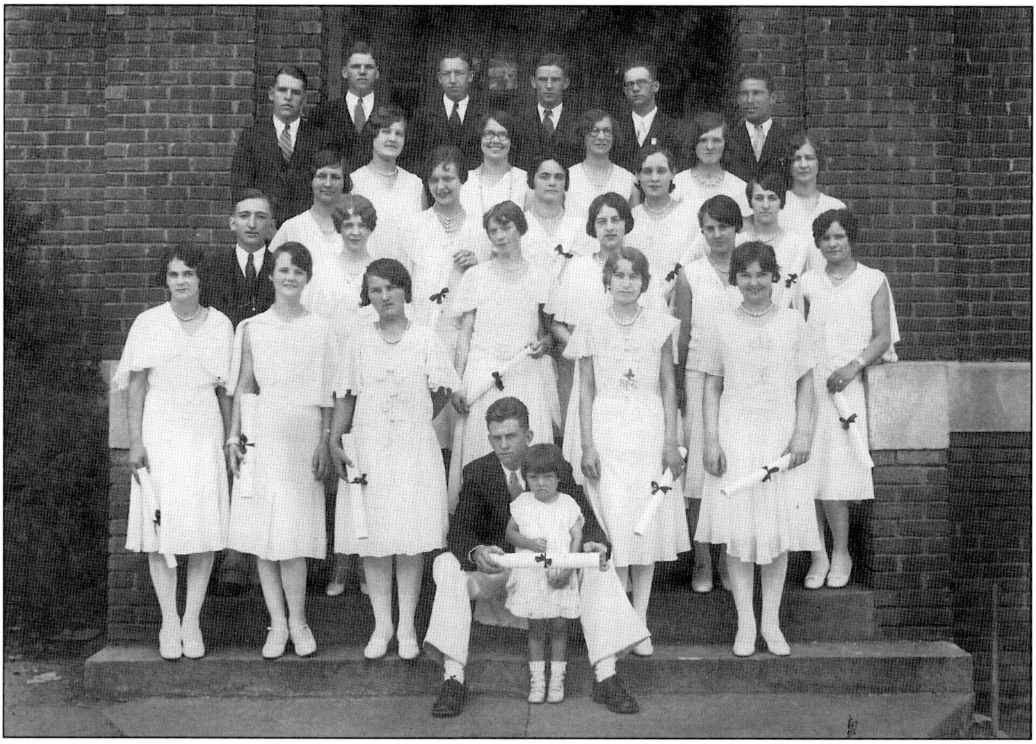

Members of the graduating class of 1930 include Dody Fesmen (upper-center left, wearing glasses); Wade McMasters (back row, far right); Max Bray (seated on step with Bill Brady's sister); Berta Bray (behind Max Bray), who later married Wade McMasters; Mark Lindley (back row, far left); Lissie M. Smith (fourth row, second from right); and Sadie Holloman (fourth row, far right).

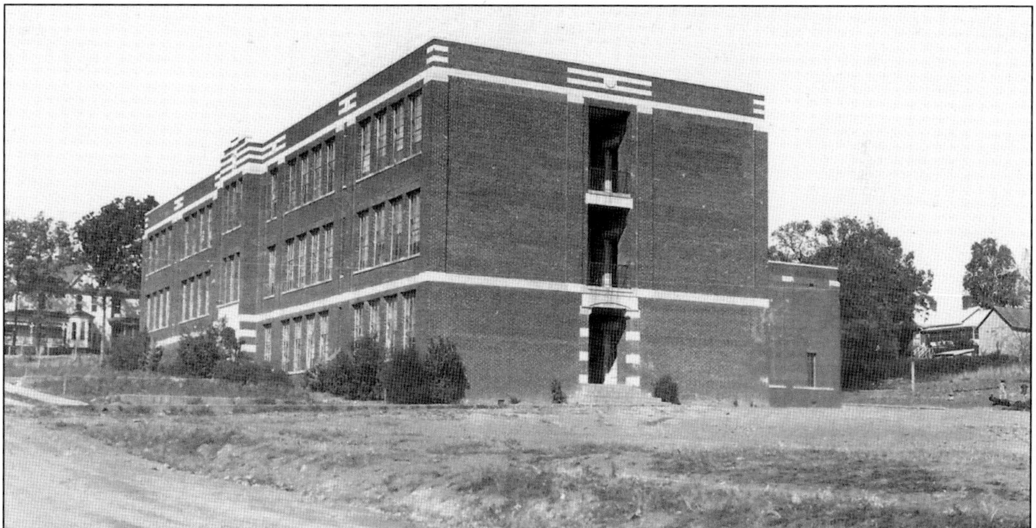

Siler City High School went into operation in the fall of 1923 in a new, three-story, brick building at 119 South Third Avenue. It served as a combined elementary and high school until Jordan-Matthews High School was built in 1956. Siler City High School was then renamed Paul Braxton Elementary School.

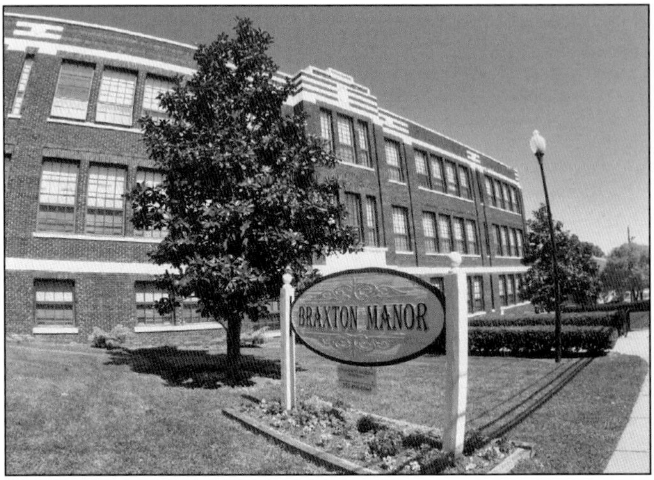

Paul Braxton's 32 classrooms were later converted by Community Housing Partners into apartments. According to an article written in the "Community and Economic Development in North Carolina and Beyond" newsletter, "Architecturally distinctive, this school is one of the few surviving civic examples of the rarely implemented Art Deco style in Chatham and Randolph Counties." (Photograph by Jeff Davis, courtesy of the Town of Siler City.)

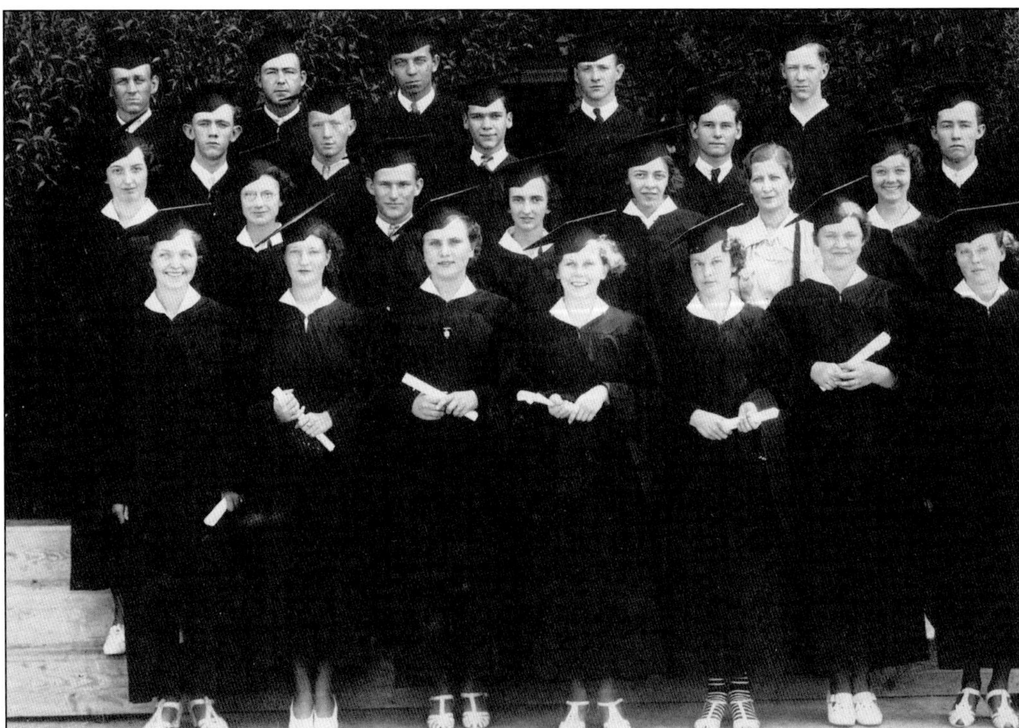

In this image of the 1936 graduating class of Siler City High School are, from left to right, (first row) Elma Kelly, Joyce Fox, Bartria Sears, Kathryn Marley, Marie Smith, Mary Decie Dark, and Golda Kivett; (second row) Olline Phillips, Mary Lee Richardson, Forrest Paschal, Kathryn Wrenn, Mary Teague, teacher Sadie Holleman, and May Pool; (third row) Charles Stone, Wathan "Red" Terry, Walter Ashe Wall, Jack Brady, and Roy Marley; (fourth row) Floyd Kennedy, Dwain Curtis, Victor Williams, John Robert Forrester, and J.C. Williams. (Courtesy of Farmers' Alliance Store and Nancy Tysor.)

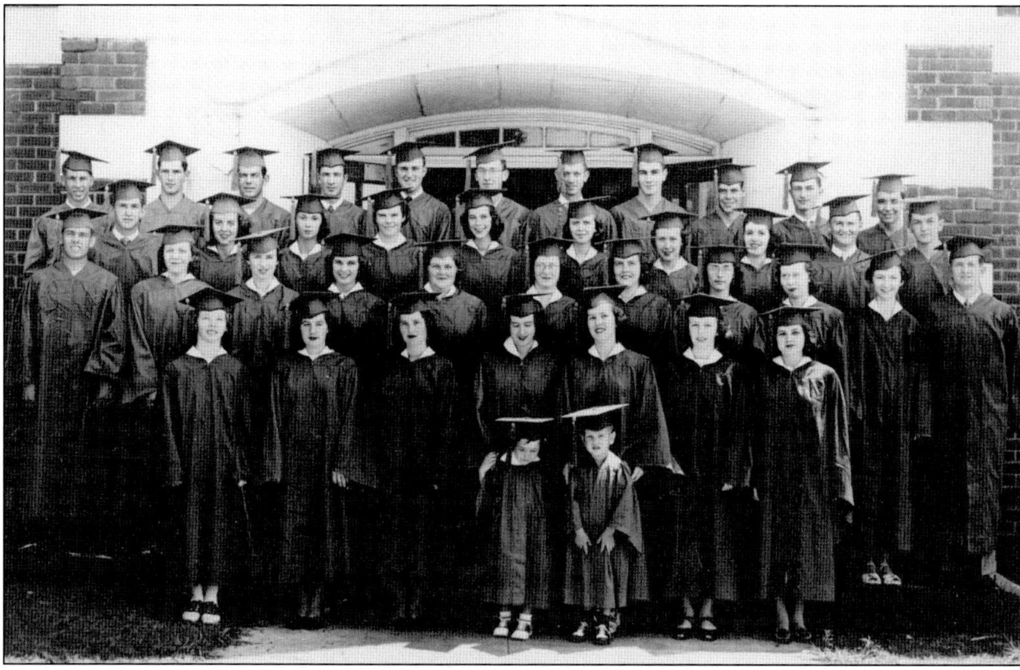

Nancy Tysor graduated from Siler City High School in 1950. In this class photograph are, from left to right, (first row) two unidentified; (second row) Anna Kathrine Holt, Jackie Hall, Lydia White, Betty Lee Jordan, Evelyn Beane, Mary Culverson, and Shirley Bradford; (third row) Bernice Gee, Peggy Smith, Ada Joe Borden, Louise Brooks, Maggie Fields, Cornelia Smith, Betty Jean Fox, Geneva Vail, Nancy Brown, Peggy Joyner, and John Jordan; (fourth row) Pat Mann, Catherine Moore, Christine Smith, Jackie Thomas, Barbara Phillips, Evelyn Smith, Lib Clapp, Nancy Price, Bobby McLaughlin, and Billy Webster; (fifth row) Harold Andrew, Jimmy Brooks, Richard Pond, Brian Oldem, Jim Clapp, Ronald Bolin, Billy Trogdon, Royce Dixon, Gerald Smith, Jack London, and Clyde Johnson. (Courtesy of Farmers' Alliance Store and Nancy Tysor.)

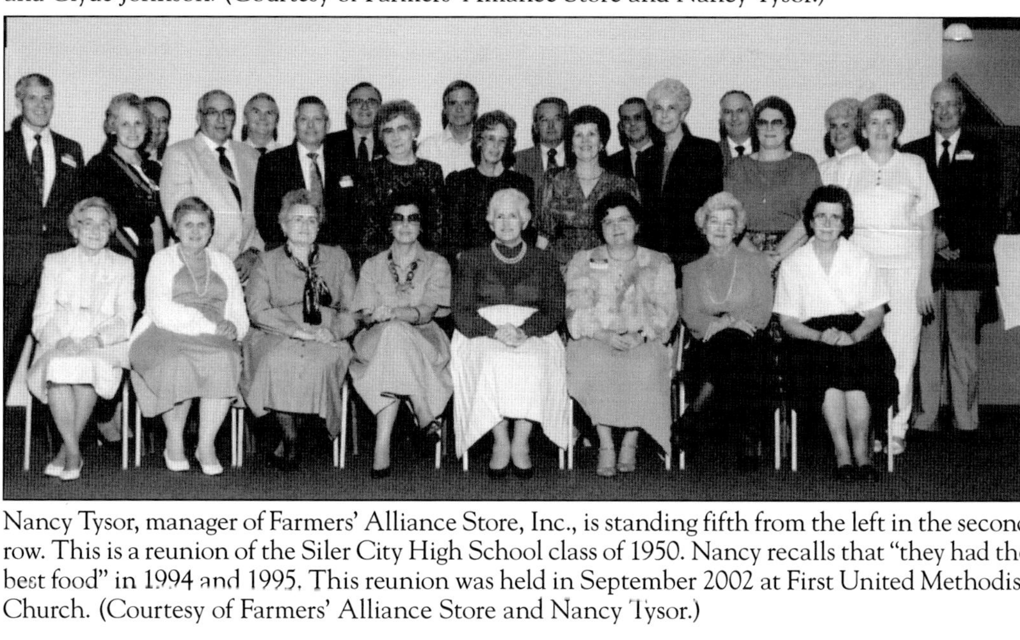

Nancy Tysor, manager of Farmers' Alliance Store, Inc., is standing fifth from the left in the second row. This is a reunion of the Siler City High School class of 1950. Nancy recalls that "they had the best food" in 1994 and 1995. This reunion was held in September 2002 at First United Methodist Church. (Courtesy of Farmers' Alliance Store and Nancy Tysor.)

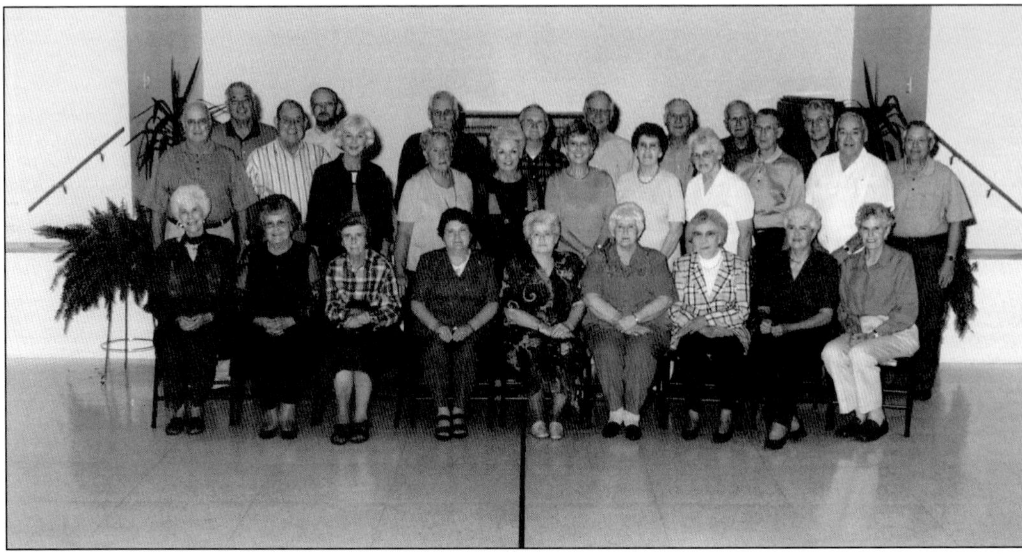

In this image, Nancy Tysor is third from the right in the first row. The photograph was taken at Lou Clark Park on October 13, 2007, for the Siler City High School class of 1950 reunion. (Courtesy of Farmers' Alliance Store and Nancy Tysor.)

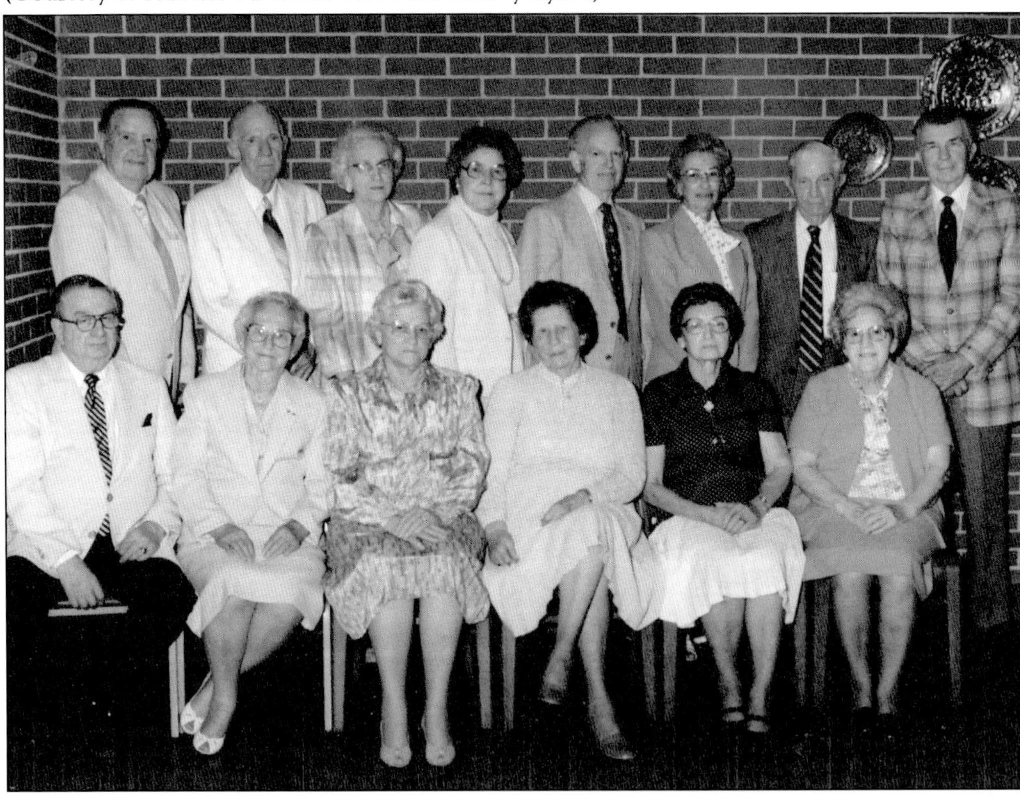

This is a reunion of the Siler City High School class of 1936. Some of the members pictured are Evelyn Marsh (first row, fourth from the left), Frank Straughn (second row, fifth from the left), Eloise Straugh (to the right of Frank), and Willard Clark (to the right of Eloise). (Courtesy of Farmers' Alliance Store and Nancy Tysor.)

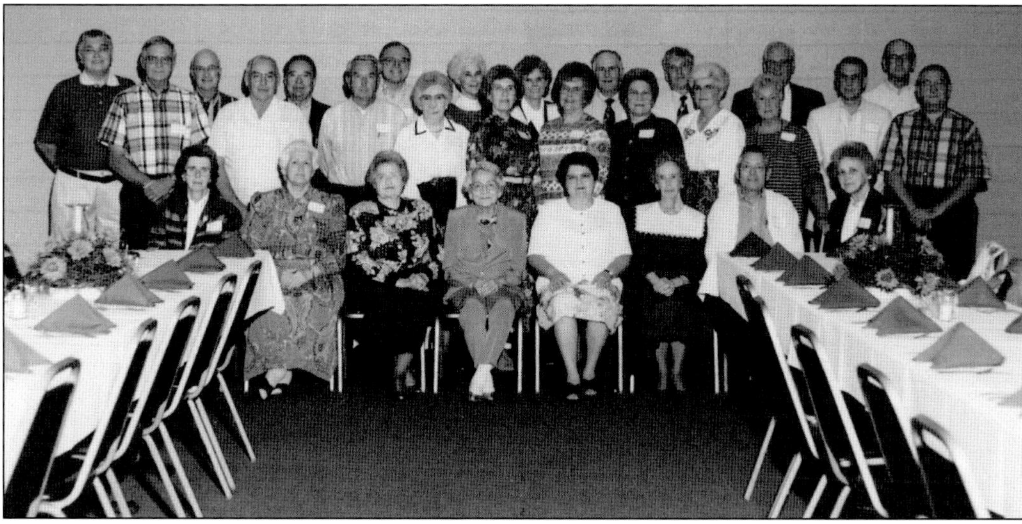

This Siler City High School class of 1950 reunion took place on October 13, 2007. Nancy Tysor is standing fourth from the left in the second row in the image above. Below, she is third from the left in the first row. The poem on the program for the event read, "Around the reunion table there are empty seats this year, the faces and smiles are missing of those we hold dear / And yet our hearts are hopeful though the days are bittersweet, because we know the ones we miss have filled another seat / For another reunion table abounds with joy and love, for who've made the journey to be with our Lord above." These classmates' love and friendship continues as they celebrate the years ahead of them. (Courtesy of Farmers' Alliance Store and Nancy Tysor.)

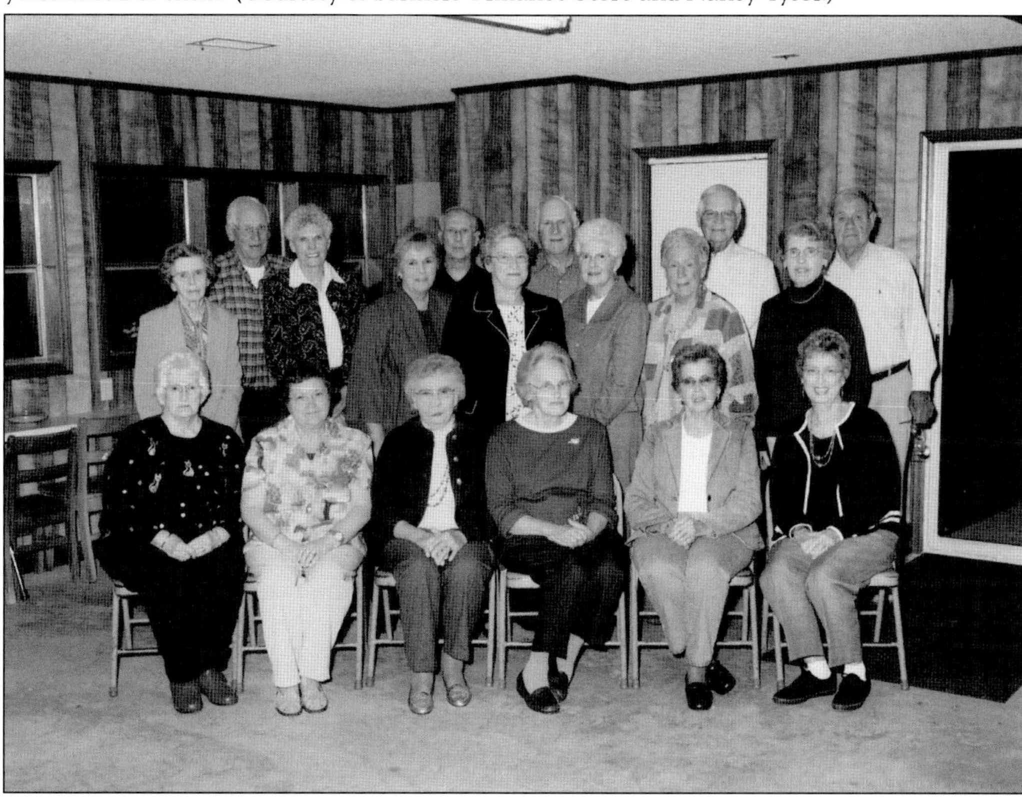

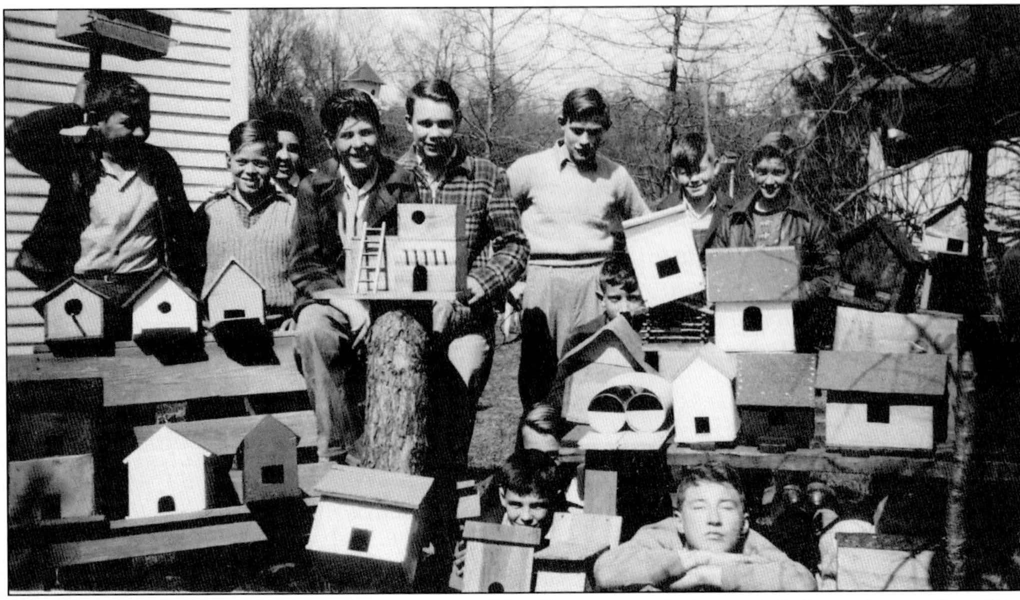

This image shows some beautifully constructed birdhouses made in an eighth-grade wood-crafting course. Pictured in the center foreground are Cleo Scott, Russell Pike, and Jack Elkin. Also pictured are Charles Campbell, Ben Clapp, and Rufus Johnson. These boys were in the 1951 graduating class. (Courtesy of Farmers' Alliance Store and Nancy Tysor.)

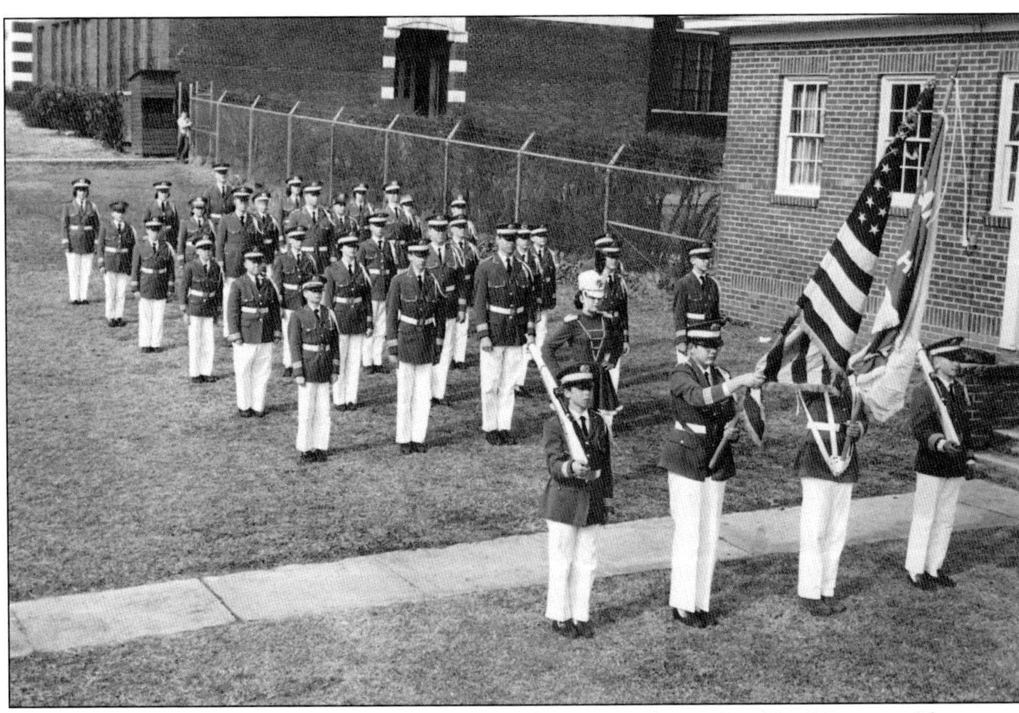

The Siler City Jordan Matthews High School Band is pictured outside of Paul Braxton Elementary School and the additional building that housed 10 classrooms a short distance east of the main structure, which was completed in December 1951. (Courtesy of Farmers' Alliance Store and Nancy Tysor.)

Members of the Siler City Jordan Matthews High School Band are pictured here in the back of Paul Braxton Elementary School around 1968. (Courtesy of Farmers' Alliance Store and Nancy Tysor.)

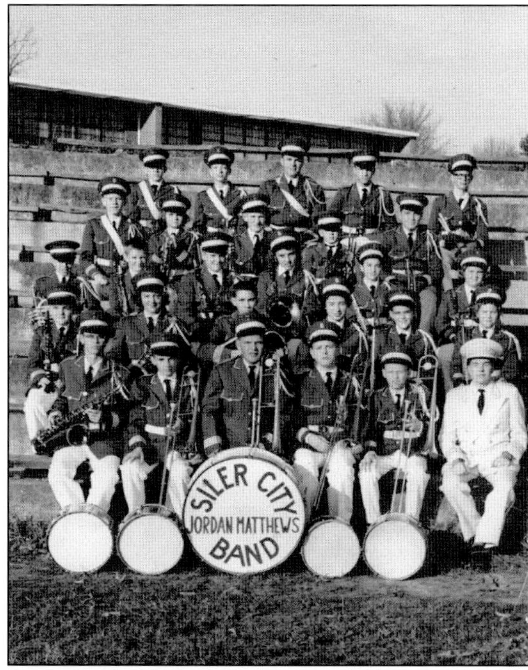

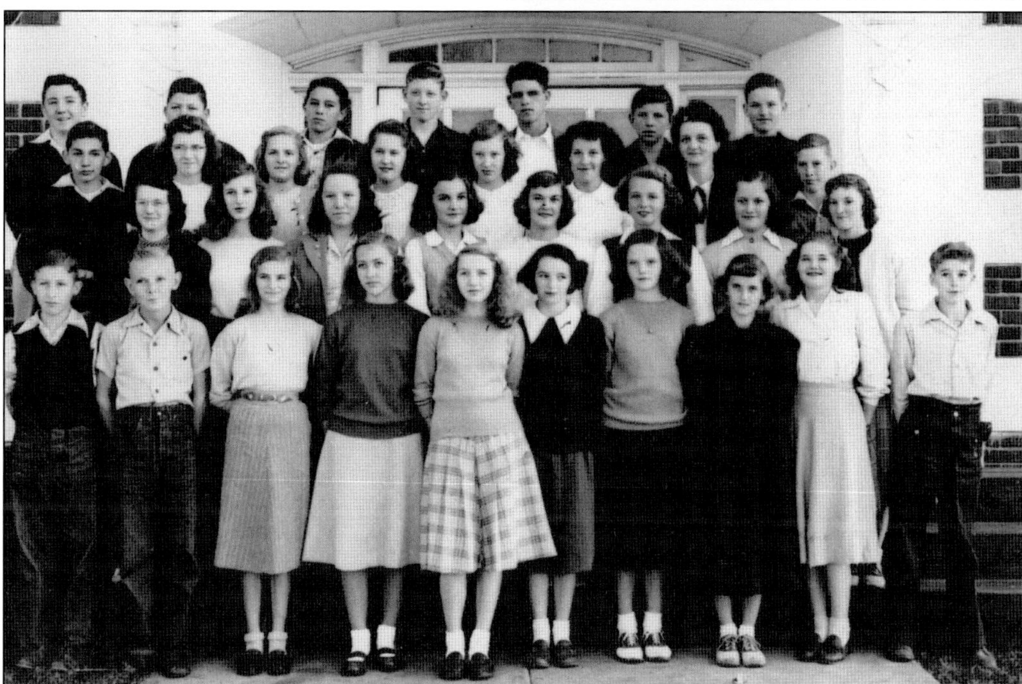

This image captures the eighth grade (class of 1953) outside Siler City High School. From left to right are (first row) Russell Oldhem, Earl Womble, and eight unidentified; (second row) unidentified, Nancy Freeman, four unidentified, Blanche Williams, and Ella Mae Francisco; (third row) Wade Darryl Jr., two unidentified, Ruth Thompson, Frances Fitts, unidentified, Ruth Smith (teacher), and unidentified; (fourth row) unidentified, Leroy Pittman, unidentified, Paul Giles Braxton, Paul Moore, and two unidentified. (Courtesy of Farmers' Alliance Store and Nancy Tysor.)

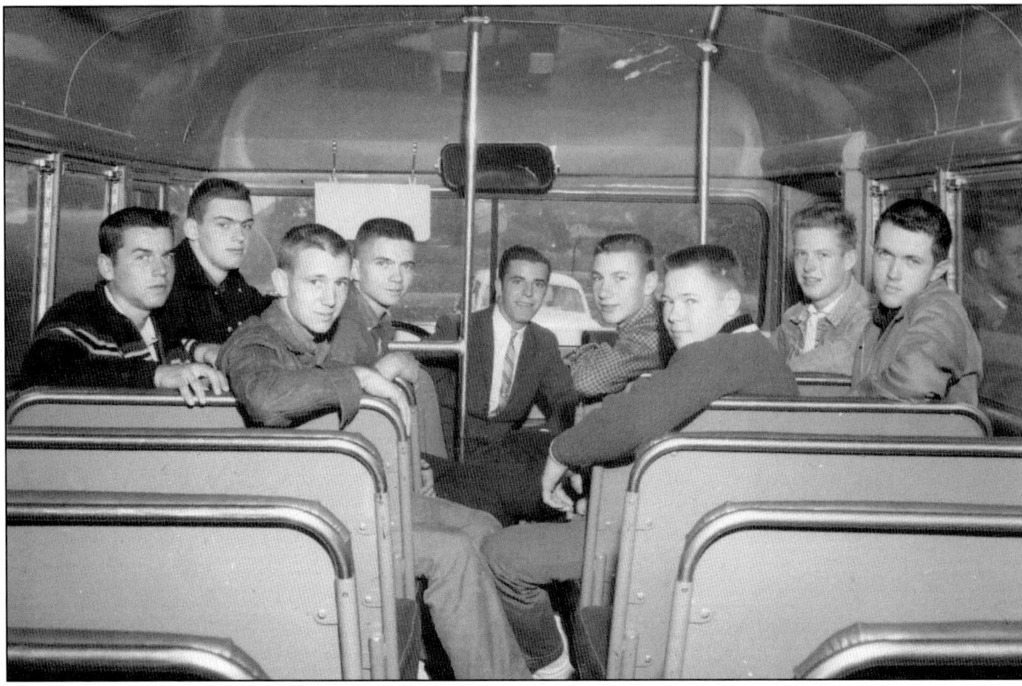

Pictured are the Siler City school bus drivers. From left to right are Newby Phillips Jr., Glen Frickie, Leo Brewer, Hurley Klass, Wayne Ellington, ? Powers, Wayne Dark, and two unidentified around 1953. (Courtesy of Farmers' Alliance Store and Nancy Tysor.)

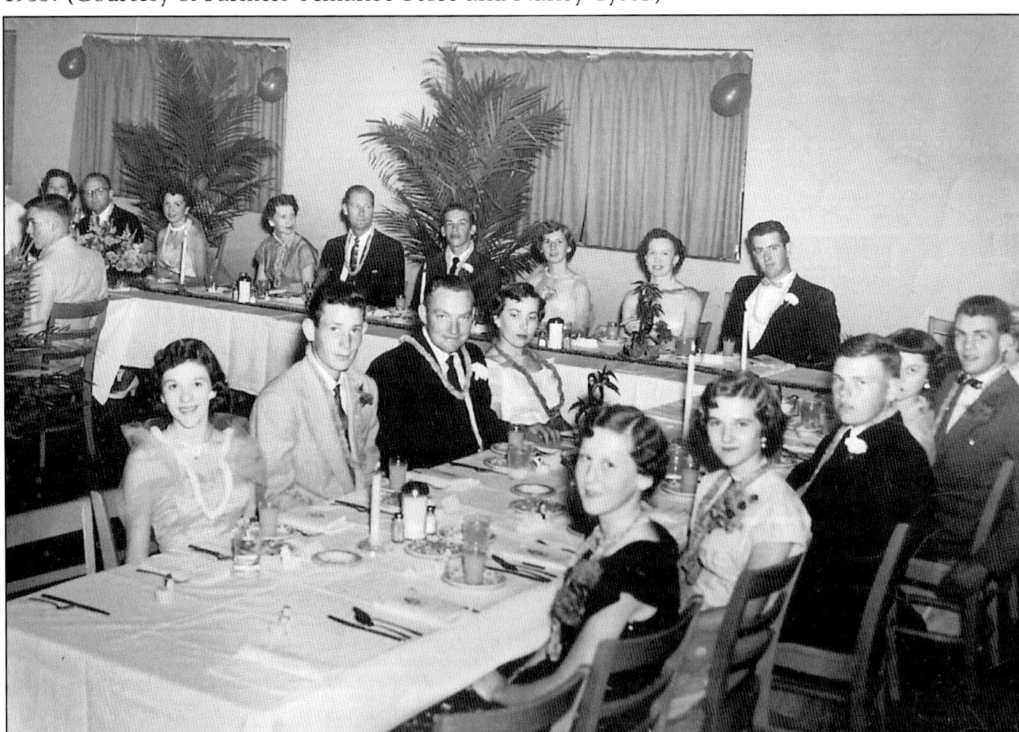

This is a high school graduation party at Club Diane in 1950s. (Courtesy of Diane Whitehead.)

The new Chatham County Training School opened its doors in 1932 and served first through eleventh grades. During the 1942–1943 school year, the twelfth grade was added. The name changed in 1952 to Chatham High School. In 1960, with two new wings, enrollment continued to increase, and from 1961 to 1962 there was a total enrollment of 989 students and 32 teachers. There were 737 students in elementary school and 252 students in high school. After the passage of the Civil Rights Act of 1964, the integration of blacks and whites began in 1965 and 1966 under the Freedom of Choice Plan. The merger of Chatham High School and Jordan Matthews High School began in 1968 and completed in 1969. The class of 1969 was the last to graduate from Chatham High School. Mary Craven, pictured here, is the secretary of the Chatham County Training School and Chatham High School Alumni Association, Inc., and Alphonso Craven is president. They are the keepers of those precious memories. (Courtesy of the Chatham County Training School and Chatham High School 1933–1969 Alumni Association.)

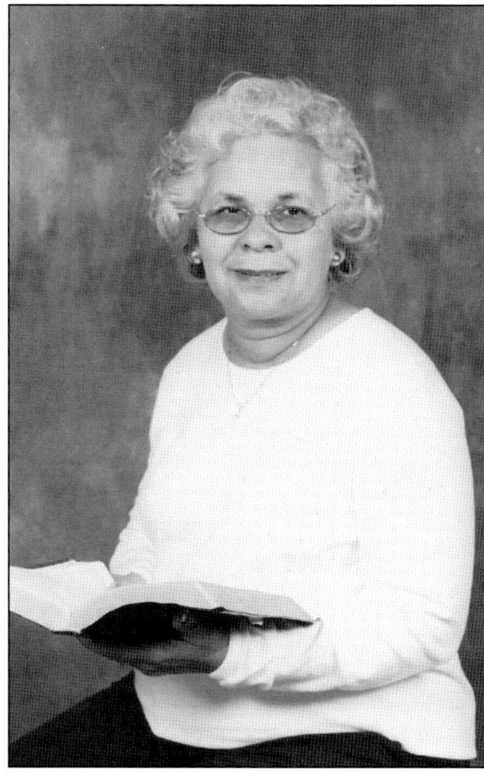

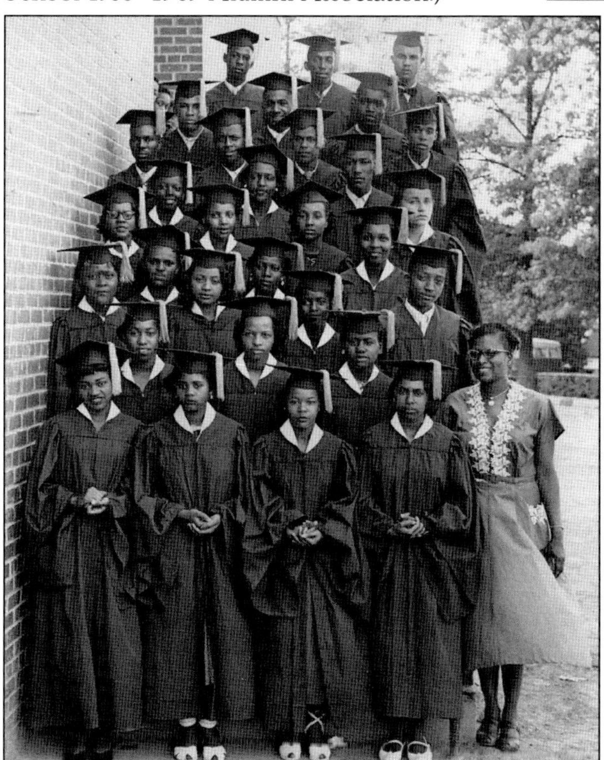

Class of 1951 included Gladys Glover, Hazel Williams, Alvester Siler, Bessie Lee, Mary Headen, Marcarida Headen, Kathrin Foxx, Annie Gladnes, Ruby Price, Martha Brooks, Katherine Siler, Fonnie Alston, Ben Marsh, Bernice Peoples, Margaret Lane, Ida Lee Johnson, Mary Siler, Dorothy Foxx, Louise Walden, Jennie Glover, Thurl Price, George Nettles, Grady Alston, Joseph Rodgers, Waddell Crutchfield, James Ashford, Wallace Mathews, Roland Brooke, Parker Price, and Bertha Joyner (teacher). (Courtesy of Madeline Foxx Moffitt.)

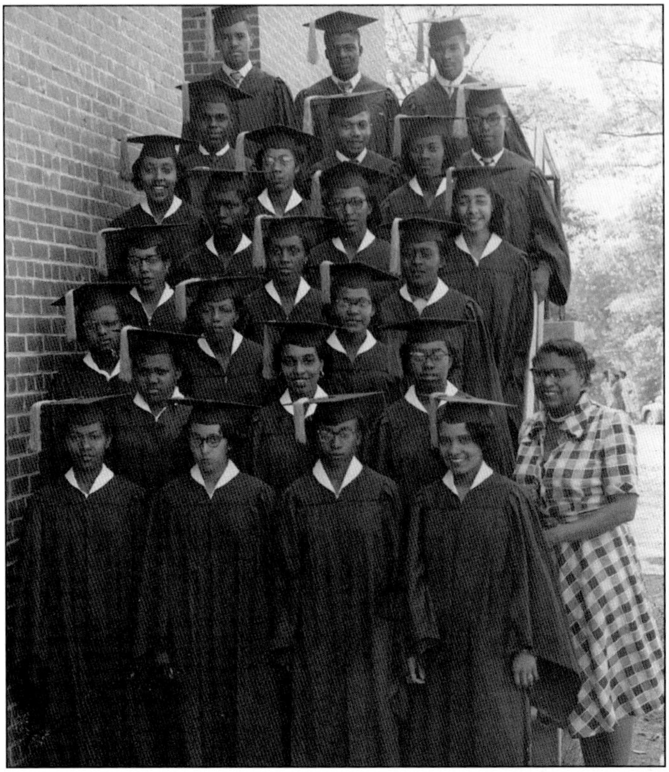

The class of 1953 included Curtis Johnson, Monroe Siler Jr., William "Billy Joe" Goins, William Moffitt, Edge Edwards, Charles Siler, Kathryn Womble, Elga Marsh, Beulah Newby, Virginia Ashford, Mary J. Horton, Madeline Foxx, Mozelle Price, Dorothy Lane, Ada Mae Degraffenreidt, Nancy Lee, Clarice Headen, Annie Cheek, Roberta Moffitt, and Bertha E. Joyner (teacher). (Courtesy of Madeline Foxx Moffitt.)

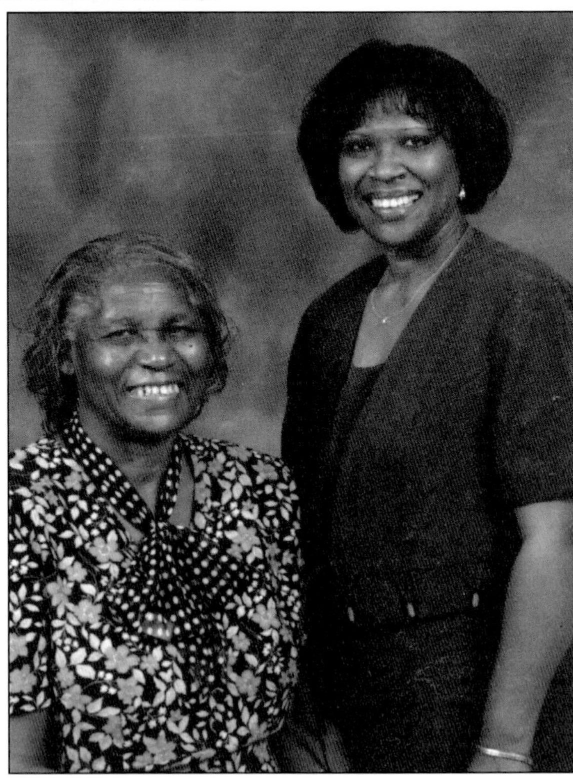

Celia R. DeGraffenreidt (standing), seen with her mother Virginia A. Foxx (seated), recalls being a part of the class of 1968 and a student of Chatham High School as the first of many students to integrate into Jordan Matthews High School. She stated, "It wasn't easy. There were riots, and it took a bit of blending, but eventually we all developed friendships." (Courtesy of Tonya Holland.)

Five

Sports and Recreation

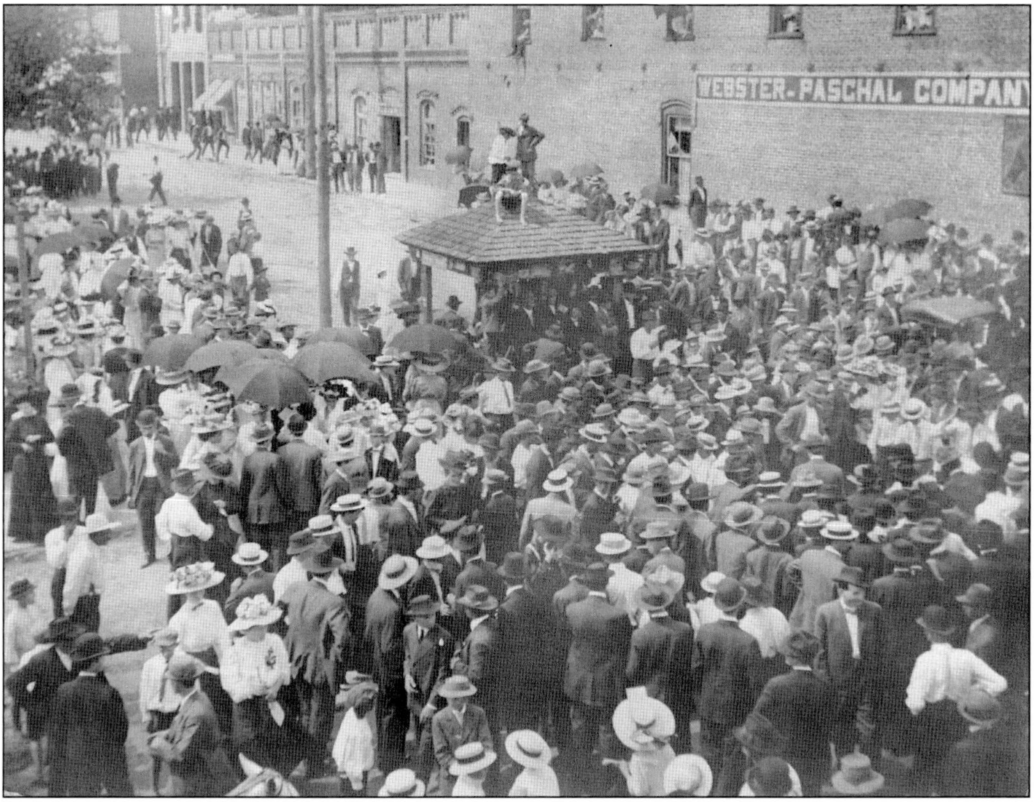

Siler City held many large, daylong celebrations, which drew crowds estimated at between 2,000 and 5,000 people. The street scene on Fourth of July around 1910 or 1911 shows a large crowd at the town well, which stood in front of what was then Buckner's Jewelry. The Webster-Paschal building on the right was at 101 East Raleigh Street.

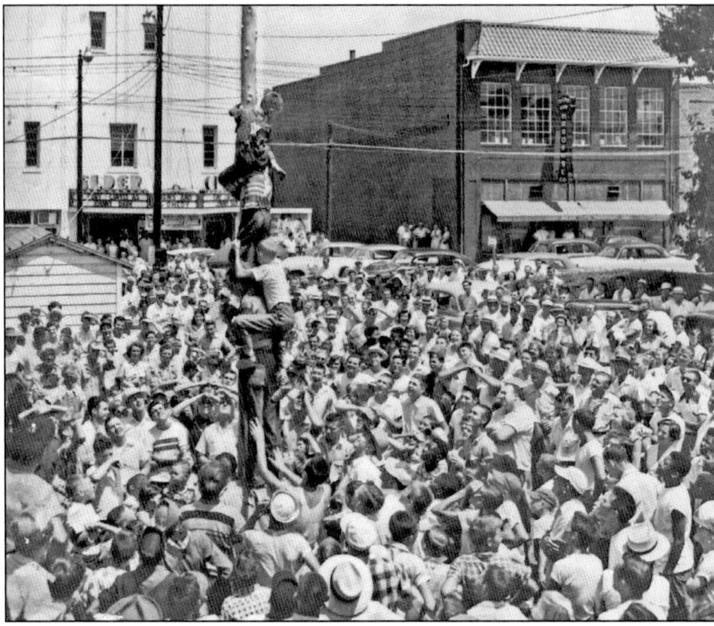

During the Fourth of July celebration in 1954, one of the activities most of the people looked forward to was climbing the greasy pole. The day's athletic events included a 100-yard dash, a sack race, a three-legged race, and the greased-pole climbing contest. A watch awaited the successful climber, but all attempts failed until just before sunset. The white building in the background is the Elder Theater.

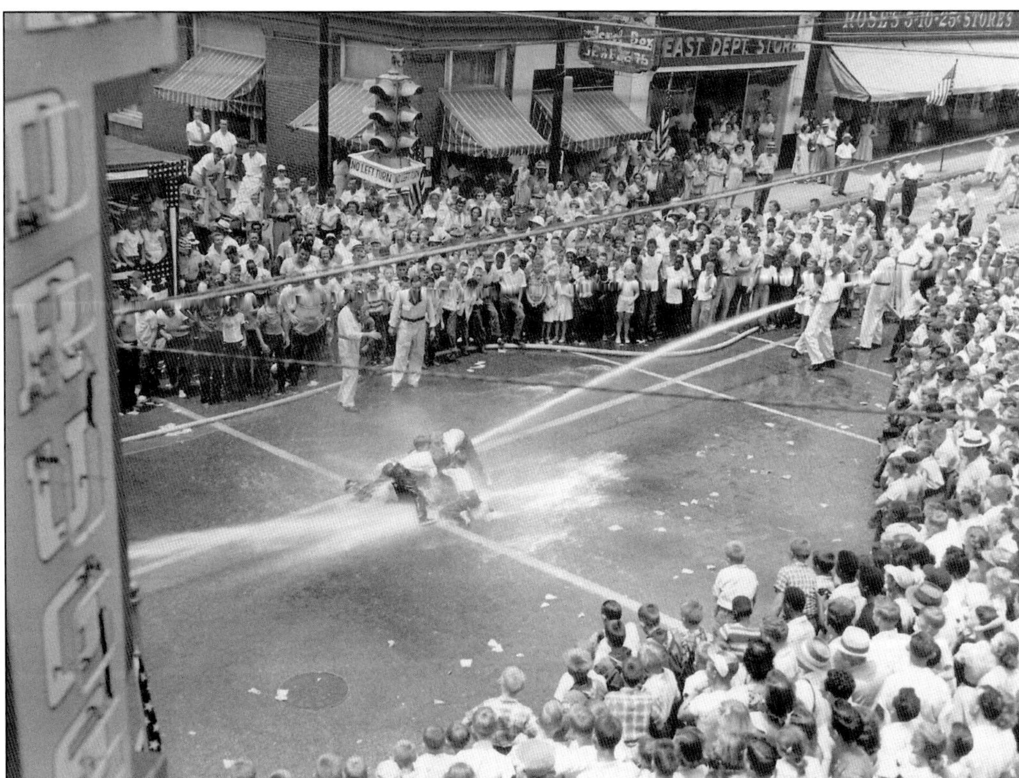

Greasing the pig for the 1907 Greasy Pig Race at the Siler City Fourth of July celebration was popular during that era. As seen in this photograph, during the celebrations of the 1950s and 1960s, the townspeople would grease a watermelon, and the town fireman would spray water while the pursuing boys would try to corral it.

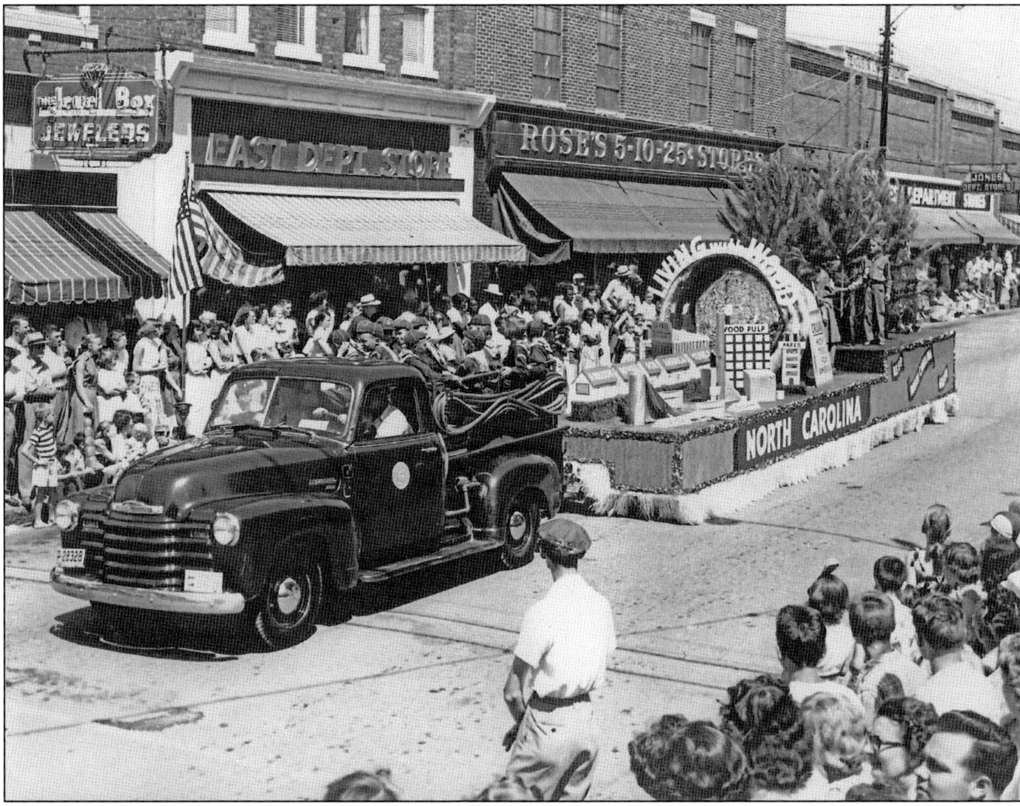

The Fourth of July celebrations in the 1950s also included a parade with beautifully crafted floats. This float, "Living with Wood from North Carolina," is pictured on Chatham Avenue in front of the Jewel Box Jewelers, East Department Store, Rose's 5-10-25¢ Stores, and Jones Department Store.

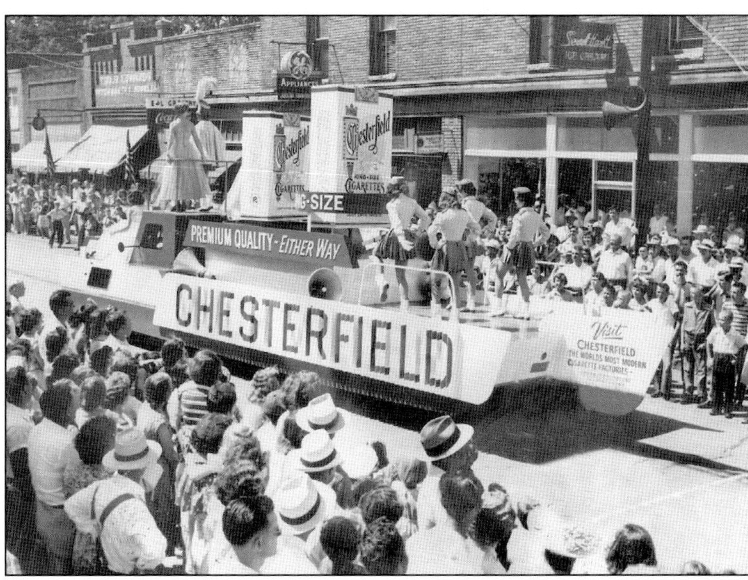

This 1950s Fourth of July Chesterfield Cigarette float travels on Chatham Avenue past, from left to right, Tod R. Edwards Watchmaker & Jeweler, E&L Grocery, GE Appliances, and Sealtest Ice Cream Shop.

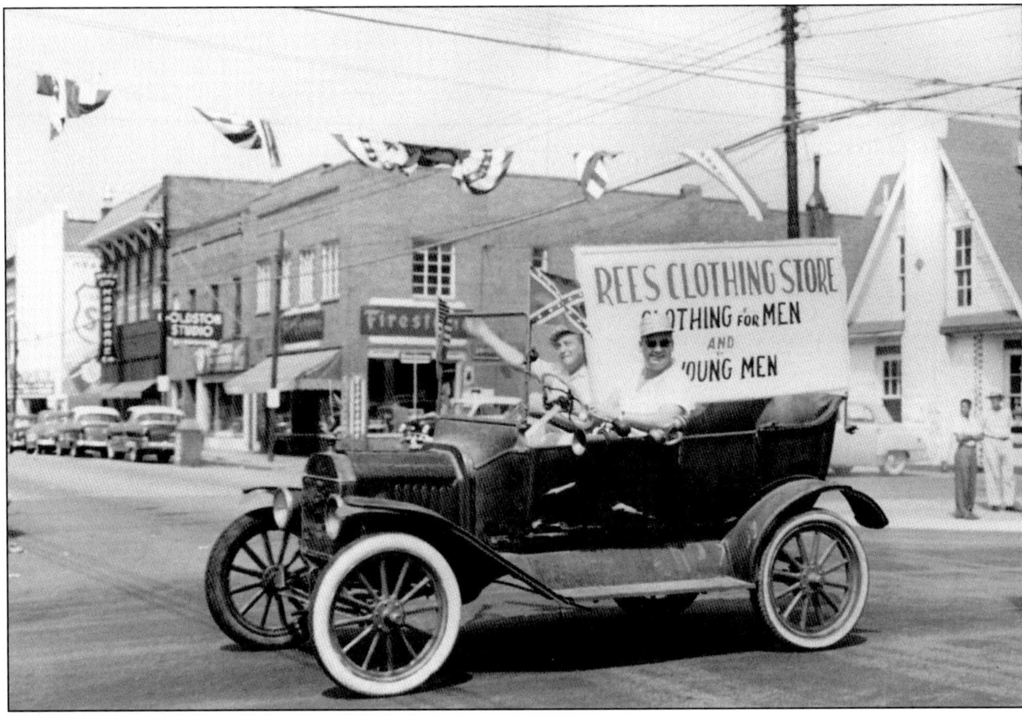

Riding in the 1950s Fourth of July–celebration car for Rees Clothing Store are Dr. George Pleasants (driving) and Sam Rees (riding shotgun). The buildings on the right are Firestone Tires, Goldston Studios, a hardware store, and the Elder Theater (white building).

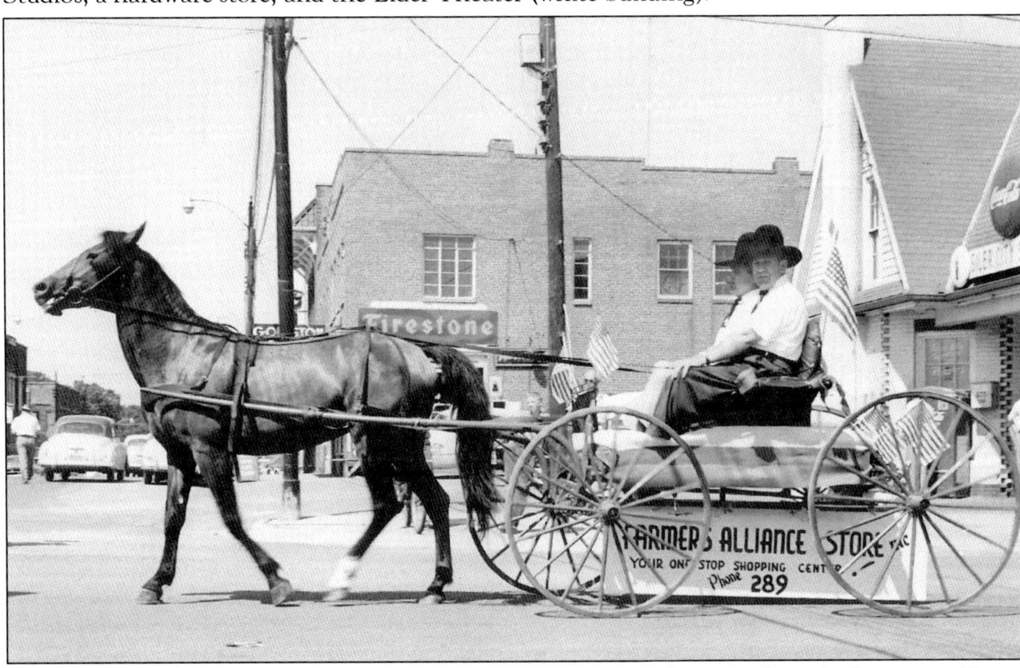

Riding in a 1950s Fourth of July horse-drawn wagon are Sam Clapp, guiding the horse, and Lester Murray, who worked for Farmers' Alliance Store: Siler City's one-stop shopping center with a three-digit phone number (289).

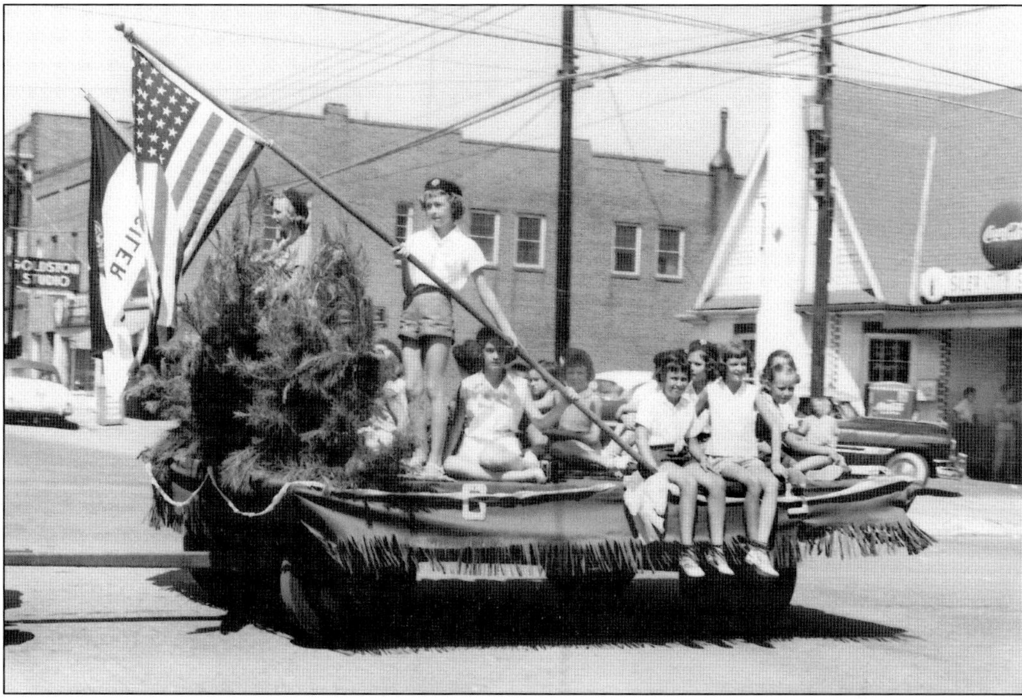

This 1950s Girl Scout troop rides in a Fourth of July celebration, holding the troop flag and the American flag.

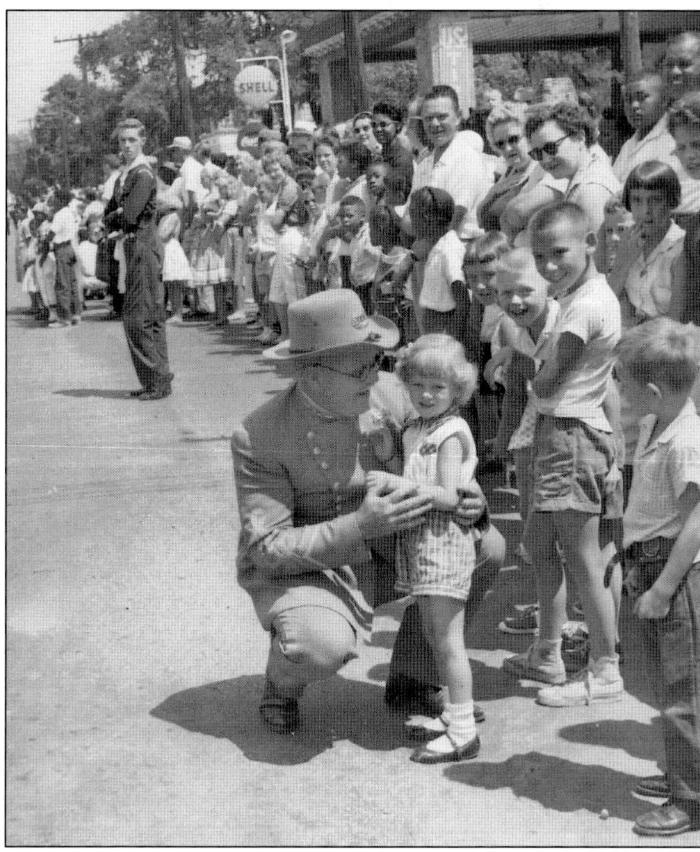

During this 1950s parade, one of the people who North Carolinians recognized instantly was Old Rebel of the *Old Rebel and Pecos Pete Show*. Old Rebel frequently participated in local parades in North Carolina.

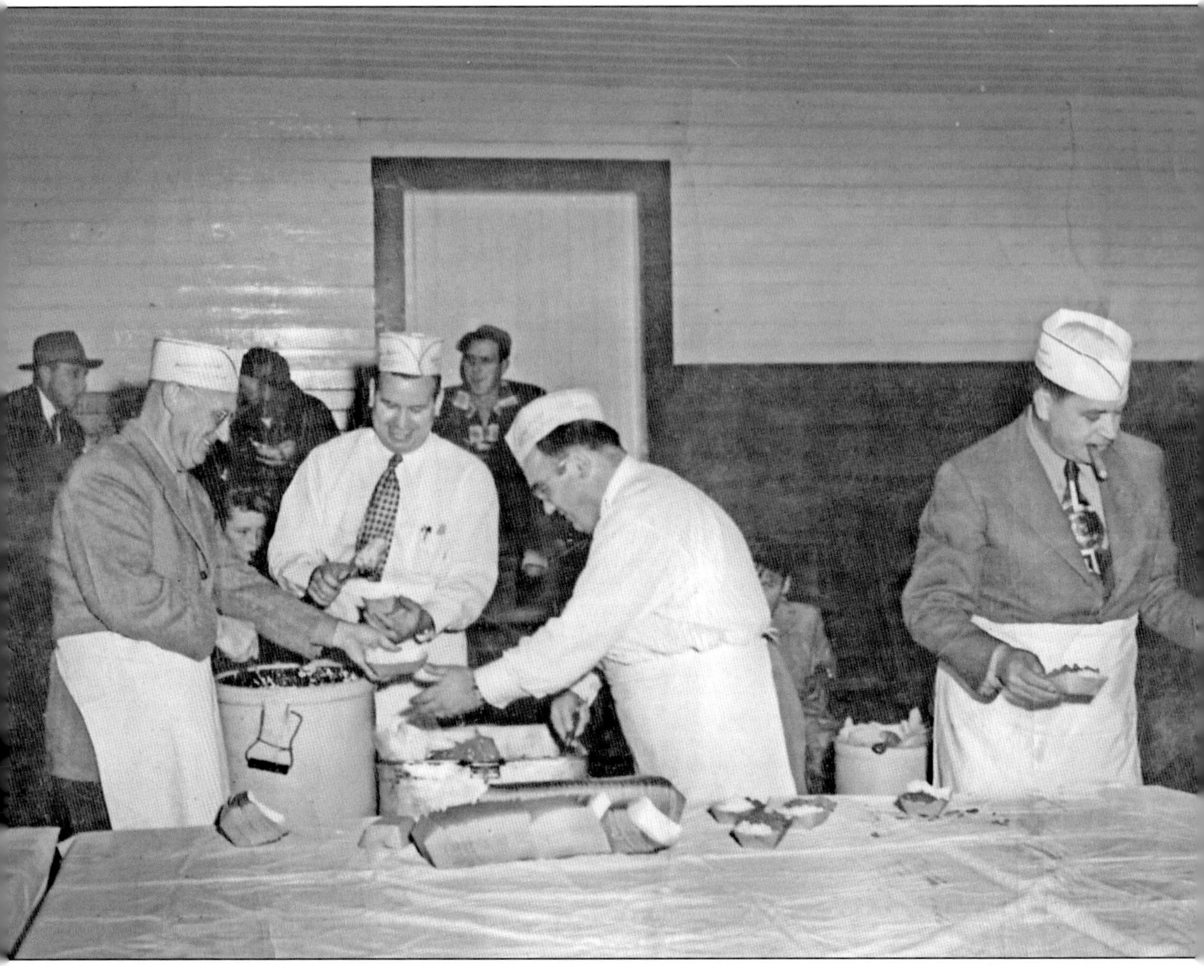

This is an early Rotary bazaar barbeque at the Paul Braxton gymnasium around 1960. Among those serving are John Bowers (second from the left) and Paul Johnson (third from left).

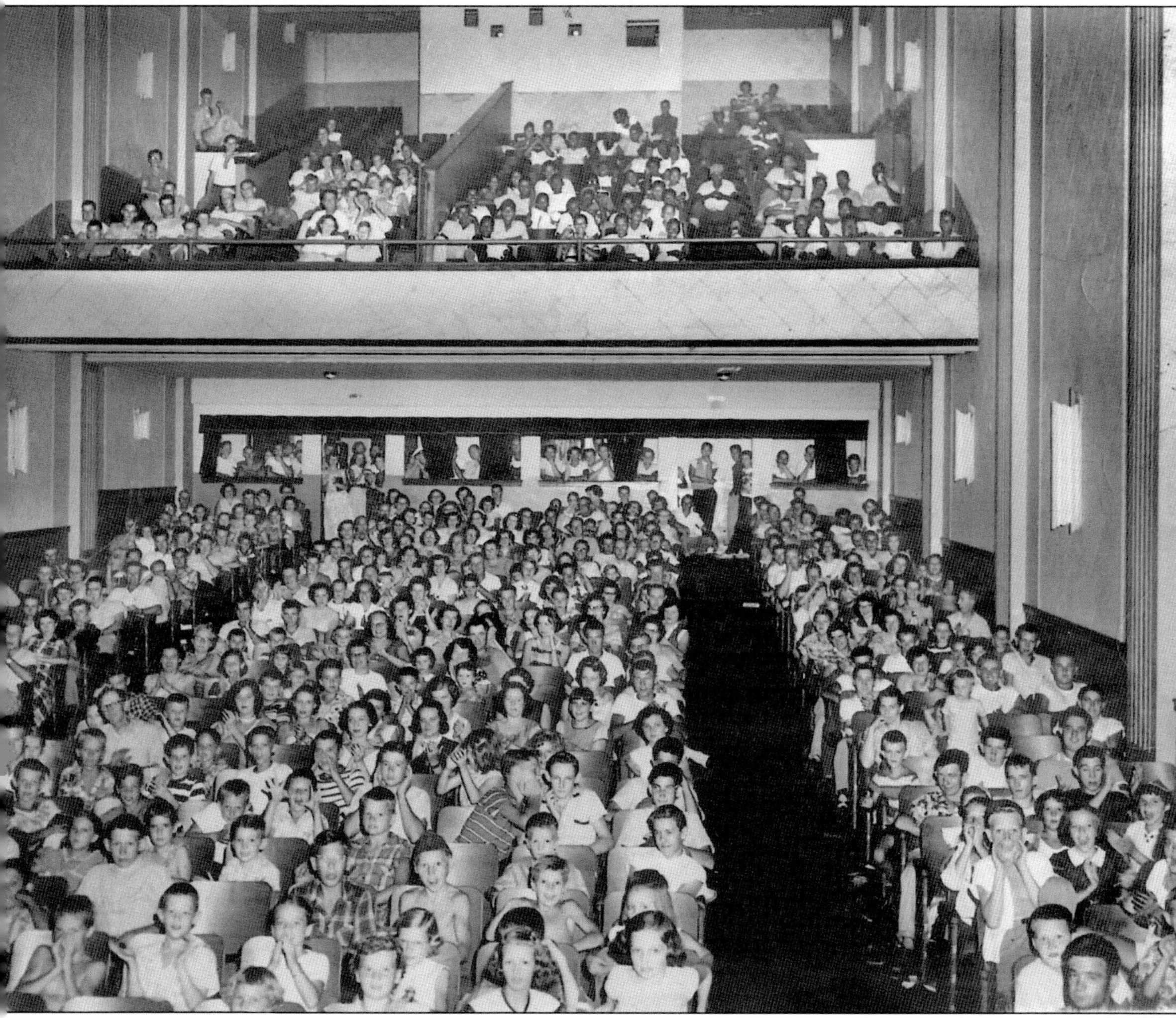

This photograph captures the interior of the Elder Theater on a hot summer day. The audience is watching a talent contest. Dickie Wright won this 1952 event with his clogging. The theater burned down in March 1962 in what was, according to the *Chatham News*, considered the worst fire in Siler City in 20 years. The building was completely gutted. A fireman and Richard Edwards (owner of the old Edwards Motor Company, now the site of the Chatham County Rescue Squad building) were coming out of the post office and spotted the smoke coming from the roof of the building. Edwards alerted the fire department, and surrounding stations responded, as did those from Liberty, Bonlee, Snow Camp, and Goldston.

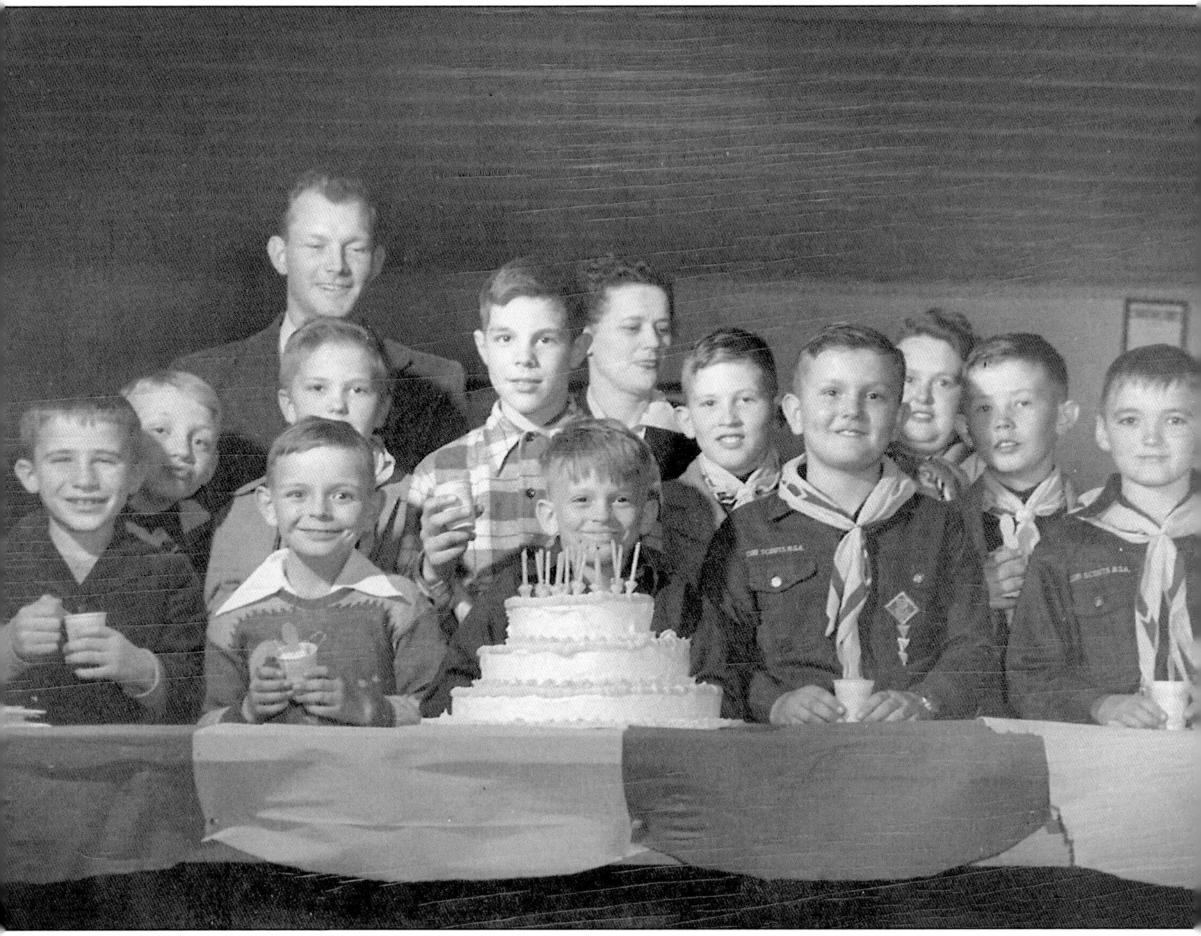

Here is the first Siler City Cub Scout troop of the 1950s. From left to right are (first row) David Harris, Jimmy Warford, Bill Patman, Charles Hicks, and Nelson Witt; (second row) unidentified, Dinky Vann, Ed Spence, Gary Stout, and Roy Stout; (third row) troop leaders Dr. Mott Blair, Ruth Buckner Johnson, and Mildred Hicks.

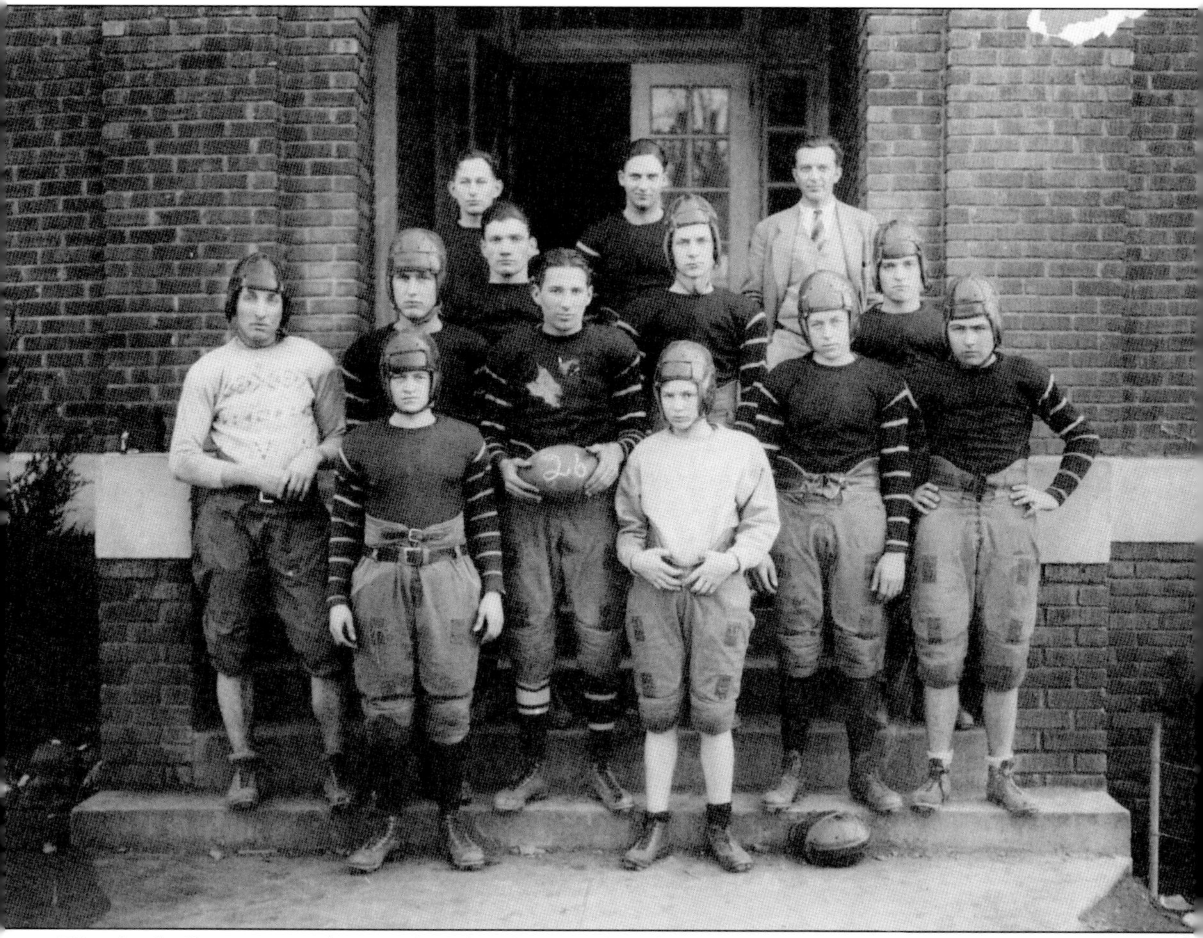

The football team stands outside Siler City High School during Career Days around 1926. From left to right are (first row) Joseph Johnson and Van ? ; (second row) Hugh Peoples, Ed Ferguson, David ? , Joe Backney, Keffer Wary, Wade Miller (captain), Joseph John, and Karl ? ; (third row) John ? , unidentified, and J. Wade Siler (coach). (Courtesy of Farmers' Alliance Store and Nancy Tysor.)

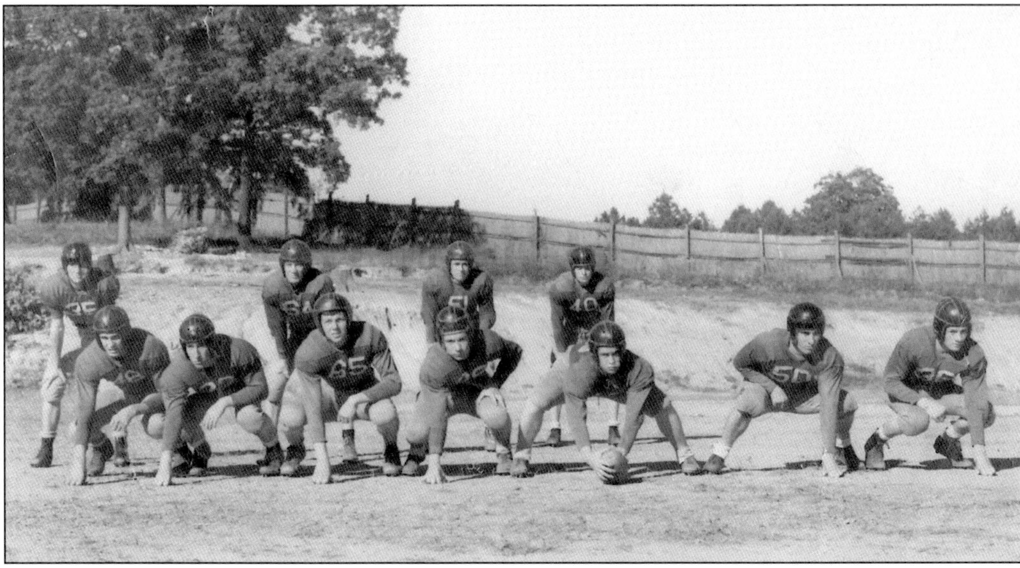

This team poses for the camera around 1945. From left to right are (first row) Emerson, Holt, Jordan, Moffit, Kan, Holt, and Allred; (second row) McLaughton, Mclead, Siler, and Harris.

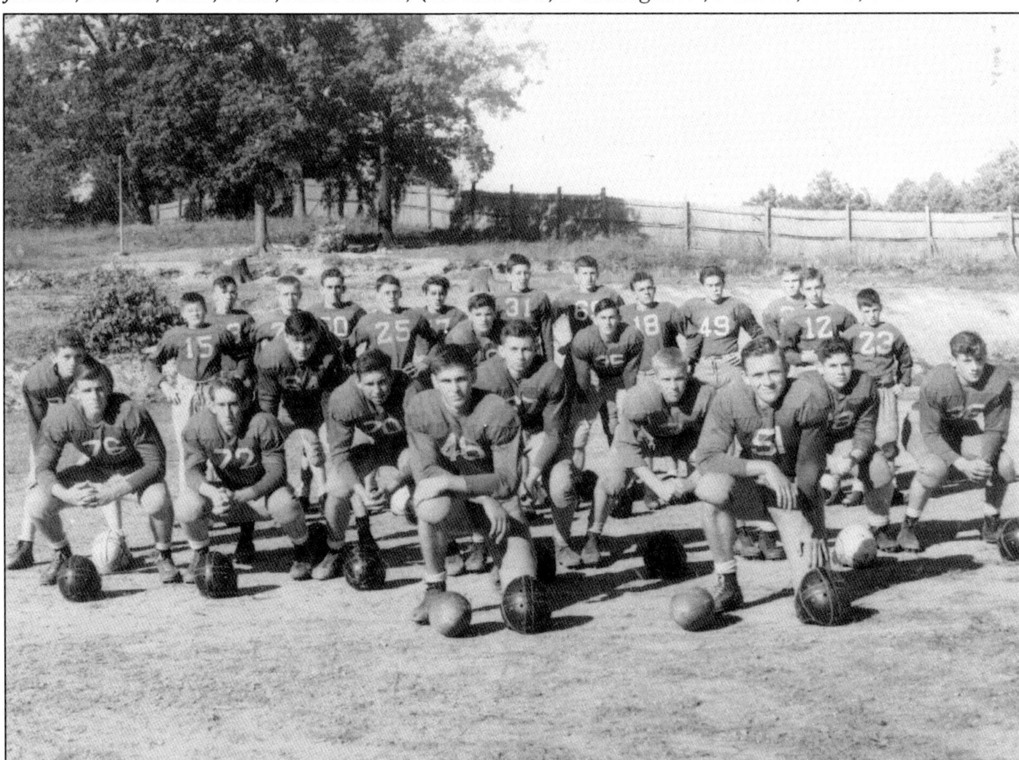

Members of the c. 1947 Siler City High School football team pictured here include Frank Fields, Milo Holt, Billy Phillips, Hudson Emerson, Richard Siler, Sandy Siler, Polly Ferguson, Jack Allred, Herman Kennedy, Bobby McLaughlin, Henry Siler, Billy Holt, Dennis Stone, Demphy McCloud, Jack Bolin, Norman Jordan, Richard Caviness, Jessie Milliken, James McManess, ? Wicker, and Robert Emerson. (Courtesy of Farmers' Alliance Store and Nancy Tysor.)

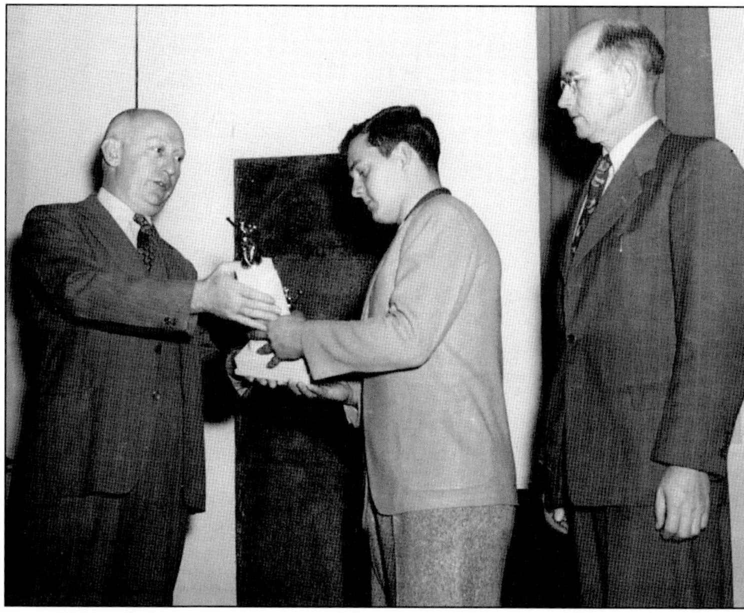

Al Resch, the owner of the *Chatham News*, presents the Most Valuable Player football award to Richard Caviness around 1950. Paul Braxton Jr., teacher, coach, and principal of Siler City High School, stands next Caviness. Paul Braxton Elementary School was named after Paul Braxton Jr. (Courtesy of Farmers' Alliance Store and Nancy Tysor.)

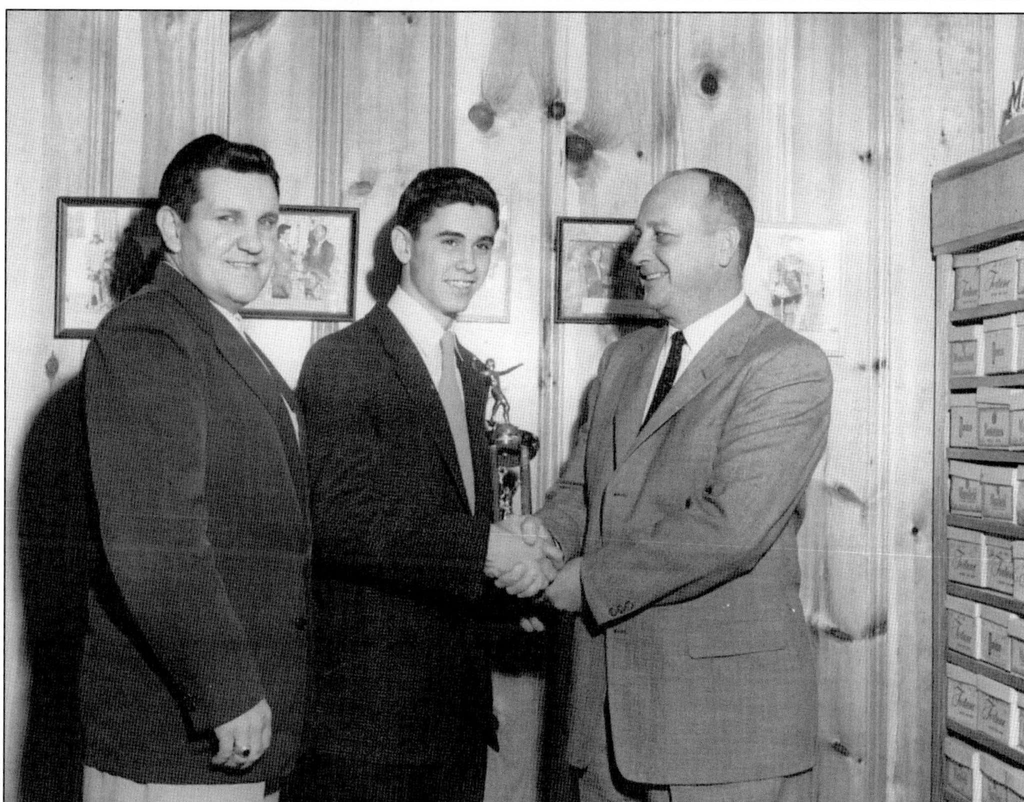

Here, the award for Most Valuable Player is presented to Thomas Jackson Emerson, co-captain and end of the 1956 Siler City High School football team. The presentation is being made by Fred Poston, a math teacher, principal, and prominent citizen (left), and Sam Reese, owner of Rees Clothing Store (right). (Courtesy of Farmers' Alliance Store and Nancy Tysor.)

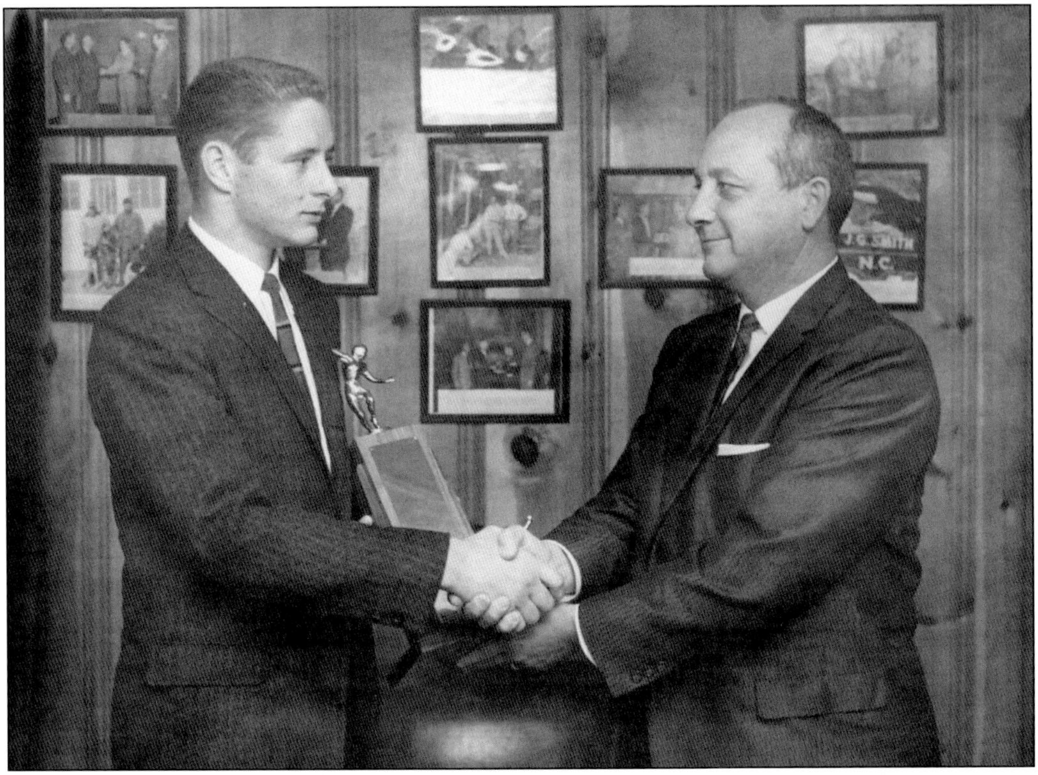

Jerry Ward (left) is receiving the Rees football trophy as the outstanding player for the 1958 season of the Jordan Matthews High Blue Phantoms. Sam Rees, the donor of the trophy, is making the presentation. (Courtesy of Farmers' Alliance Store and Nancy Tysor.)

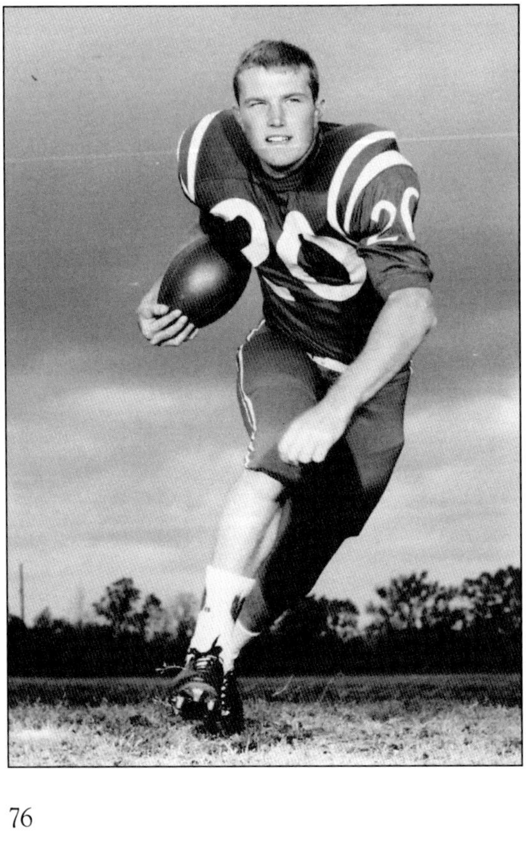

Roy Lee Marley, the son of Mr. and Mrs. Roy Marley, was the winner of the 1959 Sam Rees Most Valuable Player trophy and played halfback for Duke University from 1961 to 1964. (Courtesy of Farmers' Alliance Store and Nancy Tysor.)

Robert Headen is shown receiving the Sam Rees Trophy. The award is given annually to the member on the Jordan-Matthews High School football team that is voted Most Valuable Player by his teammates. Headen played halfback on the 1960 team. (Courtesy of Farmers' Alliance Store and Nancy Tysor.)

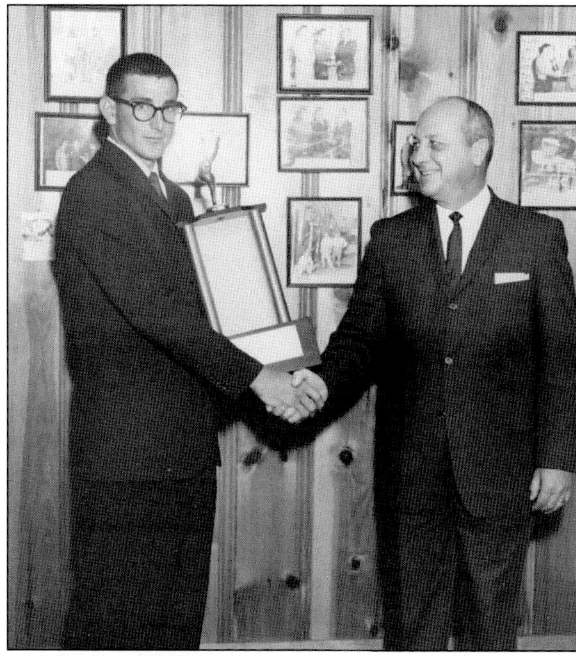

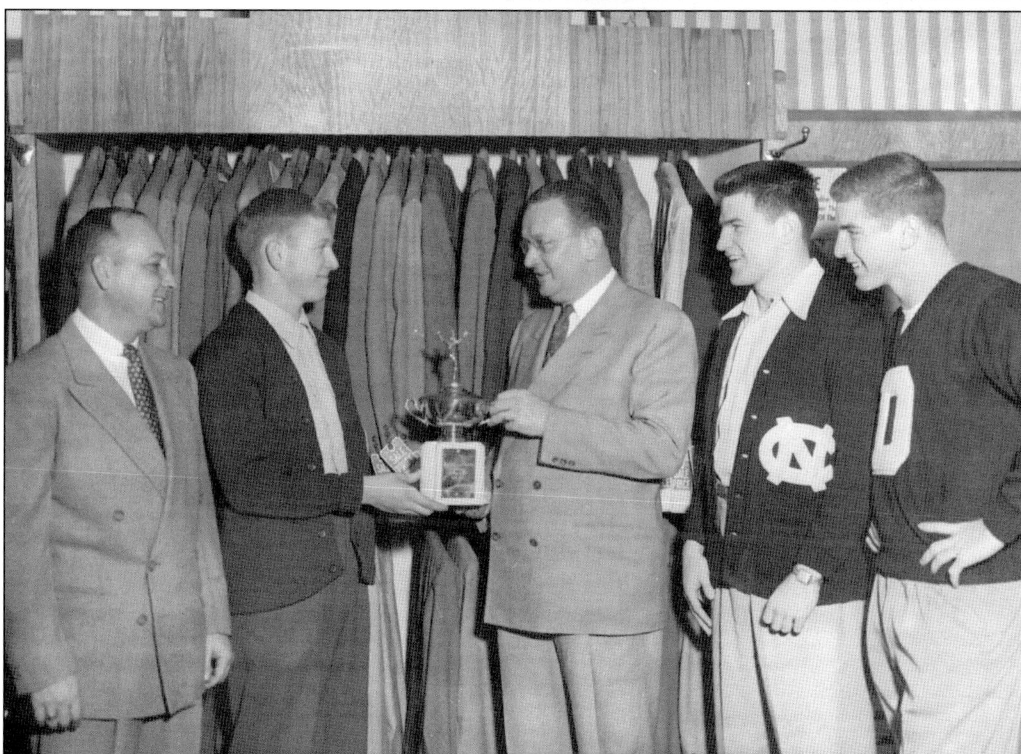

Paul Gyles Braxton (second from left) is pictured receiving the Most Valuable Player award. Also pictured are, from left to right, Sam Rees, Mayor J.B. Wood (presenting the Sam Rees trophy), Albert Long (University of North Carolina quarterback), and Worth Lutz (Duke quarterback). (Courtesy of Farmers' Alliance Store and Nancy Tysor.)

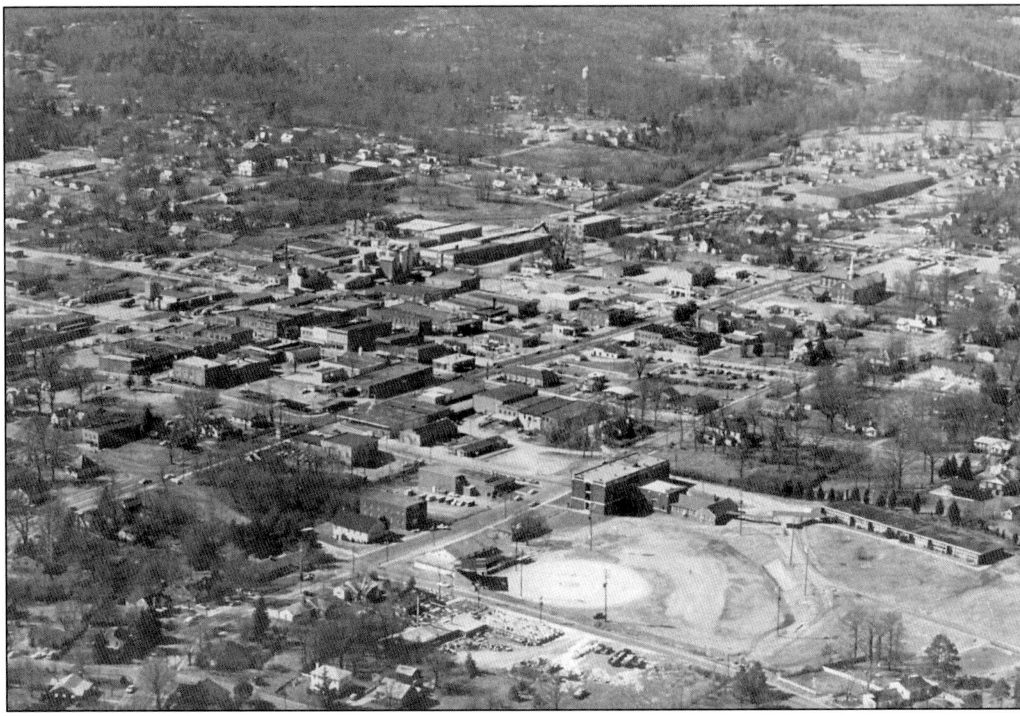

An aerial view of Siler City shows the baseball stadium. Siler City is very supportive of local athletic clubs and area middle and high school athletic programs.

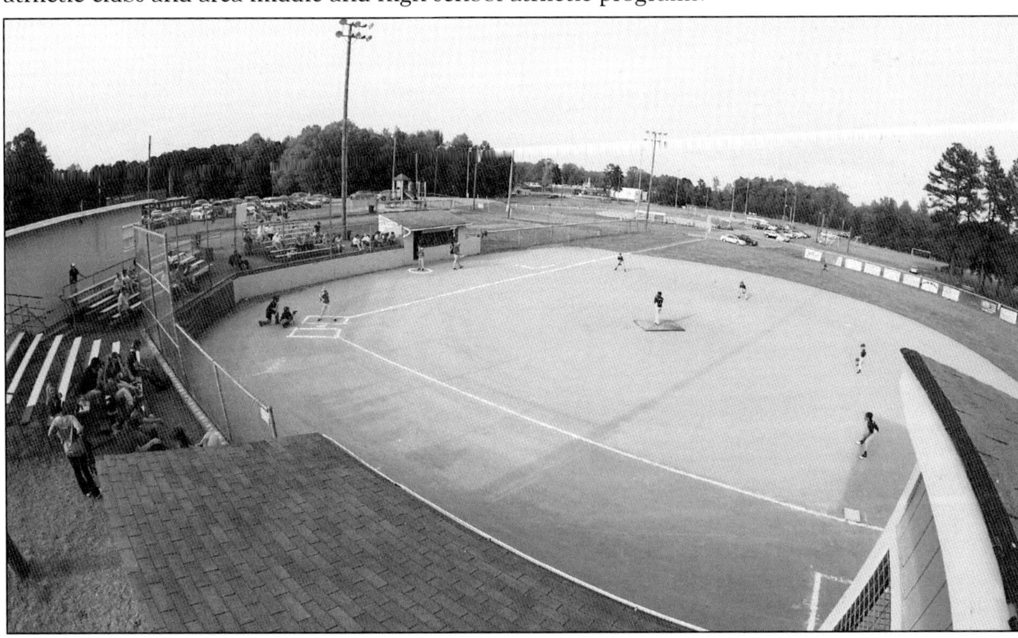

On April 5, 2013, the Siler City newsletter "Snap Shot" read, "Paul Braxton Park renovations dig in: renovations will include a new regulation-sized soccer field, a new concrete outdoor basketball court with new goals, and new grading for the baseball infield." Renovation partnerships were between the Chatham Soccer League, the Oak Foundation, and the Town of Siler City. (Photograph by Jeff Davis, courtesy of the Town of Siler City.)

This is a group photograph of the 1900–1901 Siler City Institute baseball team. Pictured are, from left to right, (first row) ? Smith, Fred W. Hadley, and Slocum R. Edwards; (second row) Frank R. Wrenn, M.W. Duncan, Jeter J. Hackney Jr., H. Grady Dorsett, and Thomas H. Siler; (third row) Kearney A. Buckner, Walter B. Owen (manager), T.V. Riggsbee, and F.D. Whitehead.

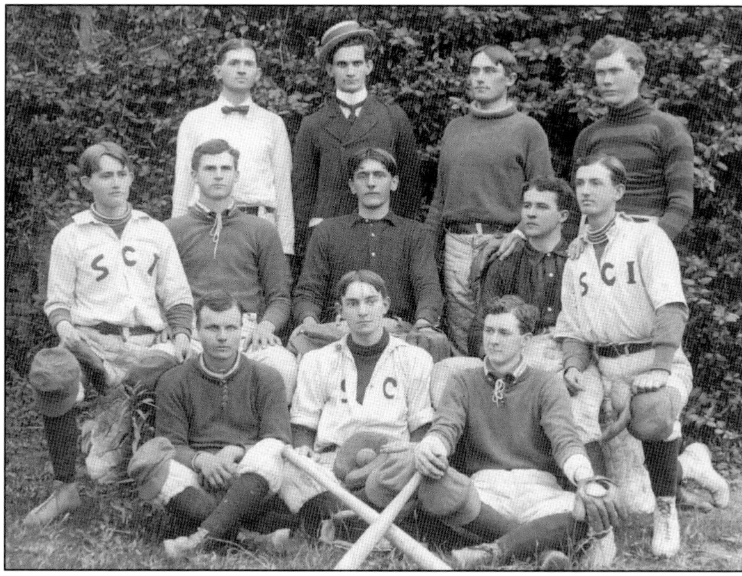

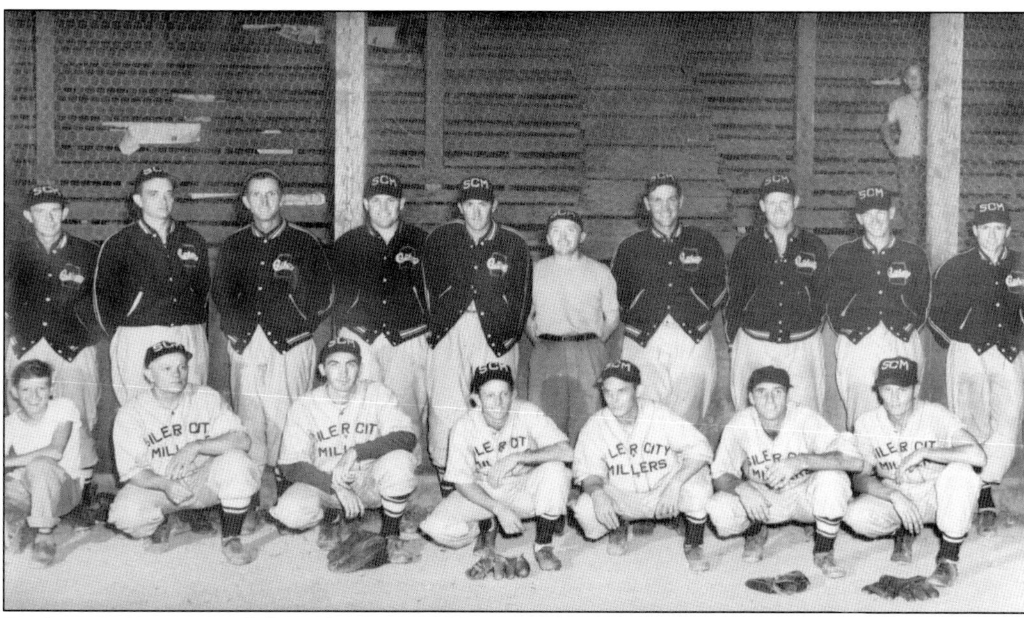

In this 1940s image of the Siler City Millers are, from left to right, (first row) Leon Buckner, Randolph Bucker, Bill Roberson, Winfred Buckner, Howard Jenkins, John P. Roach, and Earl Synder; (second row) Erwin Poe, Ossie Buckner, "Potsy" Curtis, Clyde Smith, Reitzel Payne, Obbie Budd, Norman Payne, Robert Dickson, Billy J. Daurity, and Bill Snyder; not present is Pete Brewer. The person in the back, behind the post, is Obbie Budd's son Mike Budd. The team told him he could not be in the photograph, so he hid behind the post and popped out just as the team was taking the shot.

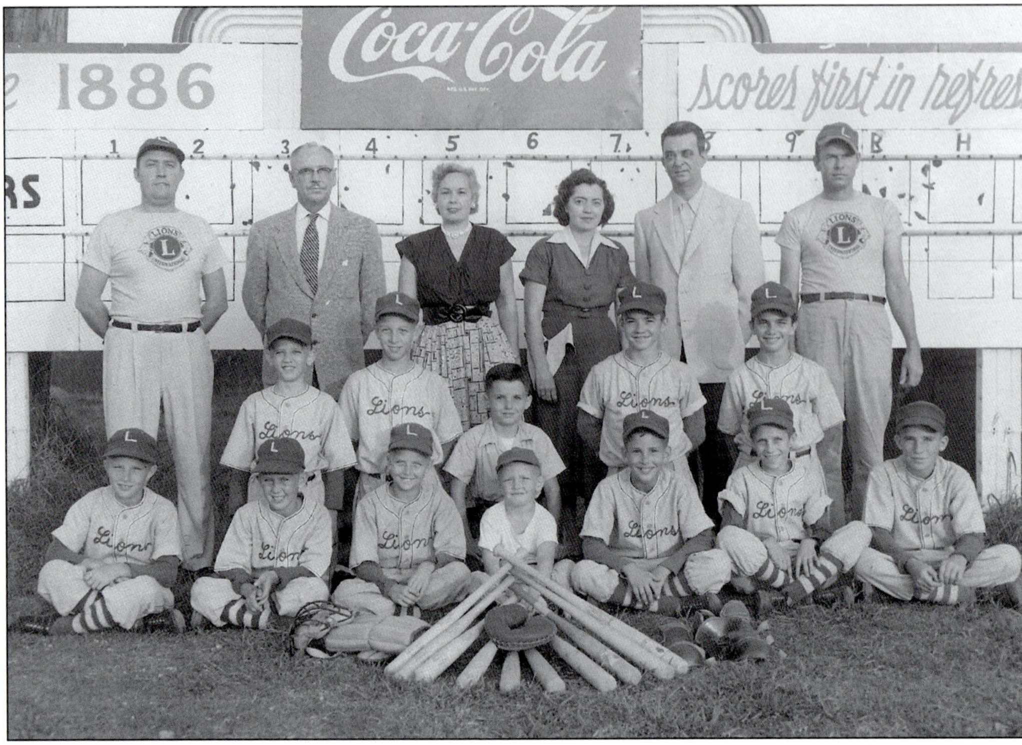

The Lions Club served youth in Siler City during the 1940s by supporting scholarships, recreation, and mentoring programs. Some of the supporters are pictured here in the third row: from left to right, they are two unidentified men, Doris Wrenn, Ruth and Ozzie Buckner, and unidentified.

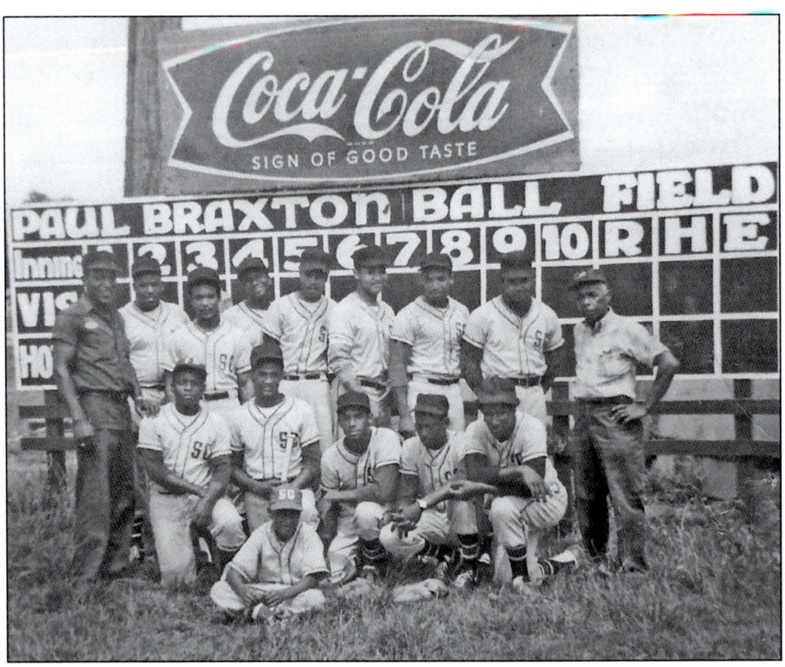

The Siler City baseball team, pictured in the 1960s, included, from left to right, (first row) Byron Horton; (second row) Bobo Pearson, Tyree "Newby" Horton, Larry Price, Thomas Horton, and Joe Goins, (third row) Tyree Horton, Clyde Fox, ? Strickland, Charles Beck, Earnest Marsh, Frankie Farrar, William "Bud" Price, Johnnie Johnson, and William Price.

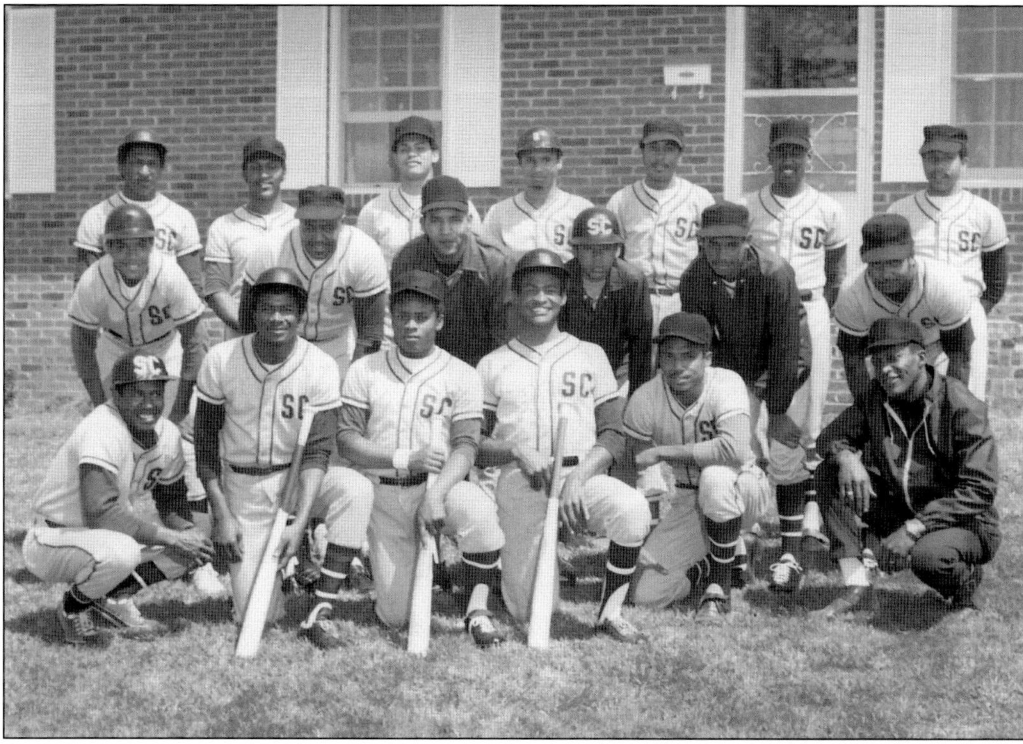

Another Siler City baseball team is shown in the 1960s. Jackie Horton is second from the left in the third row, and Tyree Horton Sr. is on the far right in the first row.

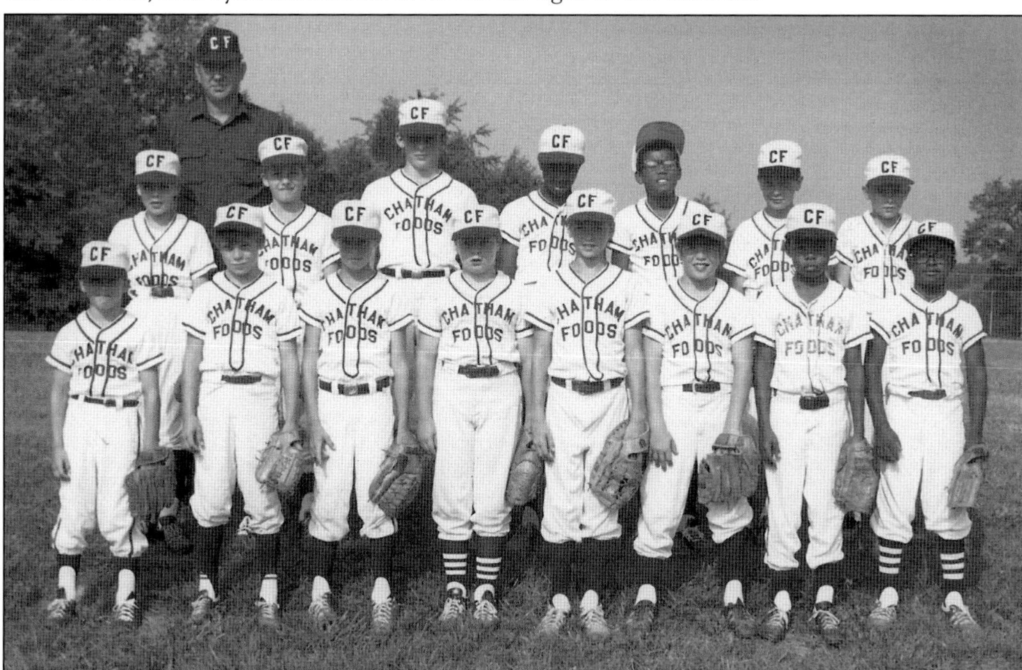

Chatham Foods represented a Little League baseball team from Siler City. Chatham Foods provided a stable payroll and made substantial contributions to the economic health of the community.

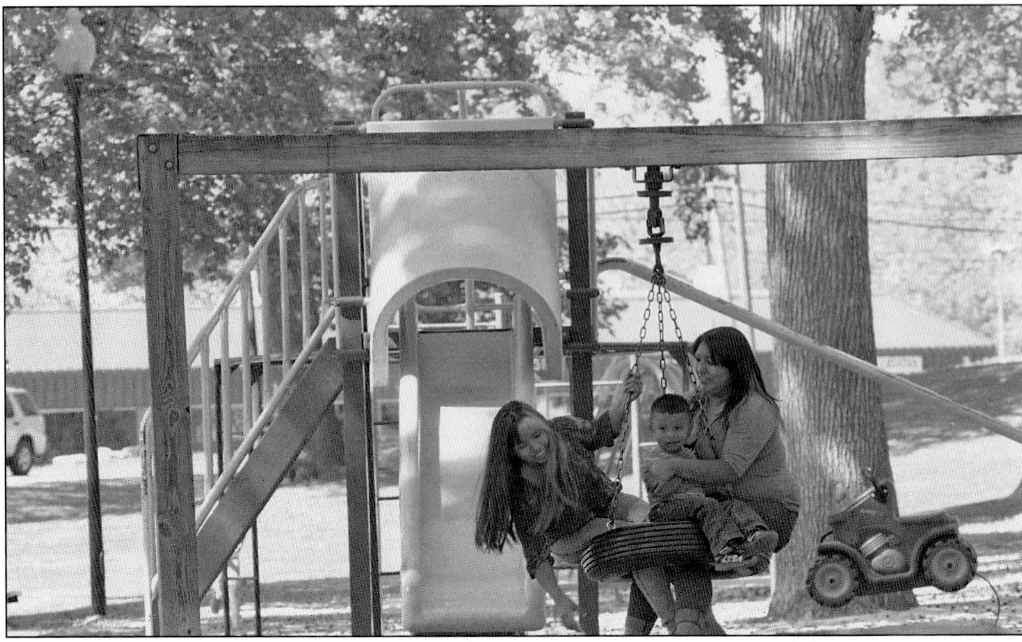

Siler City parks include Boling Lane, Washington Avenue, Bray Park (oldest) and Bray Park Pool, Paul Braxton (named after the principal of Paul Braxton Elementary School), Landrus Siler (named after a longtime post office employee), and Ernest Ramsey (named after the principal of Chatham High School, formerly Chatham County Training School). (Photograph by Jeff Davis, courtesy of the Town of Siler City.)

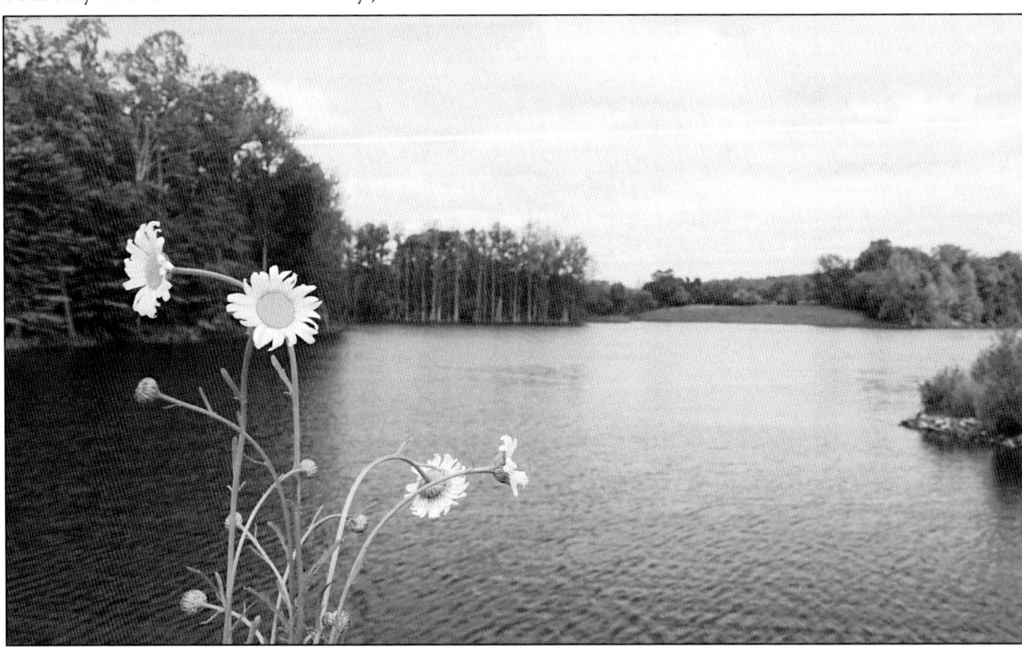

Siler City lakes and creeks include City Lake, Rocky River, Loves Creek, and Tick Creek, all good for water sports and fishing. Bear Creek is approximately nine miles outside of Siler City, and the campground at Deep River is approximately 16 miles from Siler City. (Photograph by Jeff Davis, courtesy of the Town of Siler City.)

Six

Law Enforcement and Municipalities

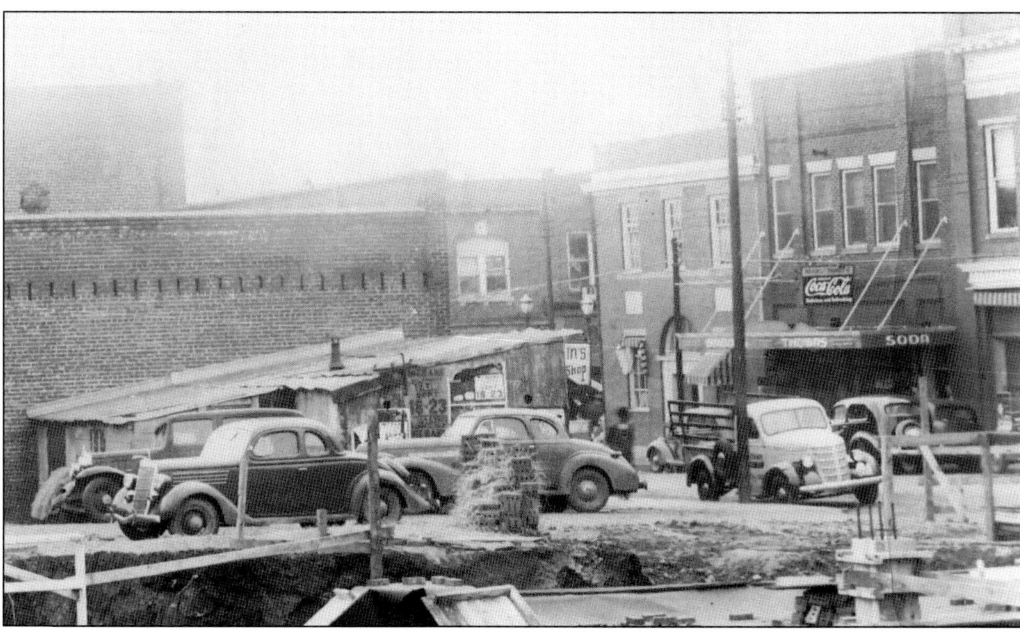

In preparation for an agricultural fair to be held on December 1–2, 1887, at Siler City, town authorities built what was described as a "commodious calaboose or lockup." By 1913, the small wooden structure with the Mebane fair announcement on it was in dilapidated condition. A new brick building was then completed, which served from 1917 to 1927.

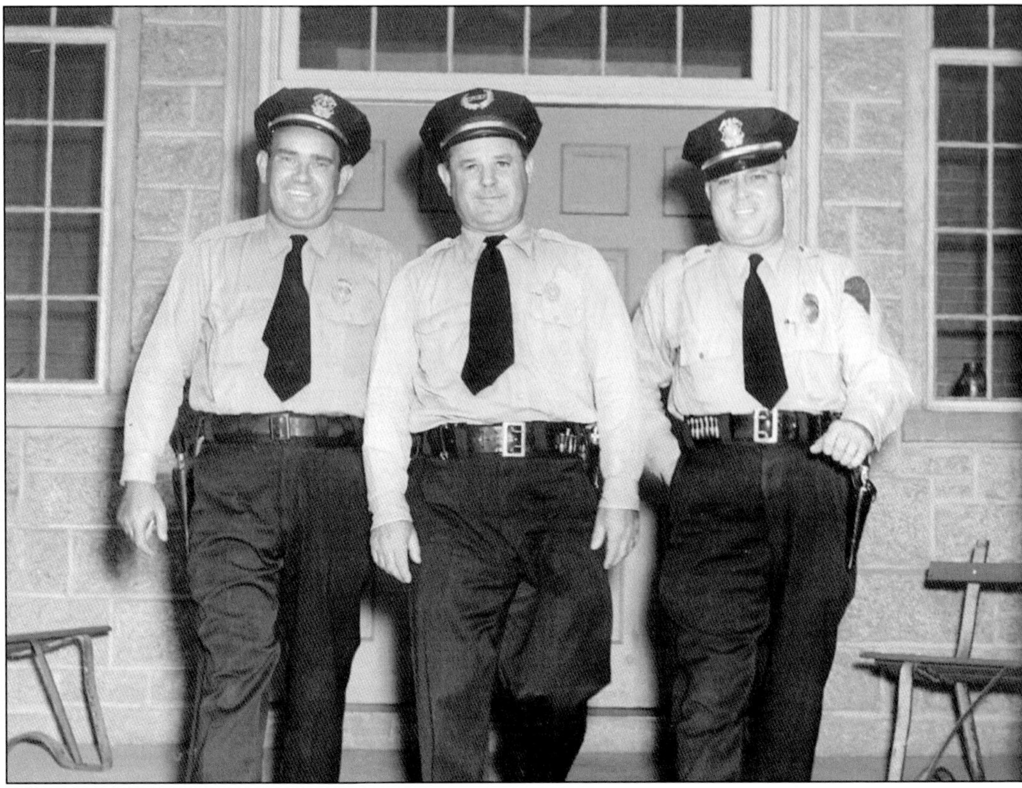

The Siler City Police force during the 1950s included LeRoy Pittman (left), ? Kimball (right), and Chief June Moody. They are standing in front of the new combination municipal and fire department building located at 311 North Second Avenue. Work on this building was underway by January 1939.

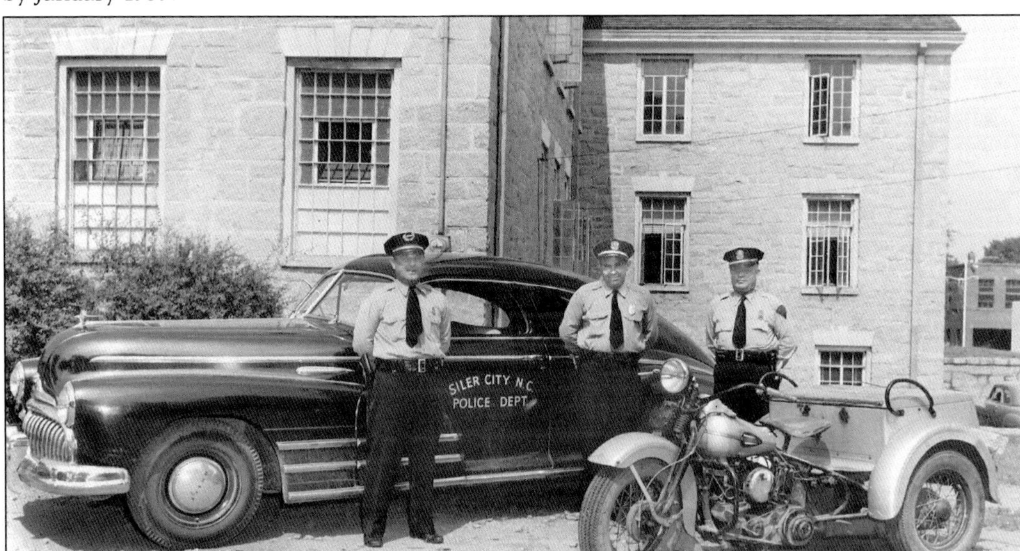

Pictured outside the city hall, which was ready for occupancy by late September 1940, are the first official Siler City Police Department police car (a 1947 or 1948 Buick) and motorcycle.

Gary T. Tyson was appointed chief of police in Siler City in February 2007 in the new police station. Chief Tyson had served 15 years with the Sanford Police Department and four years with the North Carolina Department of Corrections. Tyson and his wife, Kimberly, have three daughters: Ashly, Carrington, and Alexis. (Courtesy of Chief Gary T. Tyson.)

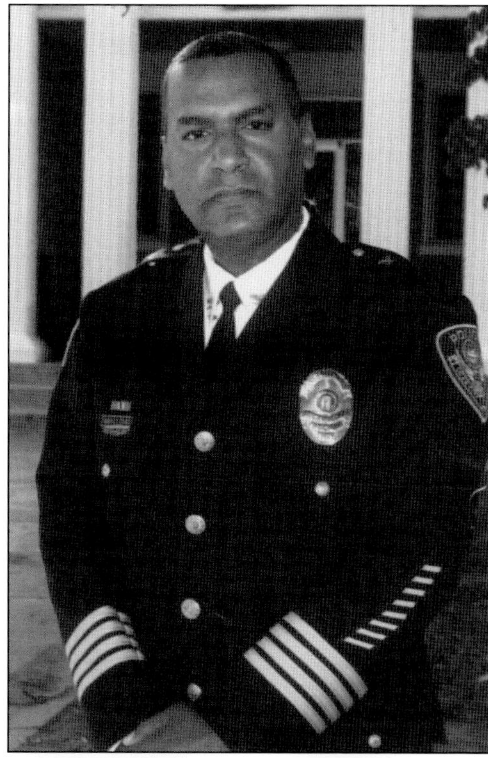

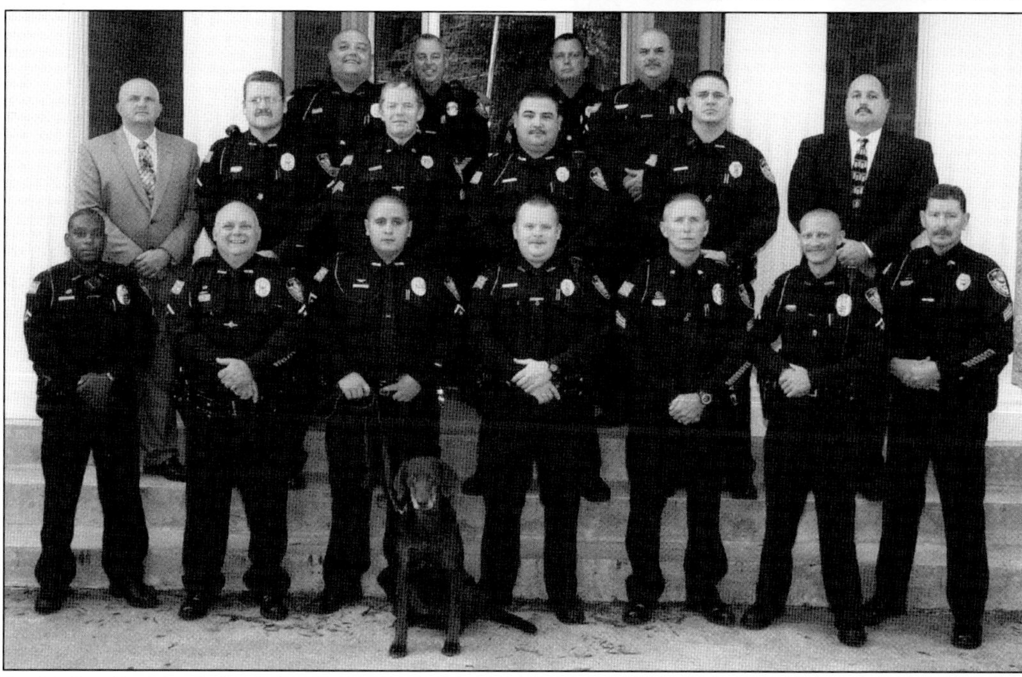

In 2012, officers of the Siler City Police Department included James Davis, Dean Johnson, Tyler Bridges, k-9 Raider, Brandon Kidd, Jimmy Bowden, Josh Moore, Larry Meadows, Shorty Johnson, Jonathan Murray, Jeff Griffin, Anthony Norton, Jacob Miles, Jay Underwood, Joe Moody, Rick Merritt, E.J. Barwick, and Todd Berry. (Courtesy of Chief Gary T. Tyson.)

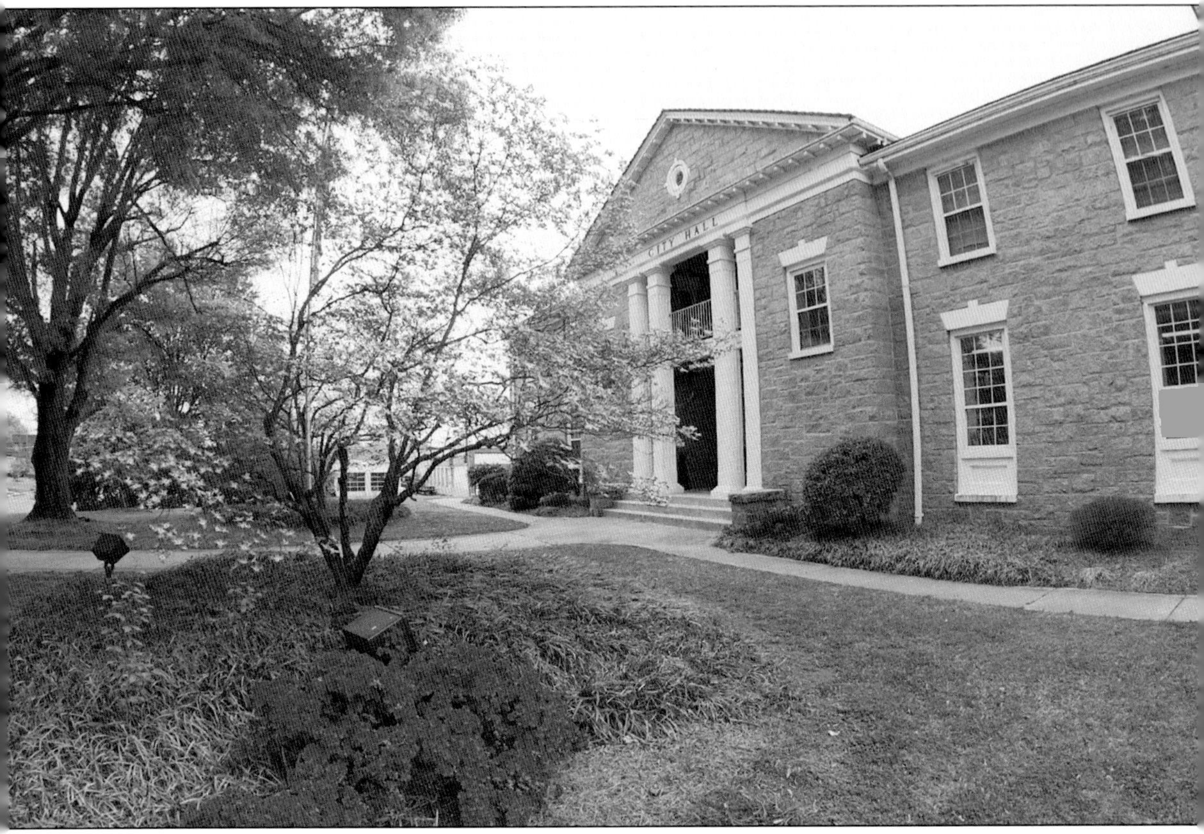

The granite used to build city hall came from a quarry located eight miles west of Siler City in Randolph County. The official dedication ceremonies were held on November 11, 1941. (Photograph by Jeff Davis, courtesy of the Town of Siler City.)

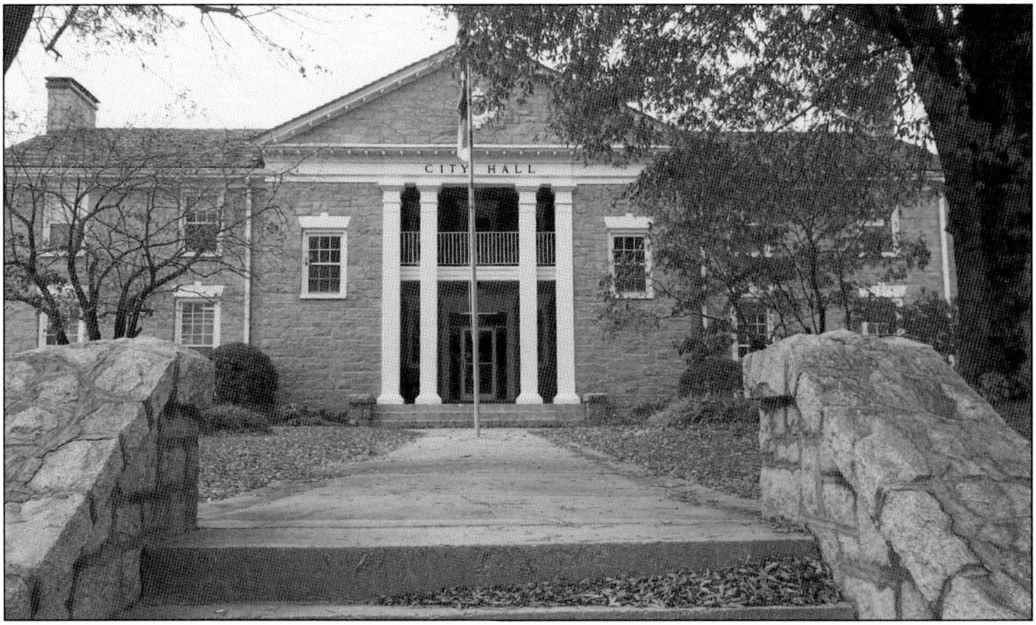

Inside city hall is the administrative head of Siler City government: town manager Bryan Thompson. The offices of Public Works director Terry Green, planning director Jack Meadows, Parks & Recreation director Donald Dones, building codes administrator Charlie McLaurin, Public Works & Utilities, and the Siler City License Plate Agency are among those also located in the building. (Photograph by the author.)

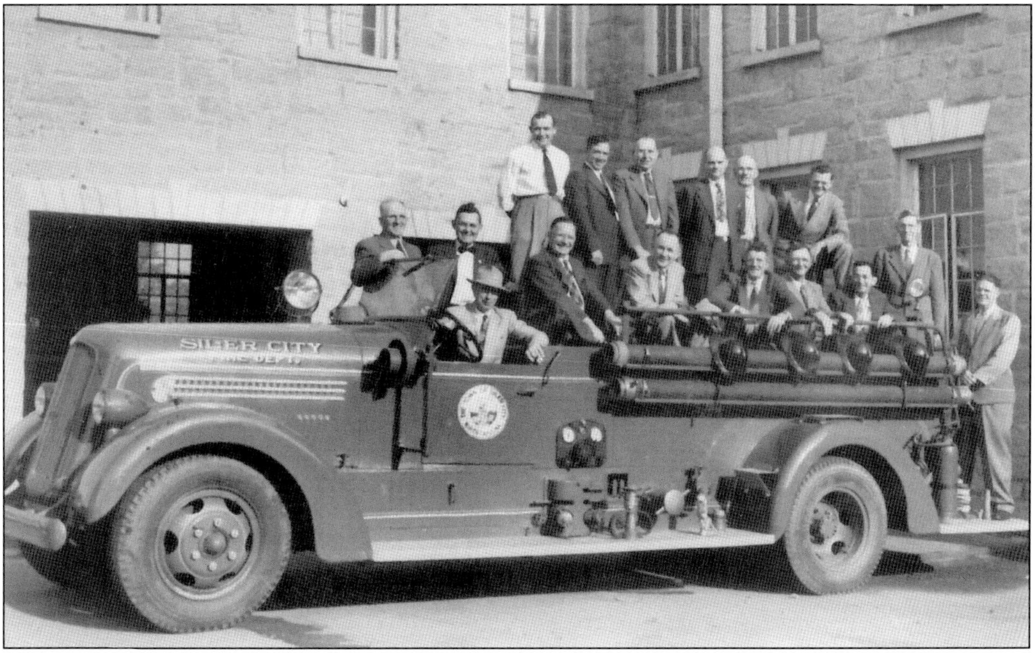

The town's first fire truck was delivered in October 1926. In this image, P.F. Reitzel sits in the driver's seat. Also pictured are, from left to right, (first row) three unidentified men, Col. Elton Stout, Ralph Blair, Randolph Lane, Wade Durham, Dewey Fox, and unidentified; (second row) unidentified, Andrew Burns, Ed Blair, unidentified, Ott Curtis, and Elwood Sharpe.

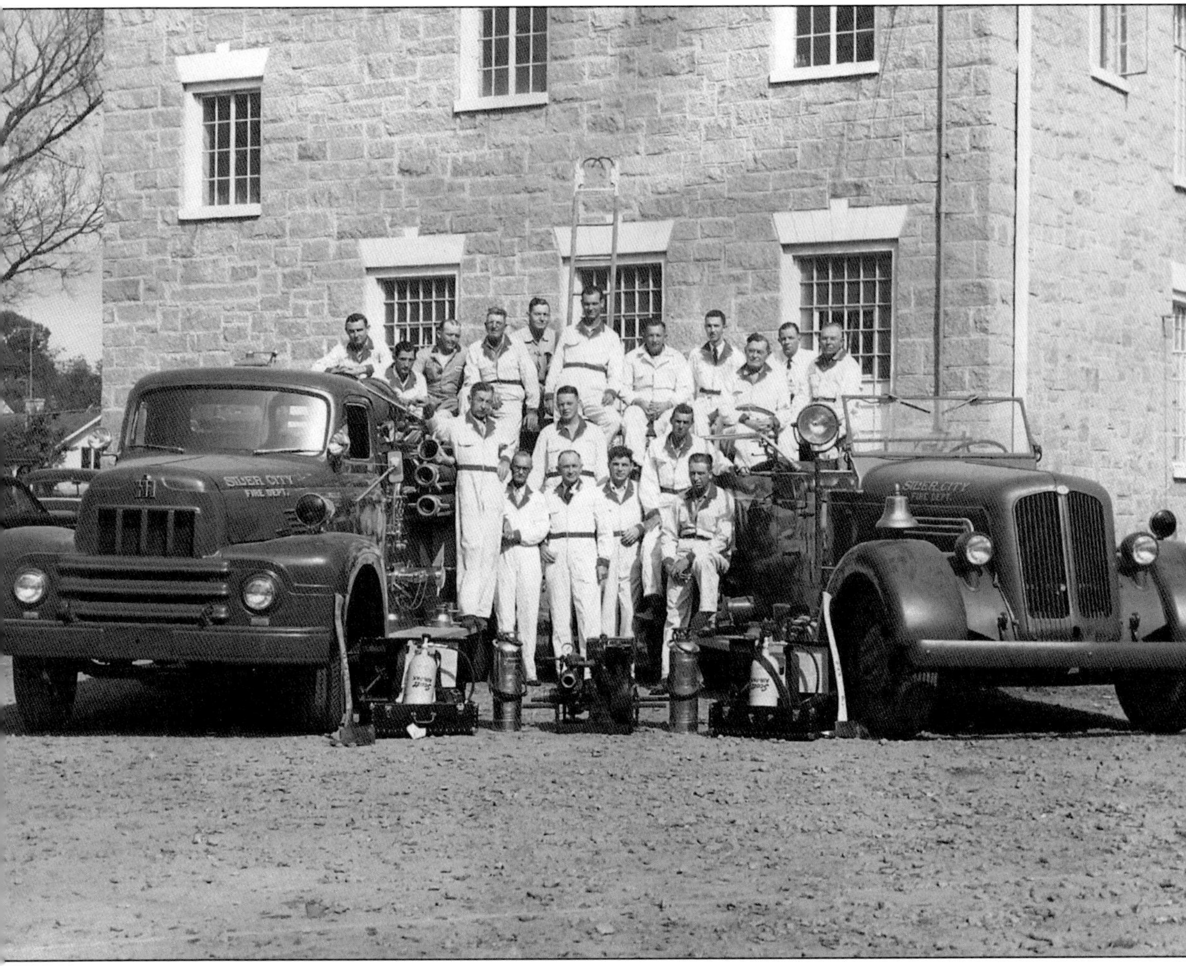

Pictured here behind city hall are the 1942 Seagrave and International fire trucks. The men are, from left to right, (first row, standing on ground) G.H. Grimes, H.E. Stout, Banks Fox, and Richard Edwards; (second row) P.J. Reitzel, Eugene Foust, and Harold Ivey; (third row) Eugene Andrews, Ervin Ellington, Ed Blair, Ralph Blair, Grady Renn, Bobby Thomas, Tommy Teague, Jerry Grimes, T.A. Burns, Russell Williams, and L.O. Curtis. This photograph was taken around 1954. Stout was the fire chief at the time, and Williams was the mayor. (Courtesy of the Siler City Fire Department and David Reeves.)

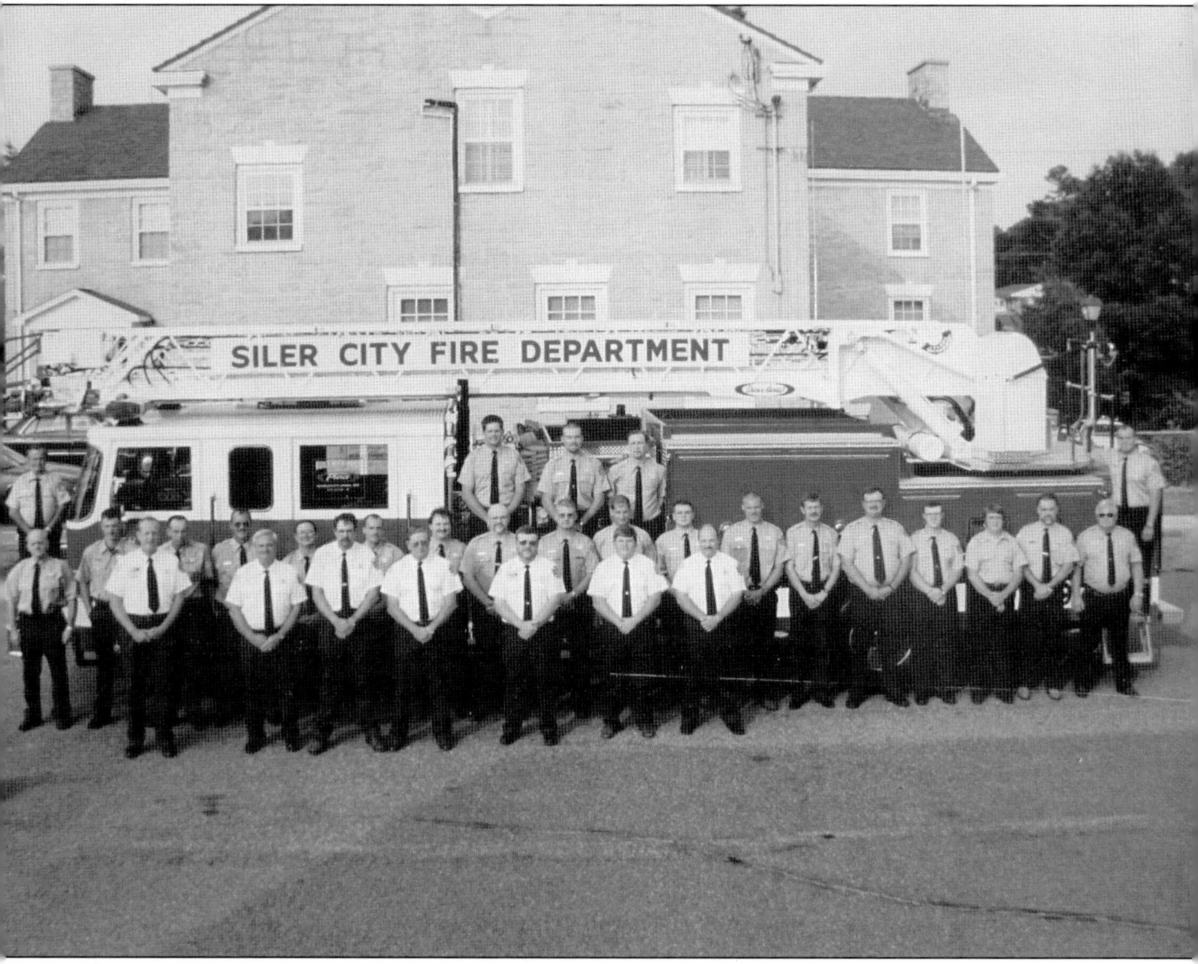

In this 1998 photograph, the men of the Siler City Fire Department are, from left to right, (first row) Steve Dowd, Darden Jarman, Mitch Dorsett, Jerry Ward, David McDonald, Eddie Dixon, and Billy Scott; (second row) Richard Caviness, Jerry Bray, Earl Dorsett, Drex Roberts, Roger White, Marty Phillips, Sam Millsap, Scott Brown, David Reeves, Ricky Henson, Nicky Starr, Wade Williams, Rocky Cook, Arliss Thrift Sr., Arliss Thrift Jr., Jimmy Tysor, Billy Williams, and Larry Staley; (third row) Clarence Gilliland, Mitch Vann, Todd Williams, Chuck Nixon, and Ron Elkins. (Courtesy of the Siler City Fire Department and David Reeves.)

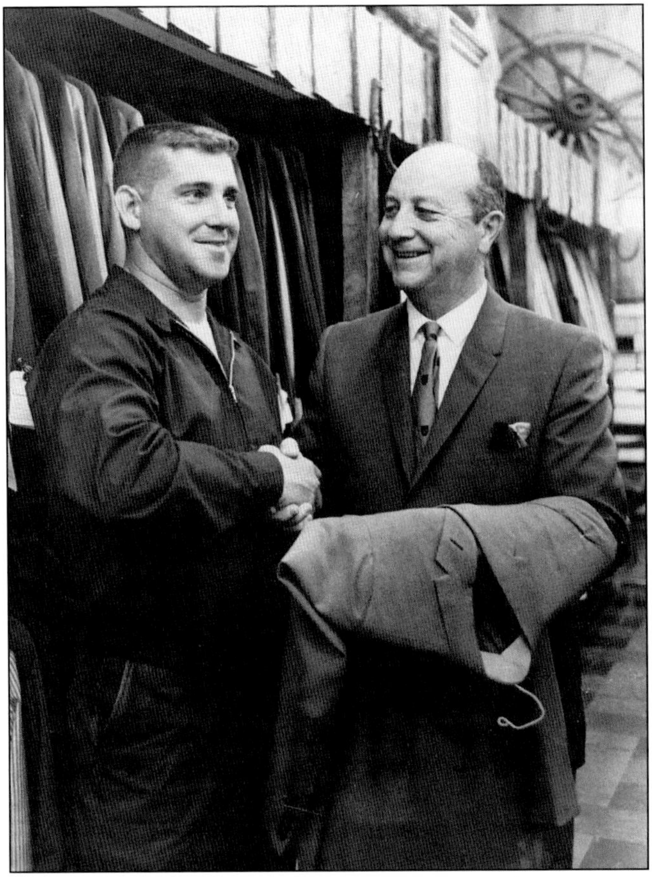

Burl Phillips is shown receiving a suit in 1967 from Sam Rees, who made the gift annually to the Siler City Fireman of the Year. Rees was the owner of Rees Clothing Store. (Courtesy of Farmers' Alliance Store and Nancy Tysor.)

Here is the Siler City Fire Department with a fire truck outside the station around 1990. In the background is the new Siler City Police Station. The fire station on North Chatham Avenue at Third Street was built in 1960 and enlarged in 1980. (Photograph by Arnette Muldrow, courtesy of the Town of Siler City.)

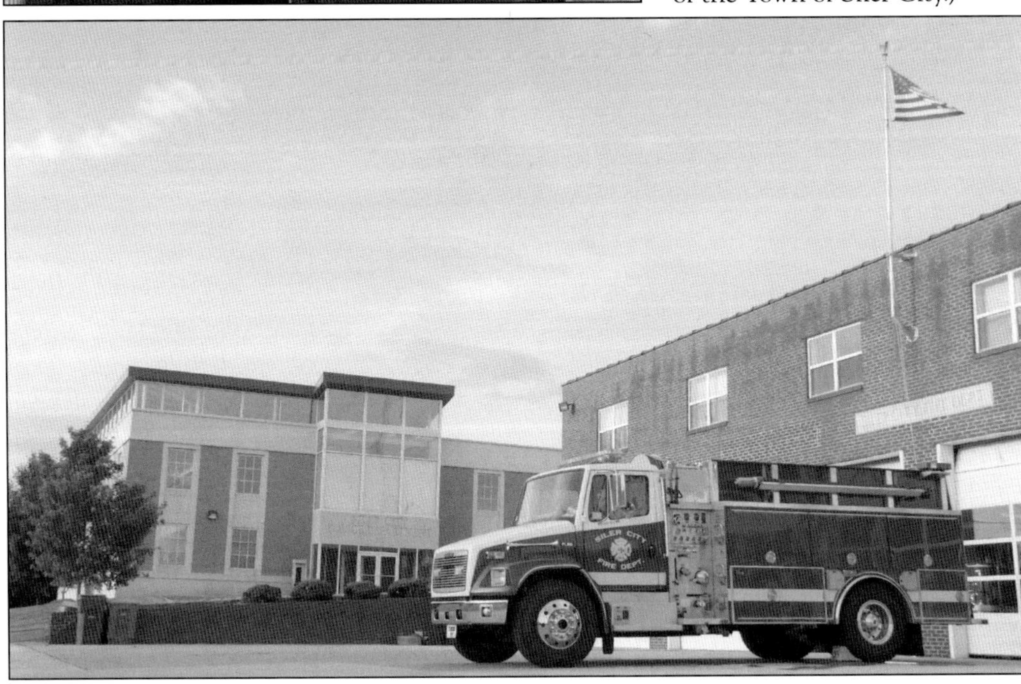

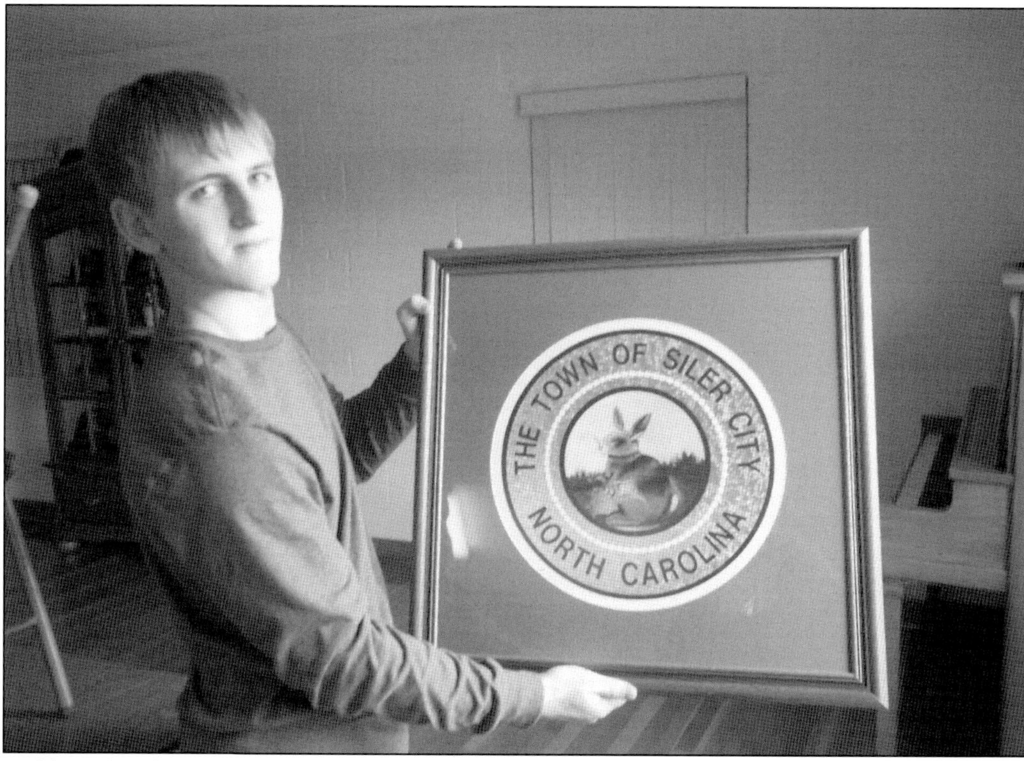

Holding the photograph of a Chatham rabbit is Caleb Reeves, the son of fireman David Reeves. The history of Chatham rabbits provoked department members to depict a rabbit on the door of the Seagrave Pumper fire truck in the early 1940s. The fire department had a modern, gold leaf–adorned rabbit seal placed on the door of the ladder truck in 1998. (Photograph by author.)

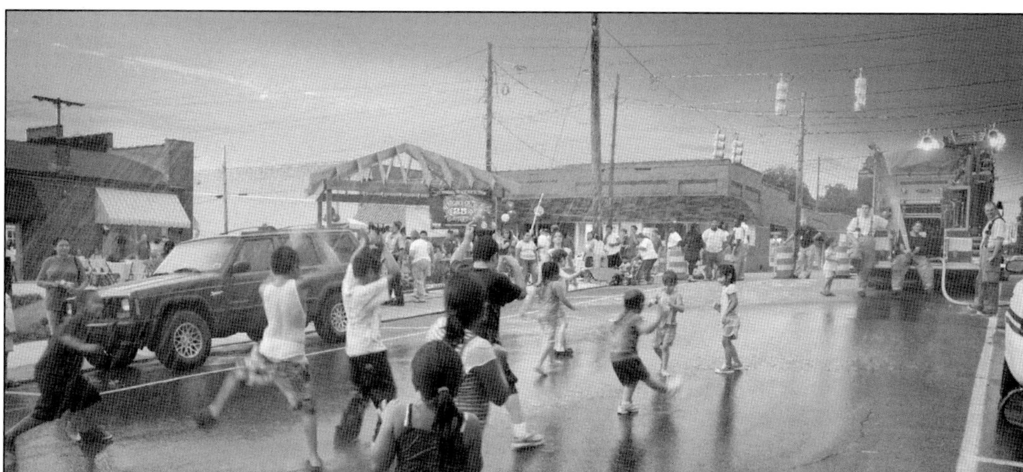

The town of Siler City North Carolina has won a National Night Out Award for six consecutive years, presented by the National Association of Town Watch. On December 2, 2013, Siler City was notified that its National Night Out program was ranked eighth in the United States for towns with populations under 15,000. (Photograph by Duane Hall, courtesy of Town of Siler City.)

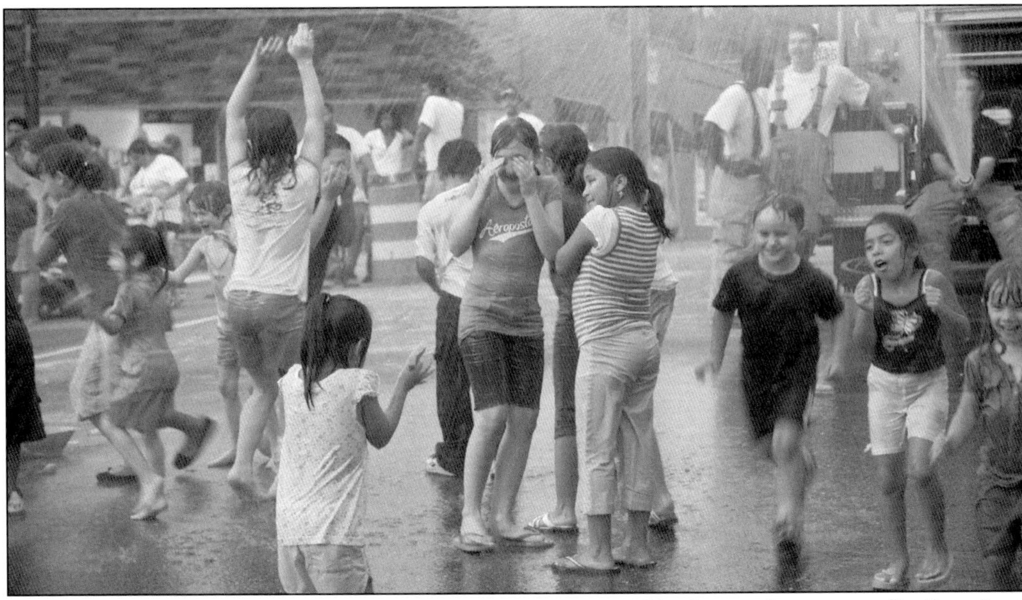

The Siler City's National Night Out program attracts over 1,000 of its residents annually. Everybody enjoys the food, music, and fellowship. This great event is a community effort between the Siler City Police Department, the Siler City Fire Department, businesses, and other governing bodies. (Photograph by Duane Hall, courtesy of the Town of Siler City.)

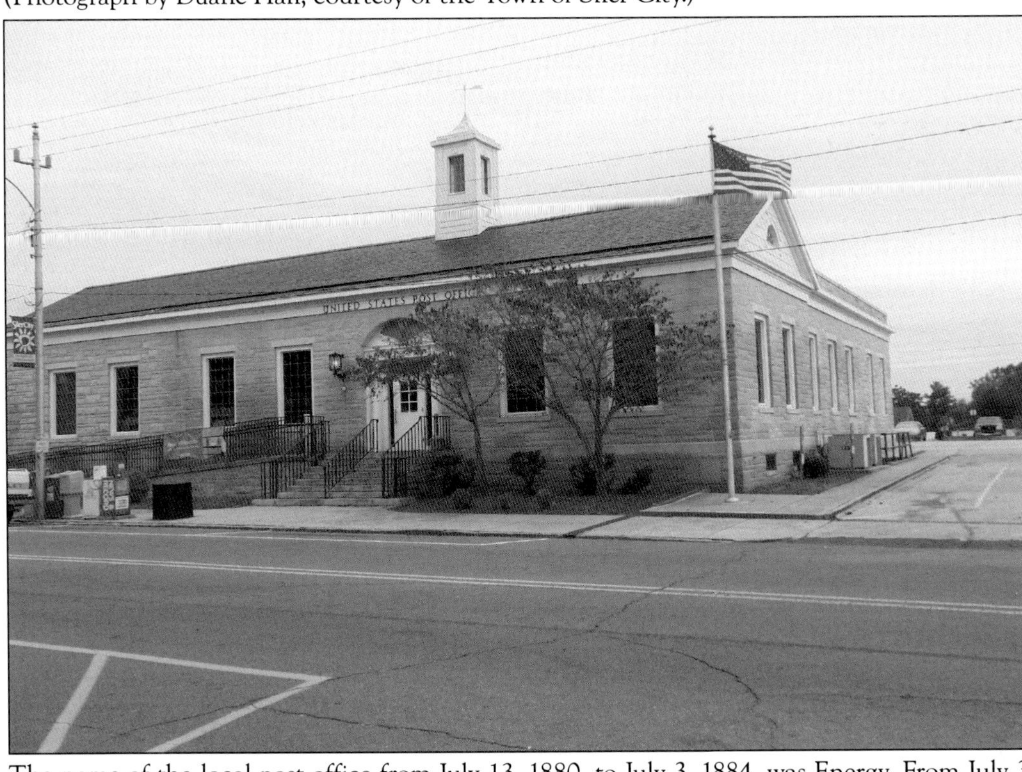

The name of the local post office from July 13, 1880, to July 3, 1884, was Energy. From July 3, 1884, to July 28, 1886, it was called Siler Station, and from July 28, 1886, to the present it has been the Siler City Post Office. (Photograph by author.)

Seven

The People of Siler City

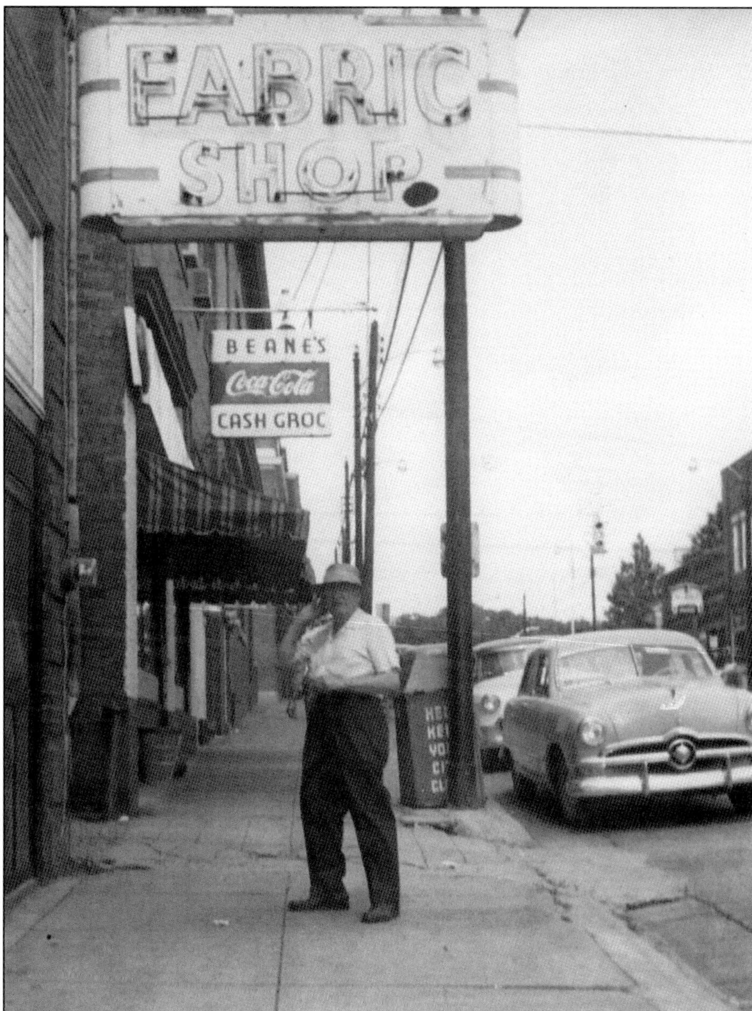

Walter "Ivey" Budd is seen here in front of the Fabric Shop located on West Raleigh Street in downtown Siler City. He and his wife, Anna, were proprietors of the shop during the 1950s. Budd was Cecilia Budd Grimes's grandfather. (Courtesy of Cecilia Budd Grimes.)

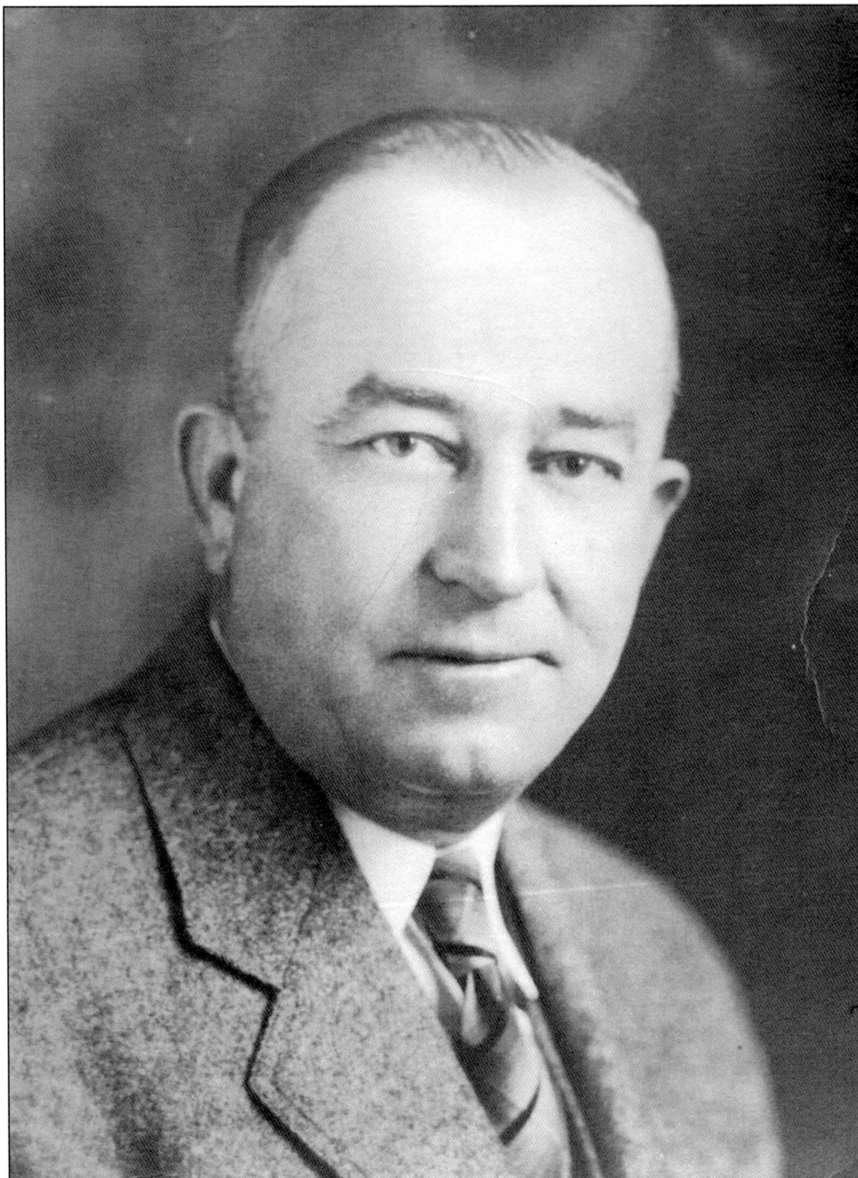

William Clyde Thomas was born on March 18, 1894, in Lee County, North Carolina, to Henderson and Barbara Isabelle Thomas. He graduated from Bules Creek Academy in 1912 and from the Medical College of Virginia in Richmond in 1917 with a doctor of medicine. Dr. Thomas moved to Siler City in 1917 after marrying Maude Herring Lillard of Staunton, Virginia, on October 21, 1916. Three daughters were born of their union. Their first daughter was stillborn; the surviving two were Barbara Ann (married to F.J. Wrenn Jr.) and Ruth Virginia (married to Cecil Budd), both of Siler City. The Thomases had six grandchildren. Dr. Thomas entered the Medical Corps of the US Army for service in World War I in 1917 with the rank of first lieutenant, and after he returned to Siler City to resume his practice. He and fellow physician Dr. J.B. Earle founded Chatham Hospital in 1937. In 1940, Dr. Thomas reentered military service as commanding medical officer for Fort Bragg Cantonment Hospital. He retired September 15, 1945, as an Army lieutenant colonel and died September 12, 1961. (Courtesy of Cecilia Budd Grimes.)

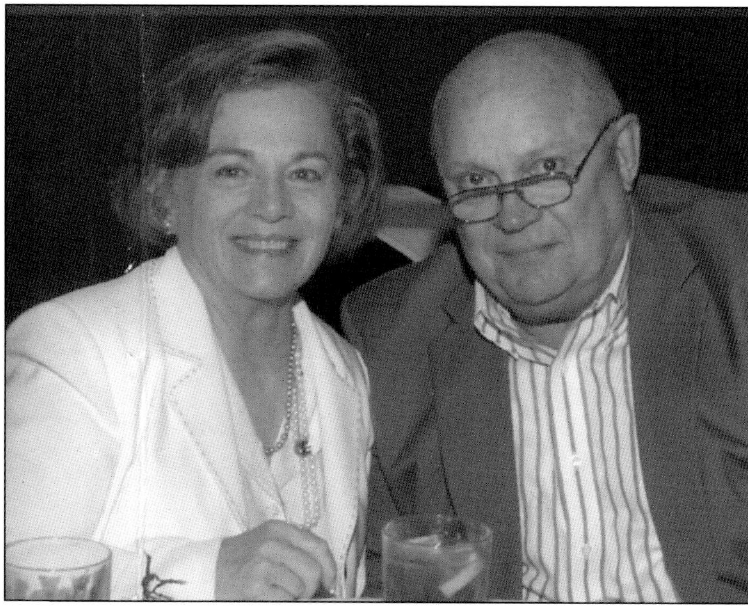

John Grimes was elected mayor of Siler City in 2013 after serving on the town board as commissioner and mayor pro tem since 1999. He is a partner in the family business Cecil Budd Tire Company, where he has worked since 1968. He is married to Cecilia Budd Grimes, and they have two sons and six grandchildren. (Courtesy of Mayor John Grimes and Cecilia Budd Grimes.)

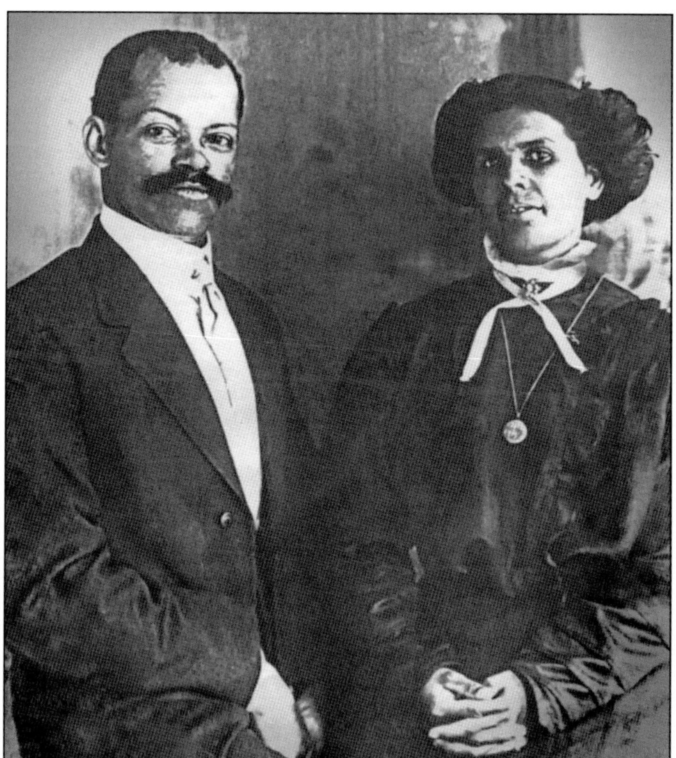

Tod R. Edwards and his wife, Ella, were the owners of a successful jewelry store around 1905 in Siler City. Tod also ran a barbershop, repaired watches, clocks, bicycles, and was a photographer. He even operated a prominent funeral home in Siler City. Tod moved to town from Bynum, North Carolina. The family continued to operate the jewelry store after Tod's death in 1951 until the business closed on September 16, 1961.

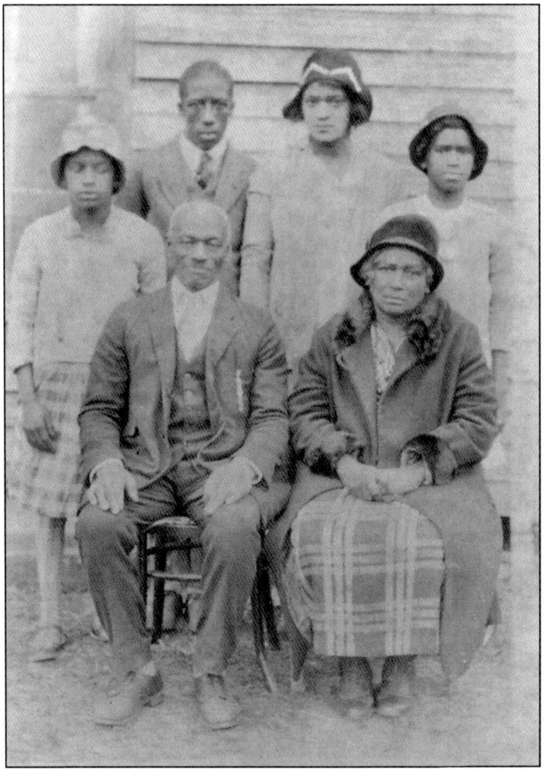

This Headen family photograph was taken around 1930. Pictured are, from left to right, (first row) William Headen and Sally Ann (Smith) Headen; (second row) Fanny Headen, John Walker Headen, Launa Headen, and Willa Louise Headen. William was the janitor at Paul Braxton High School. He raised most of his own food on a small plot of land across from Three Penny restaurant.

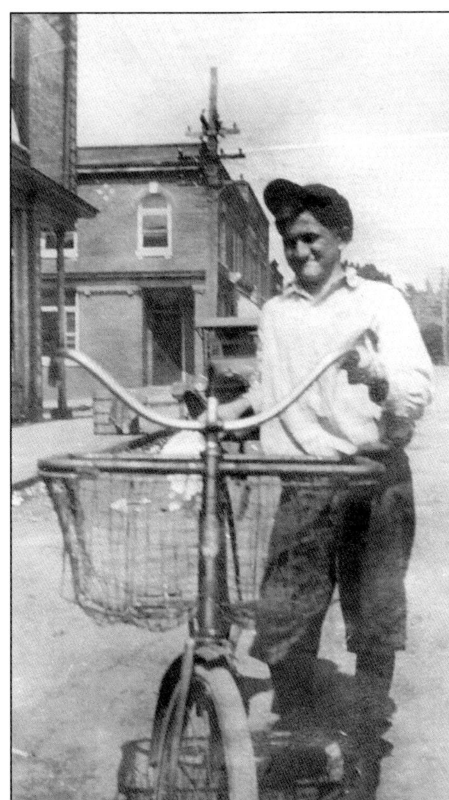

This unidentified young man on an early-1900s bicycle is enjoying posing for the camera. The vehicle behind him is said to be one of the first cars in Siler City. Dr. J.D. Edwards was reported to have bought a four-cylinder, 39-horsepower Maxwell in September 1911, according to Wade Hampton Hadley Jr.'s *The Town of Siler City: 1887–1987*.

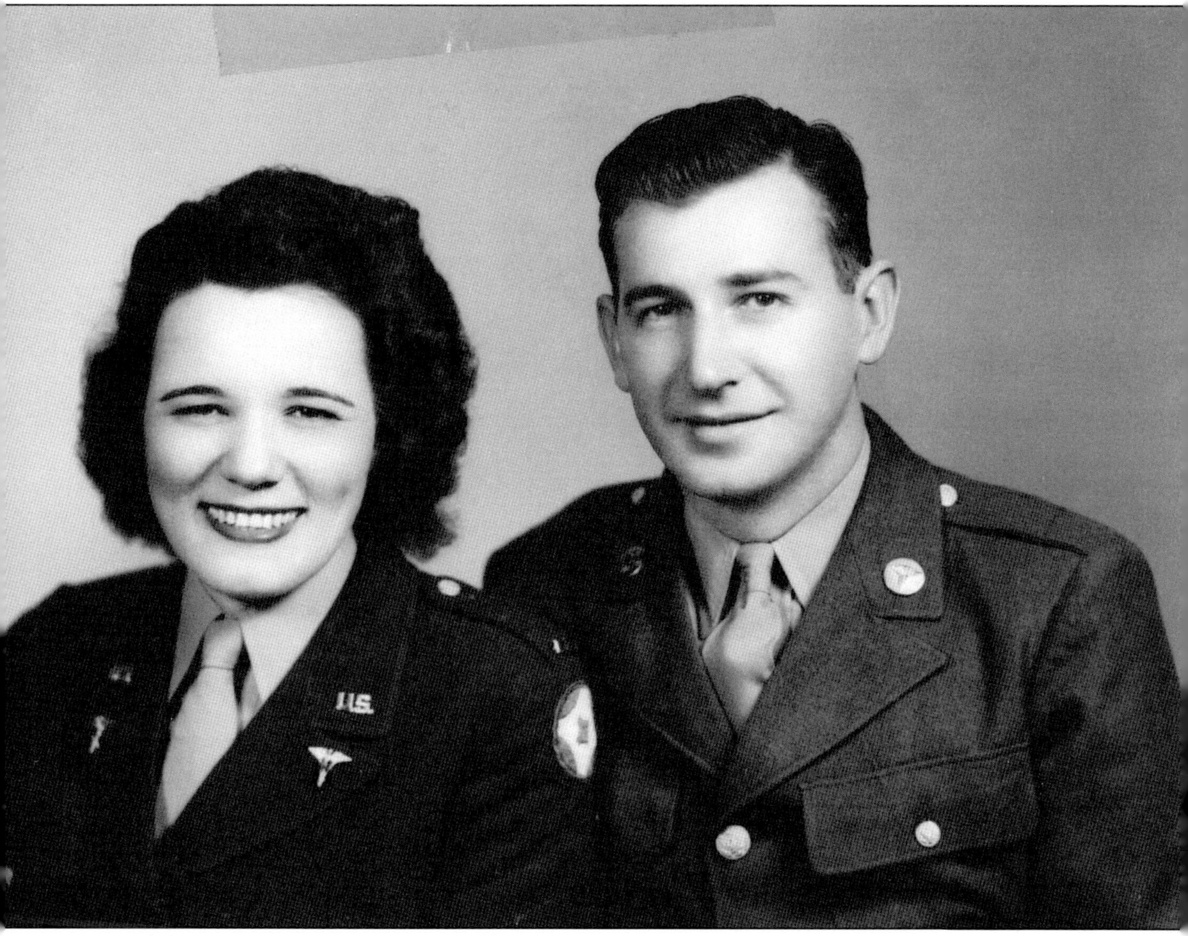

Lucy and George McMasters met in World War II. Lucy was a nurse in Atlanta during the war, and "she out-ranked her husband during the war and after," recalls her son Dan. George, meanwhile, was in Germany during the conflict. He died in 1960, leaving Lucy to raise two young boys, Dan and Joe McMasters. (Courtesy of Farmers' Alliance Store and Nancy Tysor.)

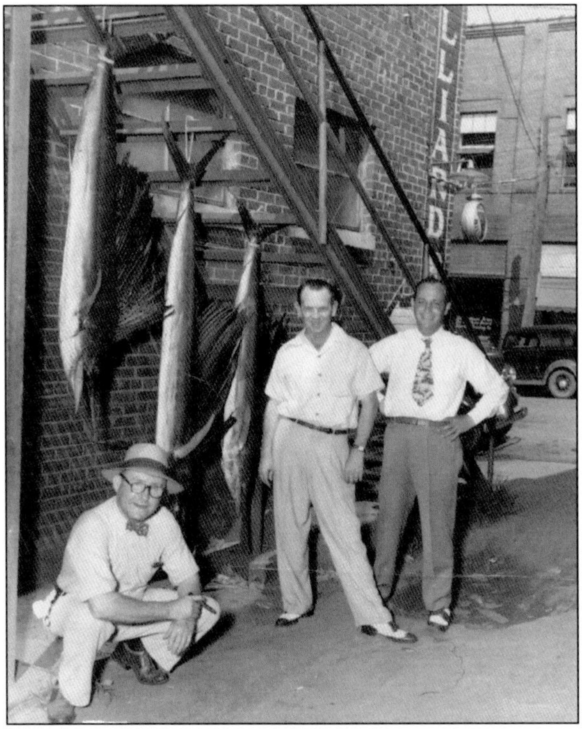

W.H. Rowland (left) owned a hardware store, Bill Vestal (center) owed a barbershop, and Sam Rees (right) owned a men's clothing store. Here, the three men show off the fish they caught off the North Carolina coast. The lengths of these sailfish were seven feet, six and a half inches; seven feet, nine and a half inches; and eight feet, two inches. (Courtesy of Farmers' Alliance Store and Nancy Tysor.)

Included in this American Legion group are Paschal Duncan, Sam Rees, Ed Goldston, and T.L. Smith (second row, far right). (Courtesy of Farmers' Alliance Store and Nancy Tysor.)

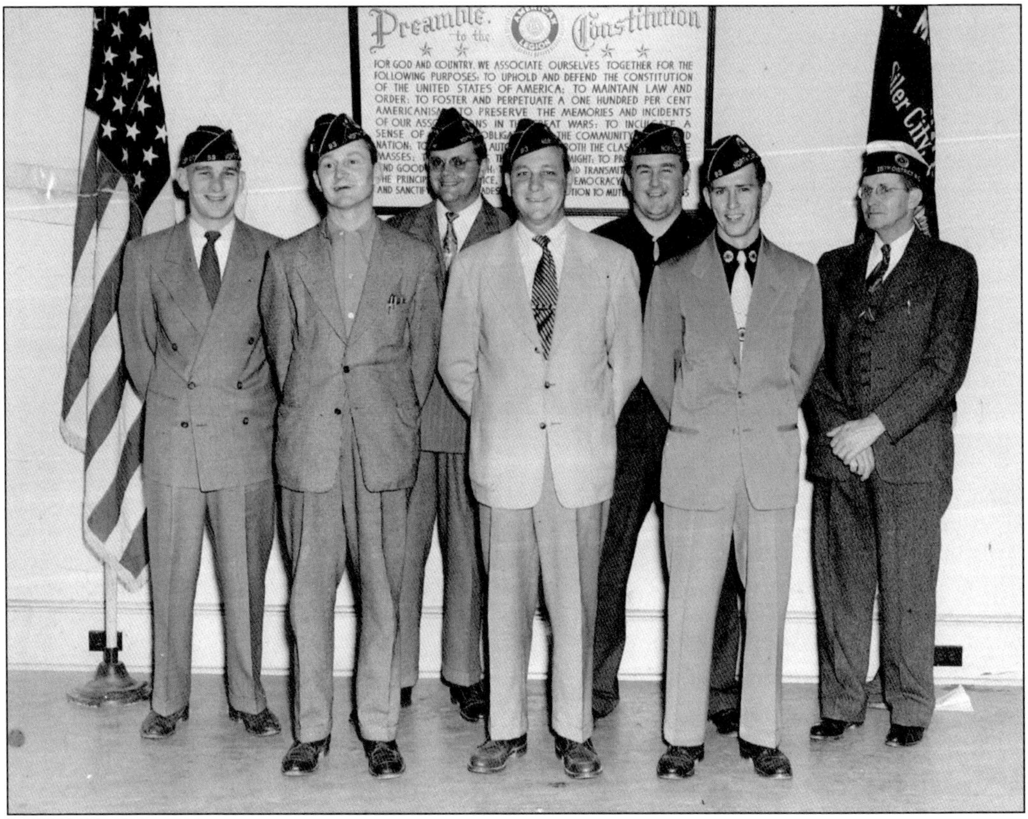

Milo Holt (front left) and Don Ferguson are in the "old swimming hole" of the Rocky River, enjoying a swim in the 1930s. The boys are swimming in the millpond at the old Hackney's Grist Mill just north of Highway 64 on the east edge of Siler City. The boys use to hike out to the pond to swim on hot summer days. Holt became one of Siler City's celebrated citizens when he started sharing his love of western movies with anyone who wanted see one. The annual Milo Holt Film Festival is held yearly and includes the Tom Mix Rangers with their stagecoach and exciting shoot-outs between the good and bad, cowboy look-alikes, and Indian chief Jay Silverheels, who is the son of "Tonto" from *The Lone Ranger.*

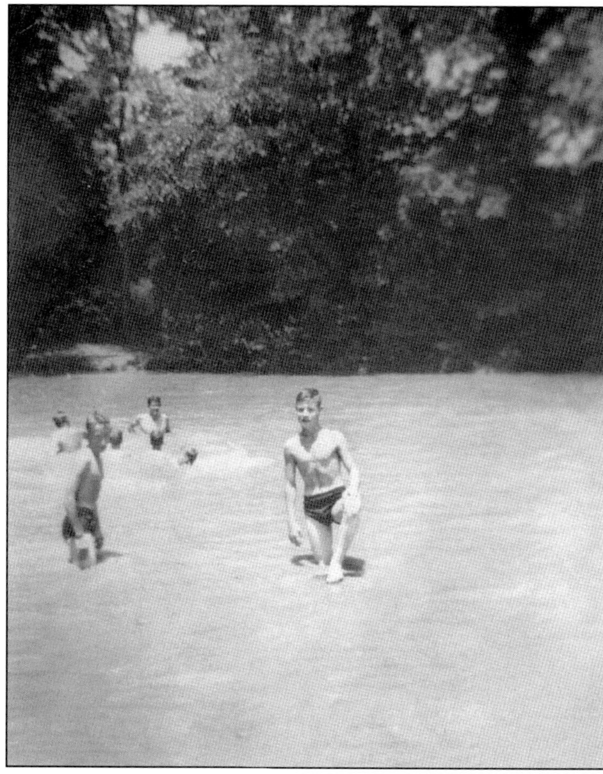

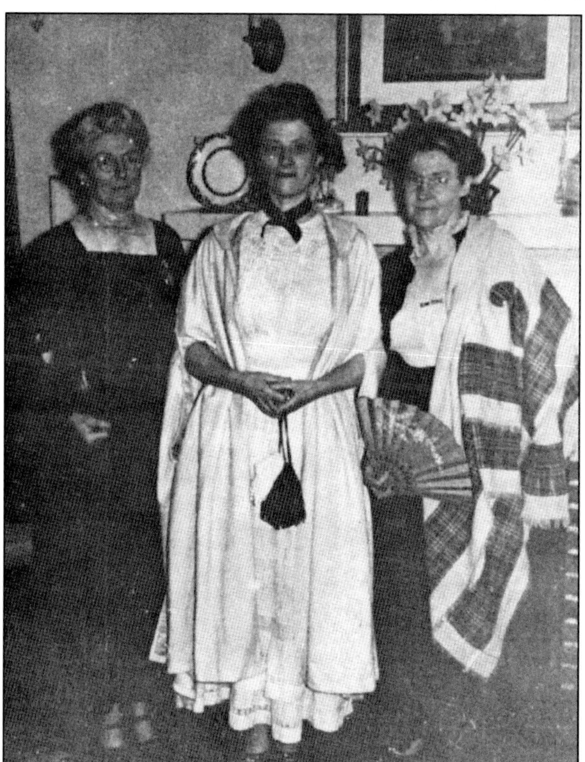

From left to right, Glenna Grimes, Hattie Dark Andrew, and Ruth Small Dixon are at the Carolina Folk Festival in Chapel Hill in June 1948. The ladies are wearing dresses handed down to them by their ancestors. (Courtesy of Farmers' Alliance Store and Nancy Tysor.)

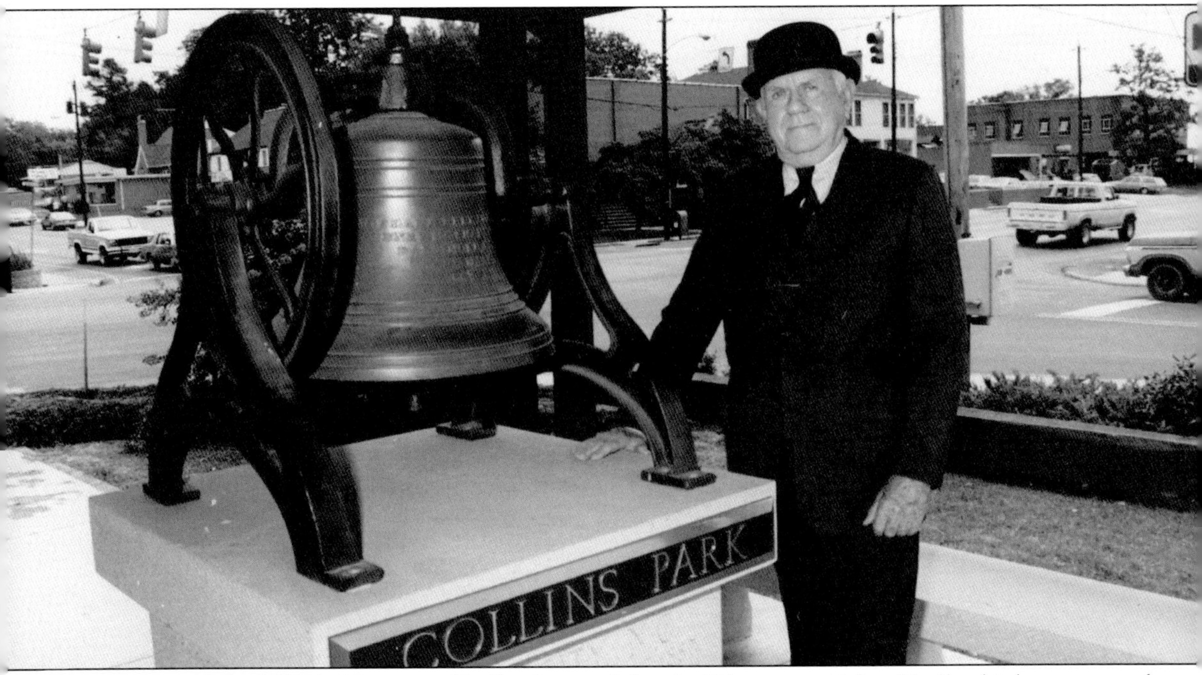

Around 1986, Wade Hampton Hadley Jr. stands by the Thompson School bell, which was moved to Collins Park. Hadley (1909–2002) returned to Siler City after a career as a geologist. He wrote *Historical Buildings of the Central Business District Siler City, North Carolina* and *Siler City, North Carolina: 1887–1987*. His invaluable research and study of Siler City was a major catalyst in the exploration of the history of Siler City within this book. (Photograph by Jeff Davis, courtesy of Farmers' Alliance Store and Nancy Tysor.)

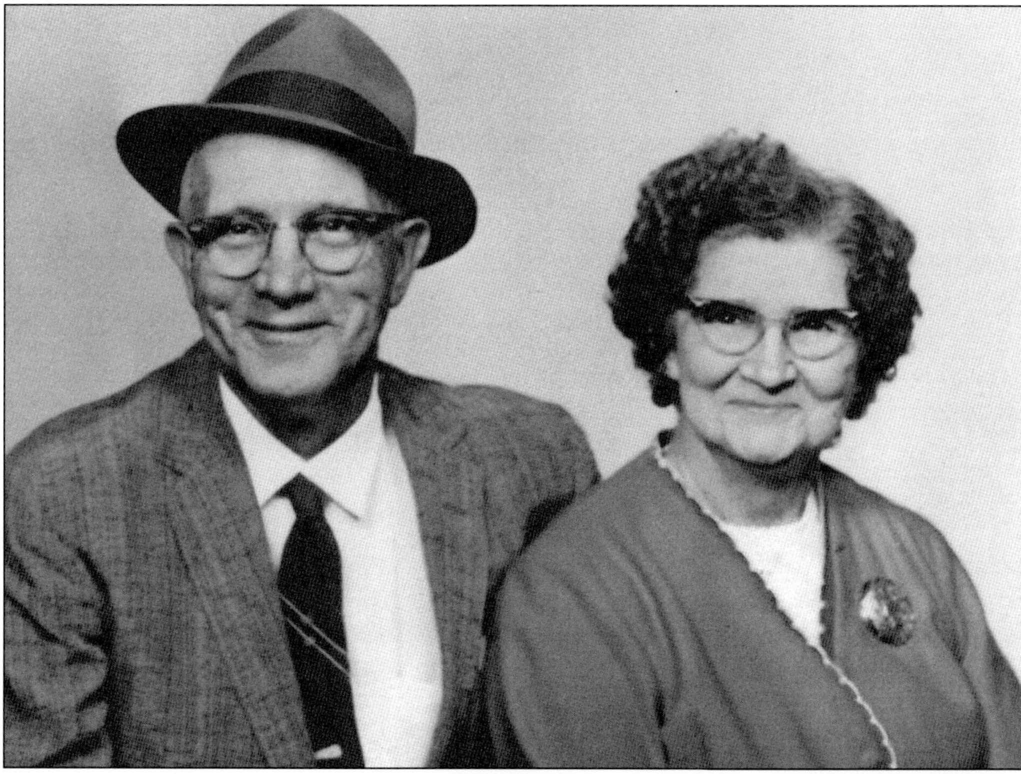

Iona Brown Wilson and her husband, Charlie "Dude" Wilson, are seen in this 1930 church photograph. Iona is an approximately sixth-generation descendant of Plikard Siler, who started Siler City. The couple's grandchild Tony Davis has done extensive genealogical research, spanning about 300 years. (Courtesy of Tony and Nancy Davis family.)

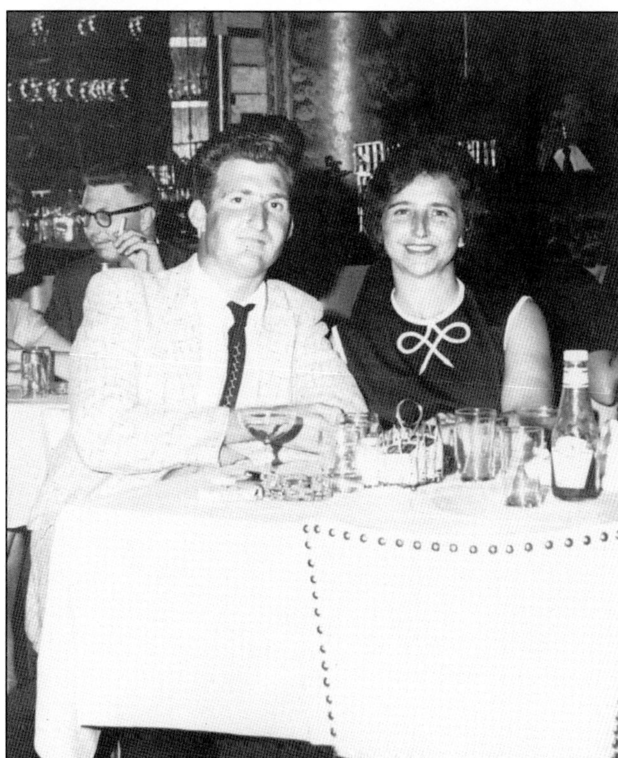

Mary E. Wilson Davis is seen with her husband, Elbert Roy Davis, on August 28, 1970, at dinner at the Barn Dinner Theater. Mary E. Wilson, the daughter of Iona Brown Wilson and Charlie "Dude" Wilson, is the approximate seventh-generation descendant of Plikard Siler. (Courtesy of Tony and Nancy Davis family.)

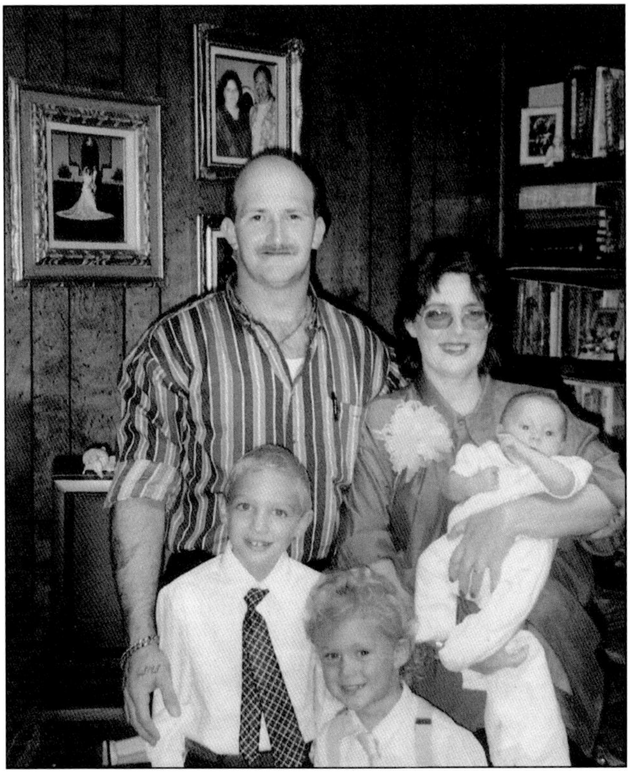

Tony and Nancy Davis are pictured with children Clayton Blake (left), Frank (center), and baby William. They lived in Ridge Top, Tennessee, at the time of this photograph but moved back to Siler City in 2002. Tony is Mary and Elbert Davis's son and an eighth-generation descendant of Plikard Siler. (Courtesy of Tony and Nancy Davis family.)

Dennis H. Sawyer was president and general manager of Siler City Mills, Inc., from 1974 to 1984. Dennis and his wife, Nina, became co-owners of Siler City Hardware. In 1987, the store became part of the ACE Hardware chain. (Photograph by author.)

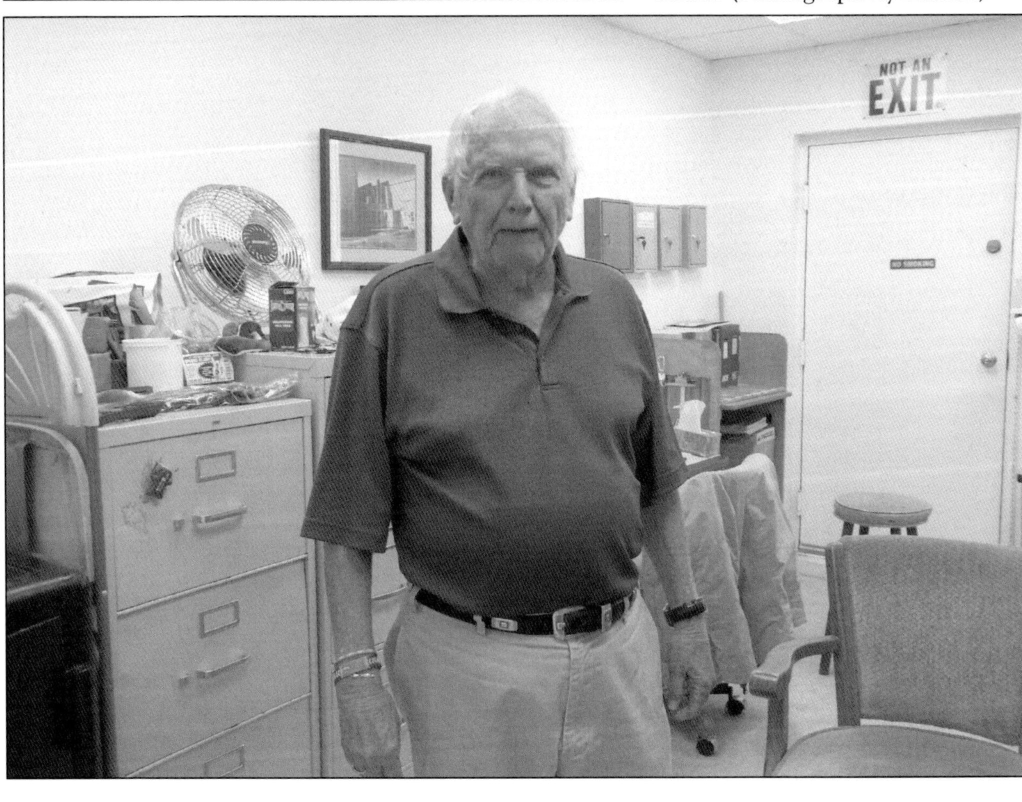

Charlie Walker Rodgers (January 13, 1890–April 13, 1965) was born in Chatham County and married Essie Williams Rodgers (July 10, 1892–November 21, 1968). The two belonged to Evans Chapel African Methodist Episcopal Zion Church. Blairton Hampton, their grandchild, is the little boy sitting between them in the photograph. He married Brenda Parker, and they have two sons, Brandon and Brent. (Author's collection.)

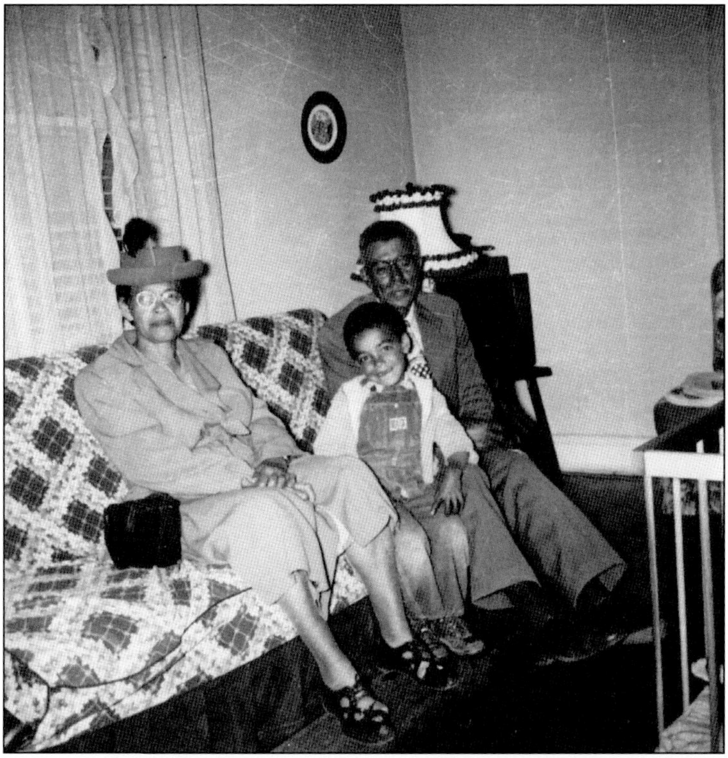

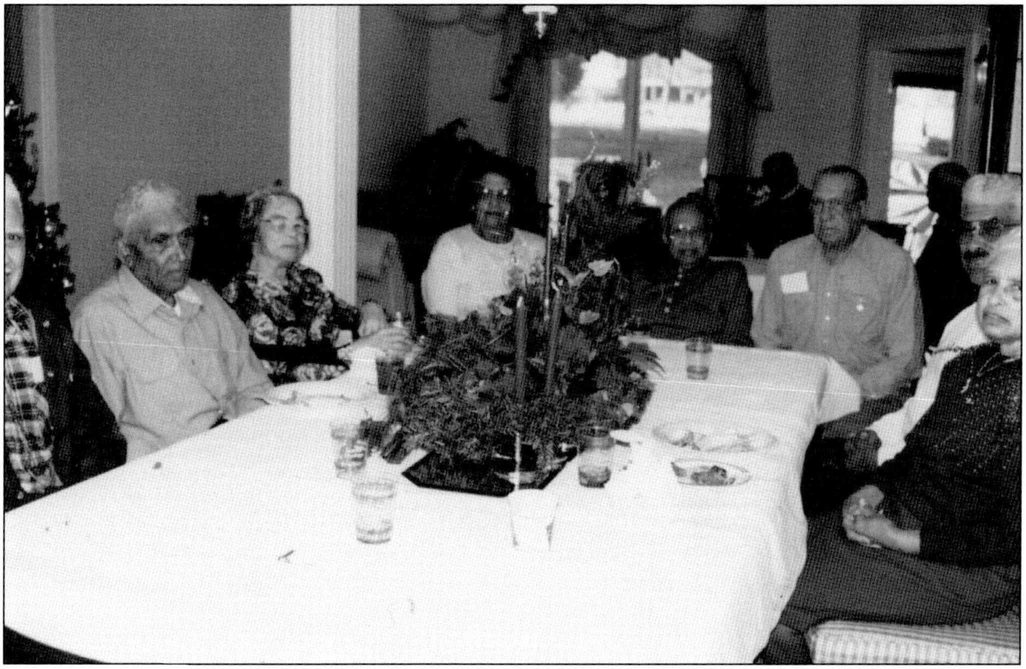

Eleven children were born from the union of Charlie Walker and Essie Rodgers; eight of them are pictured here at this table. From left to right they are Verna W. Rodgers, Edgar Rodgers, Lillian Rose Brown, Mossie R. White, Delsia R. Rogers, Examious Rodgers, Joseph Rodgers, and Ernestine R. Hampton. (Courtesy of Delsia Rogers.)

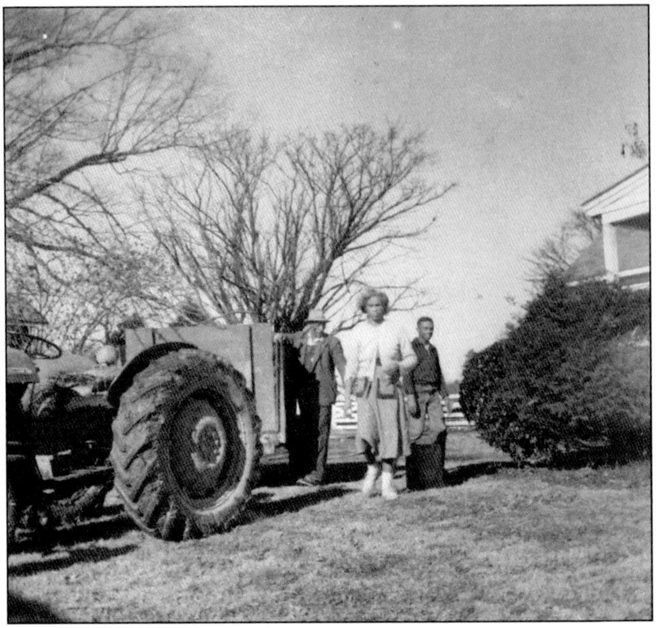

Outside their home in February 1960 are, from left to right, Austin and Delsia R. Rogers and their son Shelton. Austin conducted a tour of his farm on Thursday, November 13, 1952. Three busloads of farmers from Edgecombe and Nash Counties came to Chatham County, as reported by Chatham County's newspaper. Austin demonstrated his new milk cooler to farmers from Nashville and Pinetops. (Author's collection.)

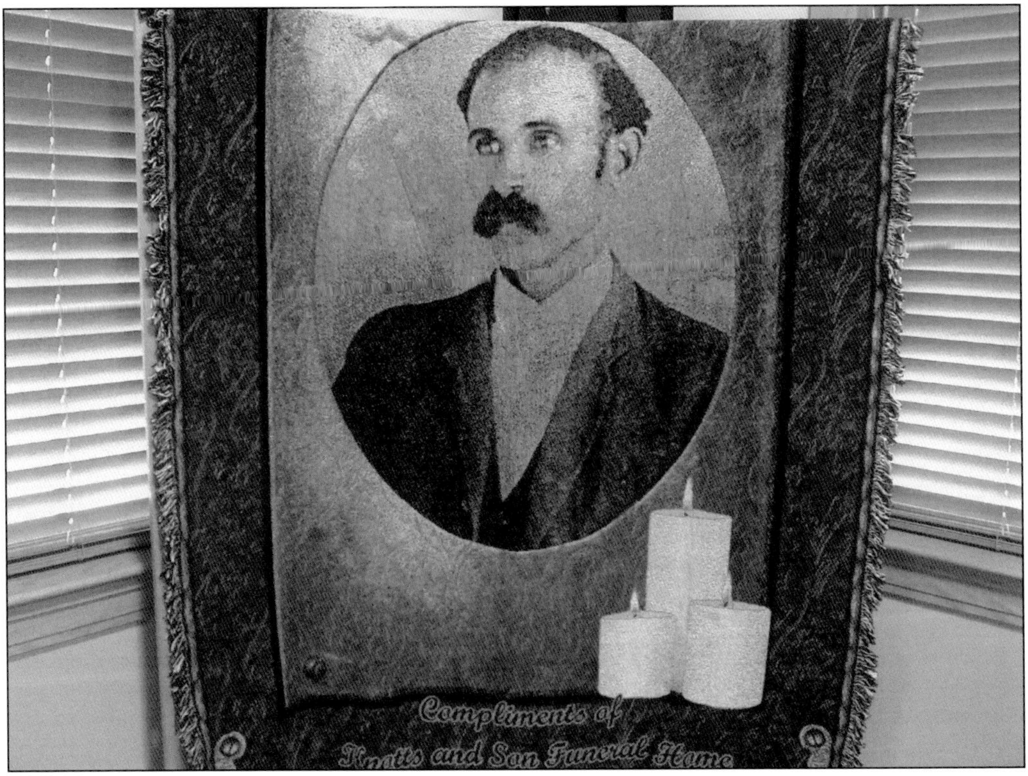

Charlie Rodgers was born 1860 in Chatham County and died in 1940. He was married three times (Eliza Smith, Sophronia Degraffenriedt, and Bertha Alston) and had 26 children, who worked on the family farm. His marriage to Eliza Smith Rogers (1867–1904) gave birth to nine children: Willie Rodgers, Arthur Rodgers, Minnie R. Burman, Lacey R. Marsh, Daisey R. Goins, Eula Rodgers, Maggie R. Price, Lizzie R. Degraffenreid, and Charlie Walker Rodgers. (Author's collection.)

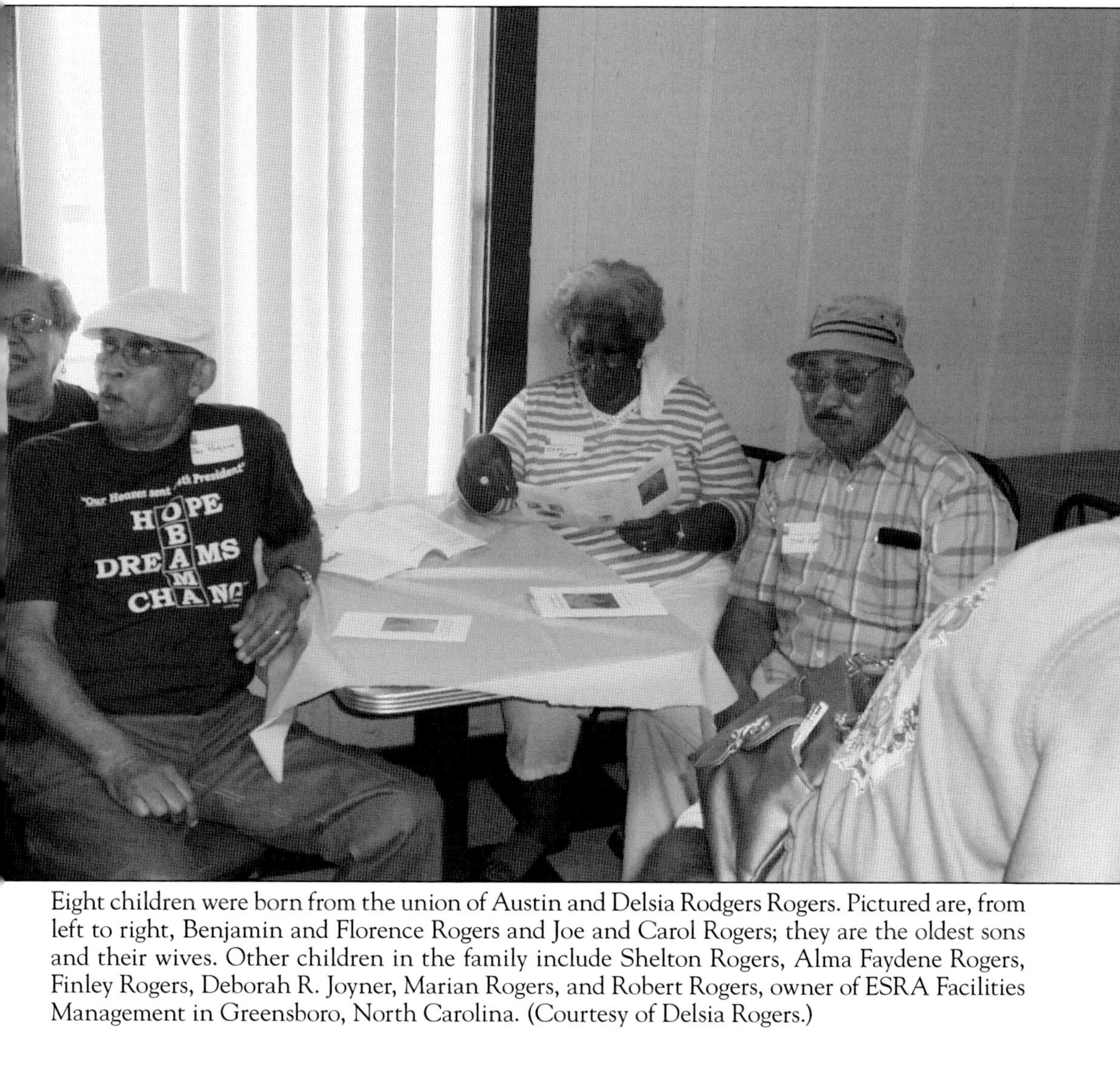

Eight children were born from the union of Austin and Delsia Rodgers Rogers. Pictured are, from left to right, Benjamin and Florence Rogers and Joe and Carol Rogers; they are the oldest sons and their wives. Other children in the family include Shelton Rogers, Alma Faydene Rogers, Finley Rogers, Deborah R. Joyner, Marian Rogers, and Robert Rogers, owner of ESRA Facilities Management in Greensboro, North Carolina. (Courtesy of Delsia Rogers.)

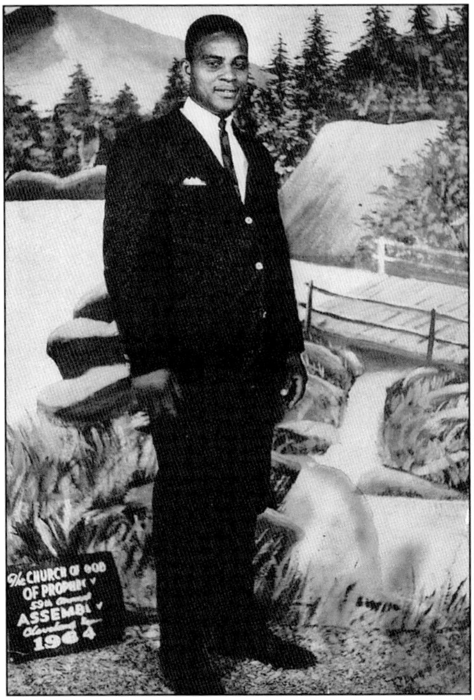

Percy "Raeford" Foxx (pictured here) married Virginia Ashford Foxx, who was born on July 26, 1933, in Siler City. Their daughter Celia married the late Wallace DeGraffenreidt. Born from this union were children Tonya, Tiffany, and Tara; the couple's grandchildren are Adrian, Ashton, Katlyn, Kristen, Kyla, and Alijah. Their family church is the Church of God of Prophecy in Siler City.

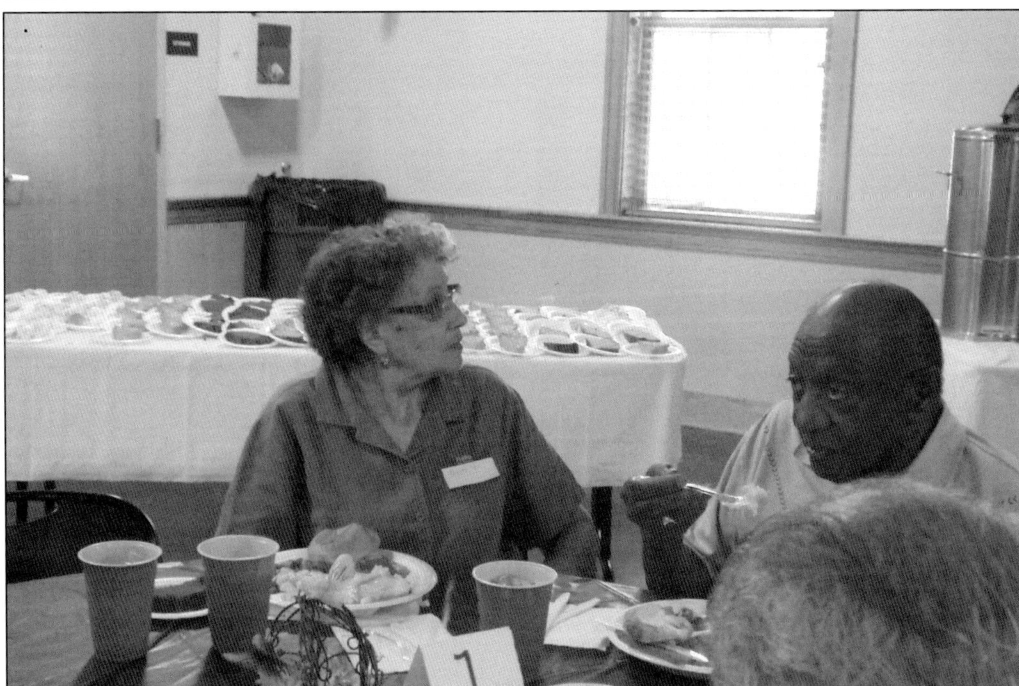

Marie R. McClain and her husband, Albert McClain, pictured here, have three children: Gregory, Deborah, and Curtis McClain. Marie is the daughter of Charles and Bertha Alston Rodgers. Her bothers and sisters include Celia Packingham, Pauline Rodgers, Julius Rodgers, Alberta Rodgers, Lester Roland Rodgers Sr., Wade Rodgers, Onnie Rodgers, Mozella R. Hooker, Worth Rodgers, Marcellus Rodgers, Vatie R. Siler, Ernest Green, and Hannah R. Alston. (Courtesy of Robert Rogers.)

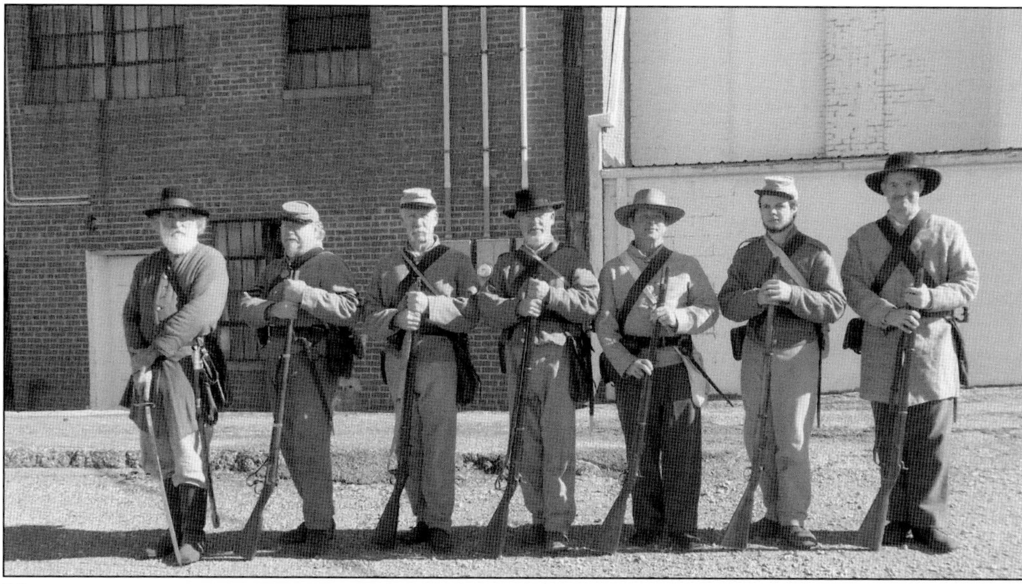

These reenactors are portraying 1861–1865 Confederate troops during a Veterans Day parade in Siler City. Pictured here in 2013 is the 26th North Carolina Troop, of which there are normally 10 members. They are, from left to right, Dennis Brooks, Neil Clack, Ronnie Lambert, Cecil Galloway, Brantley Webster, Caleb Simmons, and Jay Palmer. (Photograph by author.)

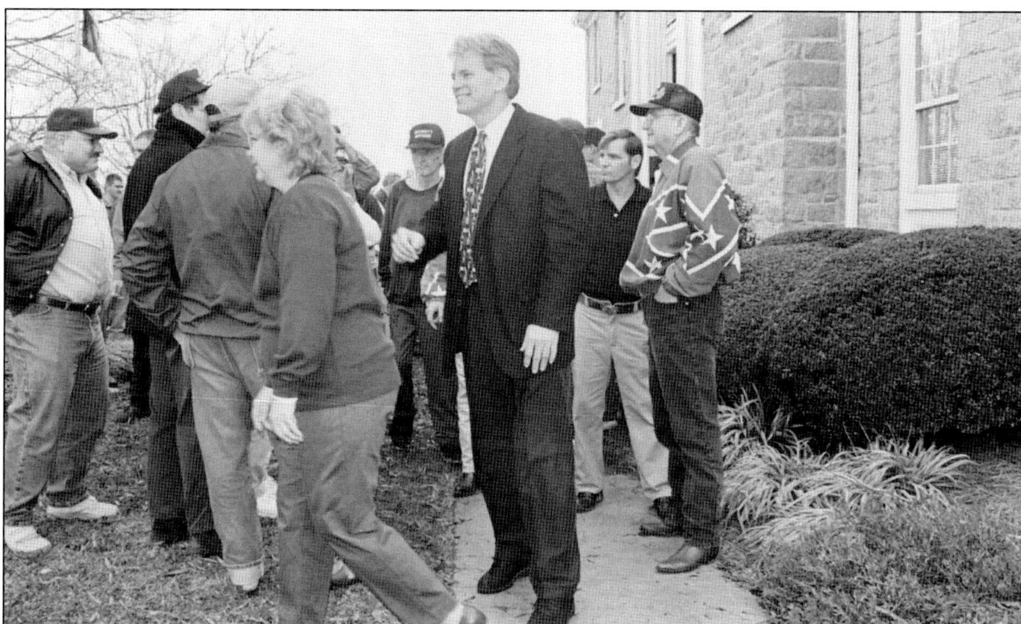

David Duke (in suit and tie) went marching into Siler City on February 19, 2000, when some community members became uneasy about an influx of Latinos, but when the former Republican Louisiana state representative and one-time grand dragon of the Klu Klux Klan immersed himself into the situation, some community members began to worry about the price of hate. (Courtesy of North Carolina Collection Photographic Archives, Wilson Library, University of North Carolina at Chapel Hill.)

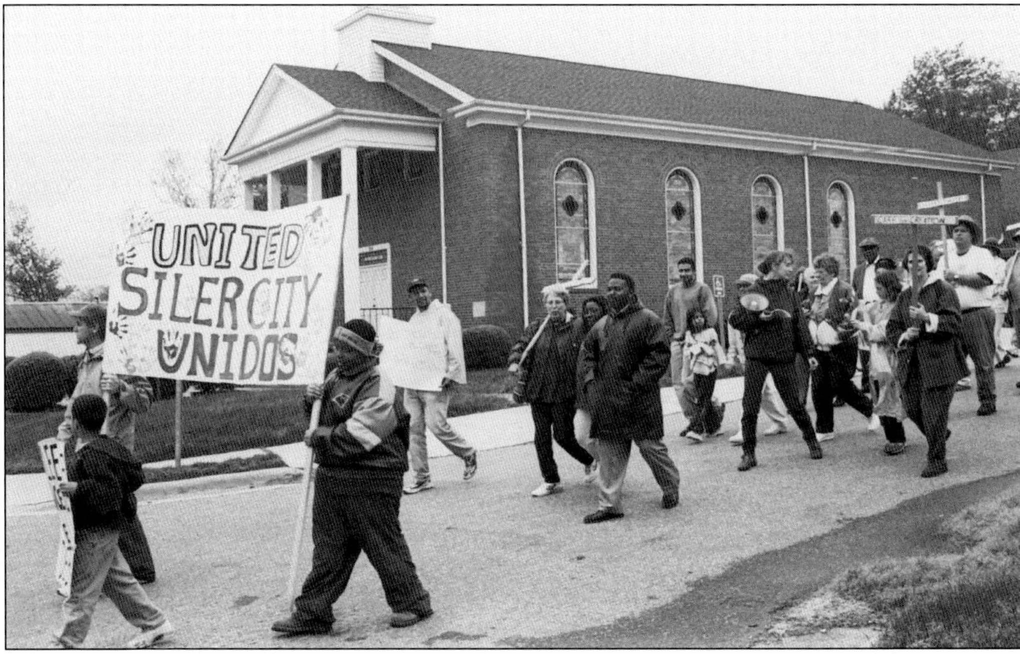

The Reverend Barry Grey of Missionary Baptist responded with rallies in support of uniting Siler City against racism. Duke did not gain much new local support at the February rally. Latinos are now helping to revitalize a once-dying town. (Courtesy of North Carolina Collection Photographic Archives, Wilson Library, University of North Carolina at Chapel Hill.)

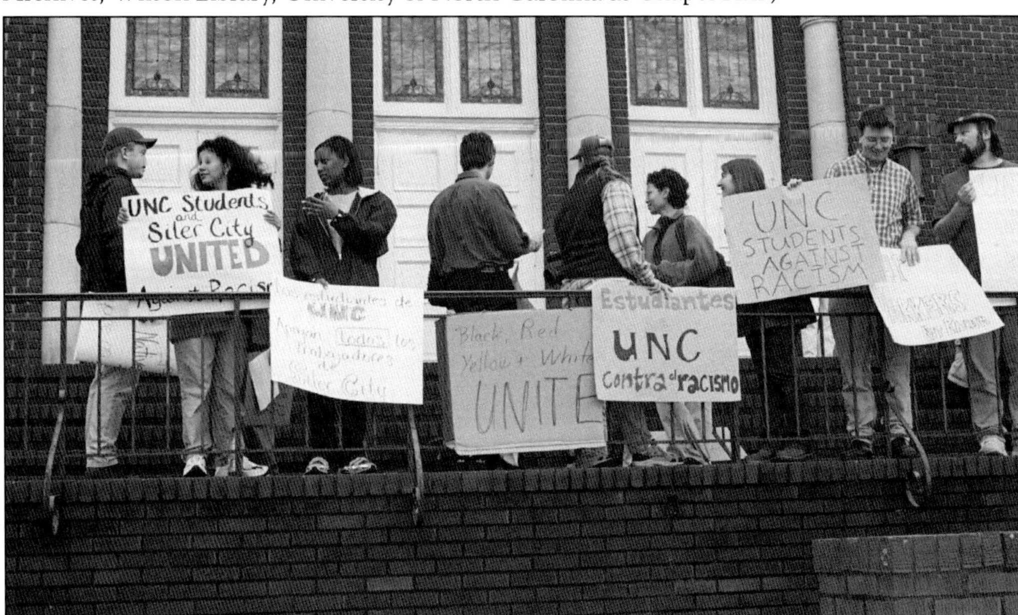

University of North Carolina students organize on the steps of First Baptist Church in support of uniting Siler City against racism. The David Duke rally in Siler City caused efforts to accommodate the Latino population. Longtime residents—both black and white—have found common ground with their Latino neighbors in small-town life. (Courtesy of North Carolina Collection Photographic Archives, Wilson Library, University of North Carolina at Chapel Hill.)

Eight

Town Murals

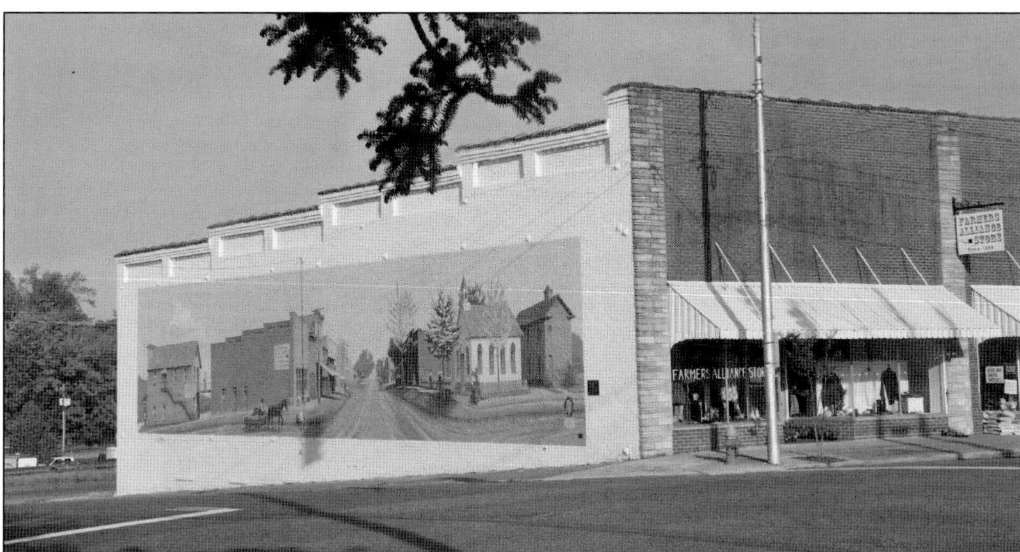

The Farmers' Alliance mural is painted on the Farmers' Alliance Store building, located on West Beaver Street and South Chatham Avenue. The painting was completed by Stacye Leanza in 2006 and depicts life in Siler City in the 1910s. (Photograph by Jeff Davis, courtesy of the Town of Siler City.)

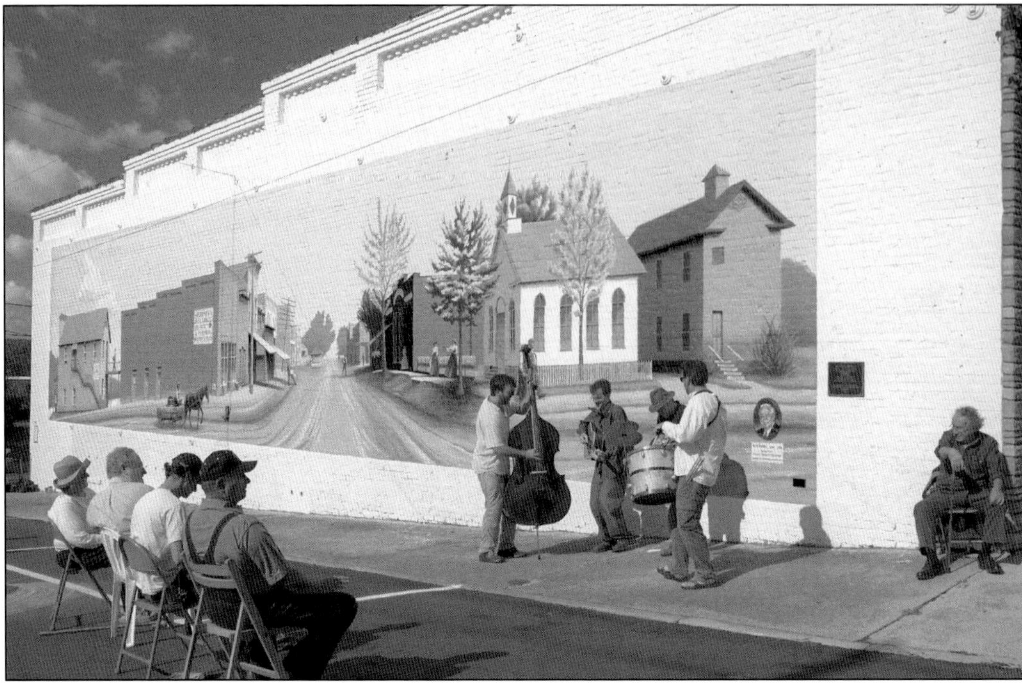

The backdrop of the Farmers' Alliance mural provides a unique place for musical performances from area musicians and artists. During the Third Friday ArtWalks, visitors are invited to explore downtown Siler City's art and culture. Shops and galleries stay open late, while live music plays at the courtyard.

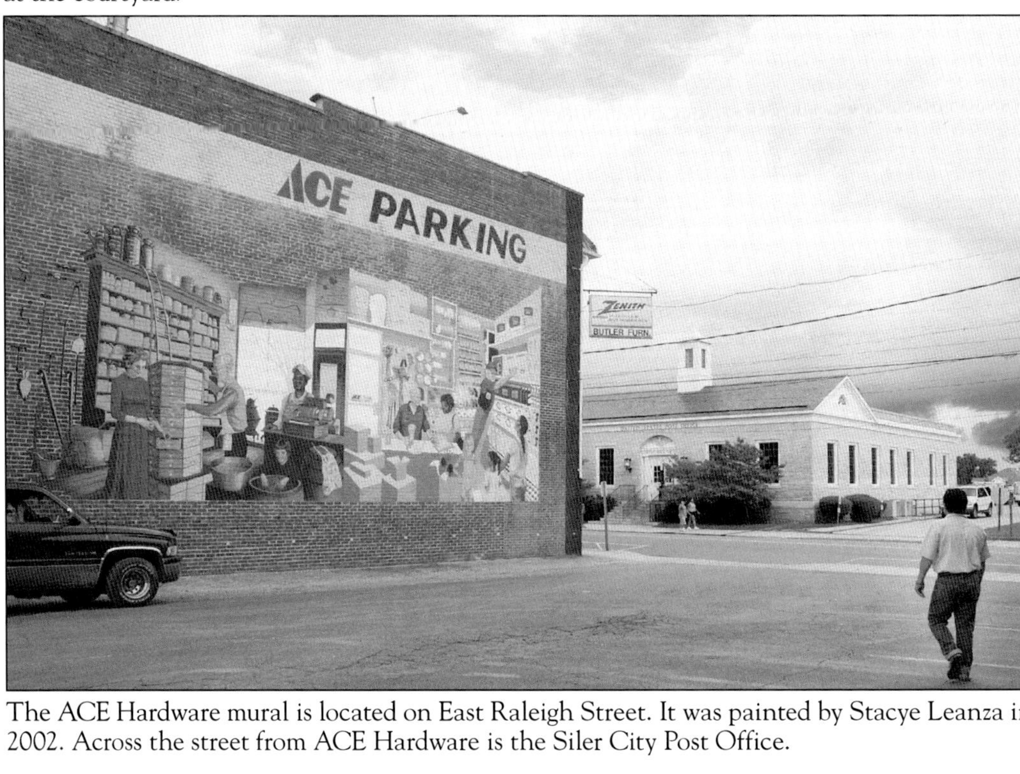

The ACE Hardware mural is located on East Raleigh Street. It was painted by Stacye Leanza in 2002. Across the street from ACE Hardware is the Siler City Post Office.

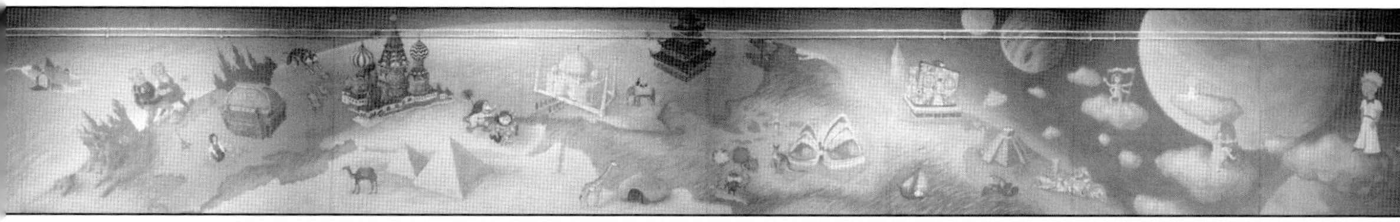

The Wren Library children's mural exposes the children of Siler City to the vast world around them, real and imagined. It includes examples of architecture and flora and fauna from every continent. Commissioned by library staff Tom Kenlan and funded by the Wren Foundation, it measures 34 feet by four feet, six inches. (Courtesy of Stacye Leanza.)

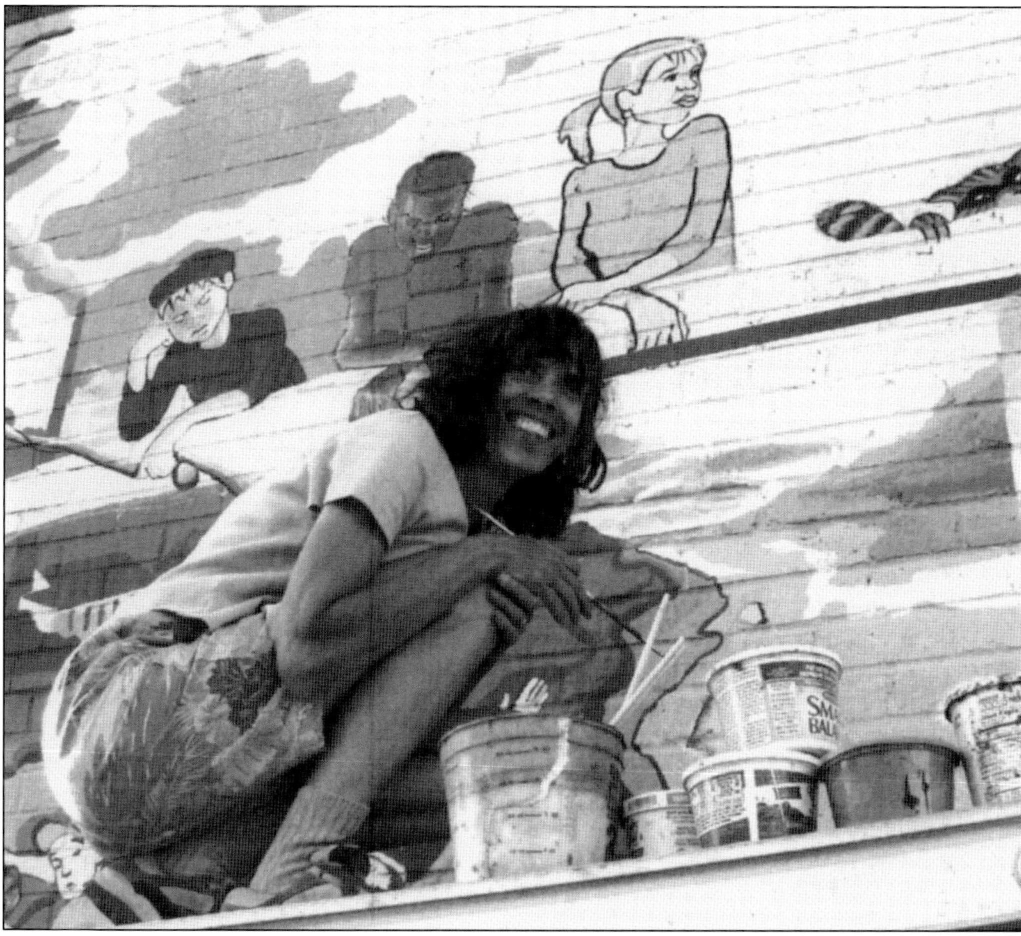

Stacye Leanza became immersed in the practice of painting murals when a friend of hers convinced the Siler City Mural Society that they should hire a local artist to complete the murals in Siler City. Though only a few miles from her Pittsboro home, Siler City was culturally speaking, "a world away." Being up on the scaffold and out in the streets day after day gave her real insight into the heart and soul of the town. People constantly came by with juicy stories about the people she was painting or what it was like back in the day. The stories were often told with a delightful brand of local humor. She said, "It's hard to say what was more fun: climbing the walls and painting, or listening to those entertaining stories!"

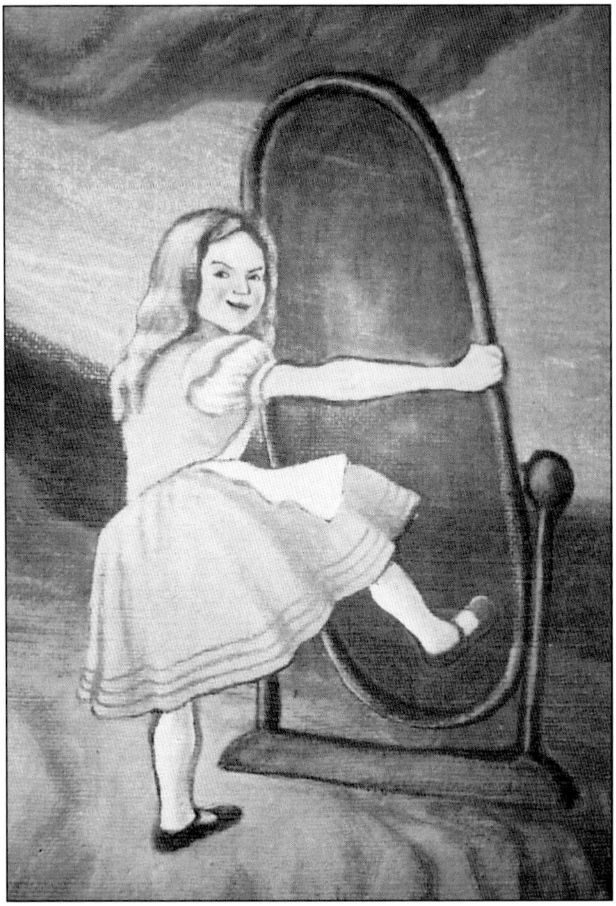

Included in the details of the Wren Library children's mural are a few characters from children's literature, like Alice from *Alice's Adventures in Wonderland.* (Courtesy of Stacye Leanza.)

The mural also contains an example of some outer-space architecture that is modeled after the actual library building. (Courtesy of Stacye Leanza.)

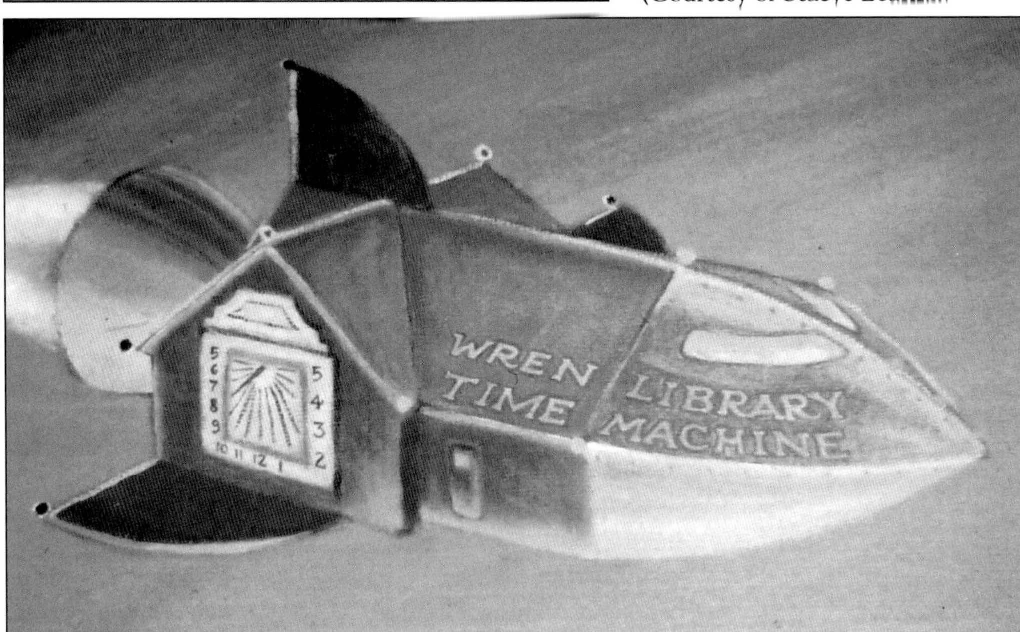

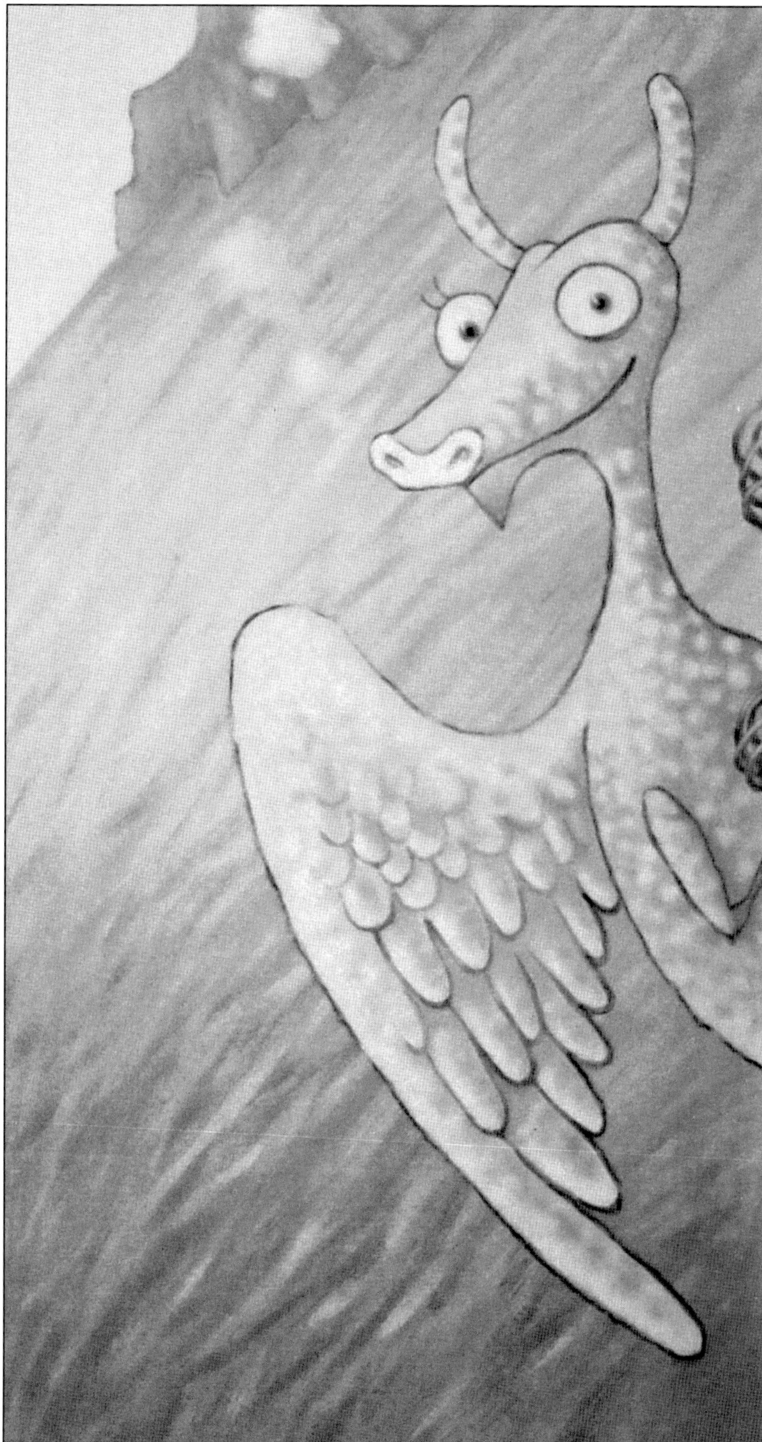

This dragon is about the size of the average four-year-old, about the size of many who enter the Wren Library children's area. The mural was completed by artist Stacye Leanza in March 2004. (Courtesy of Stacye Leanza.)

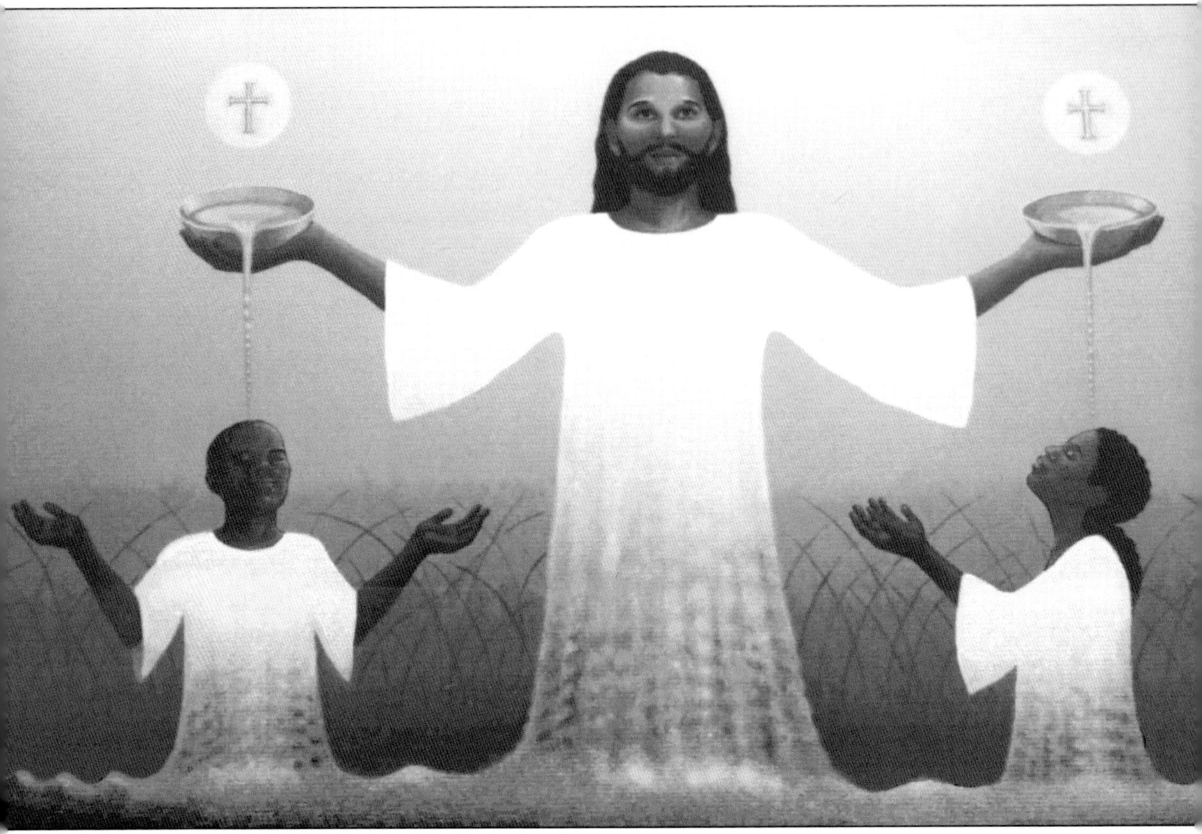

The Holy Trinity Church Baptistery mural can be found in the sanctuary just above the pool. It depicts St. John the Baptist baptizing members of the congregation. Completed in May 2002, the size of the mural is 10 feet, six inches by nine feet, four inches. Reverend Obie asked for an image churchgoers could relate to. (Courtesy of Stacye Leanza.)

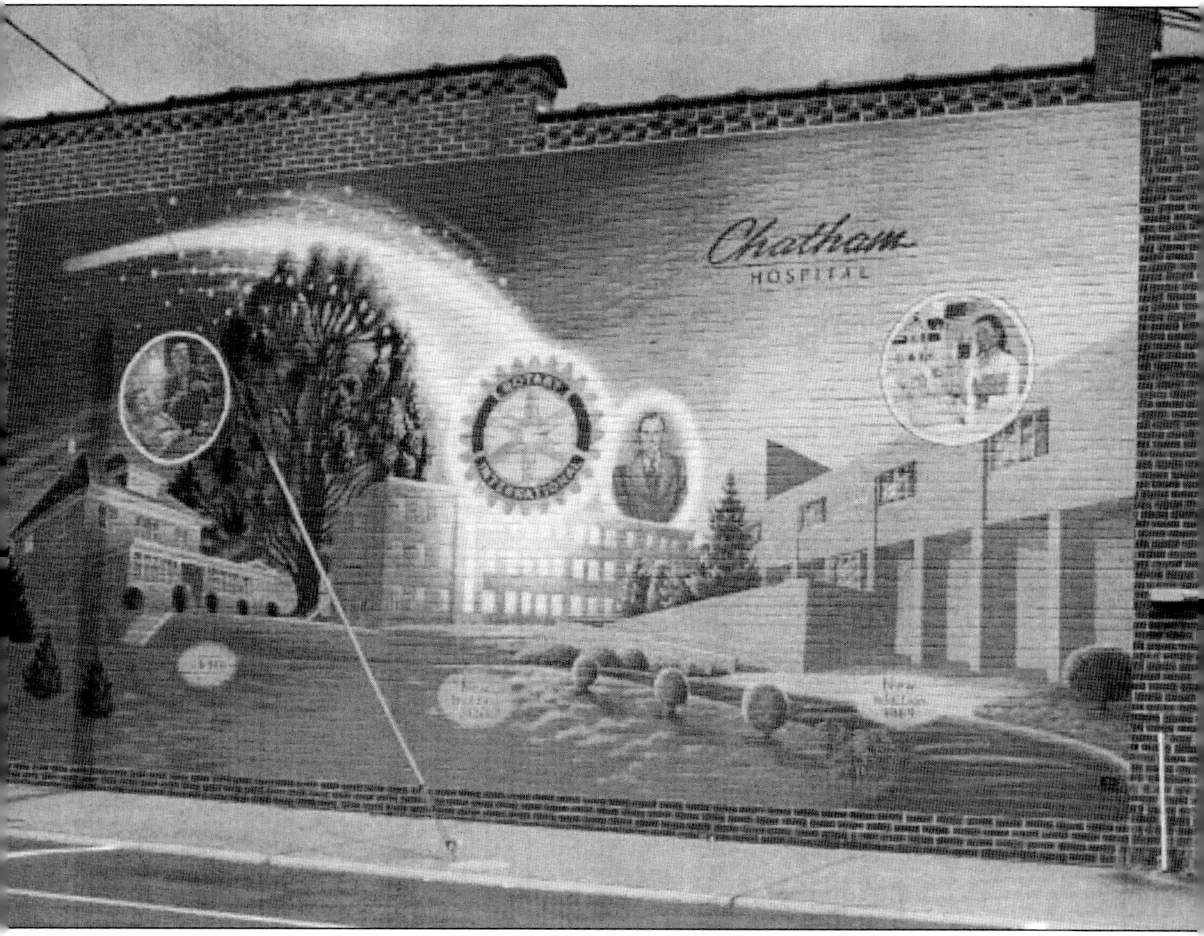

The Chatham Hospital mural at 125 West Raleigh Street was completed in October 2003. The mural was done for the Siler City Mural Society and depicts the history of Chatham County's first and only hospital and pays tribute to the significant contributions to its development. There are 10 hidden objects painted in the mural. (Courtesy of Stacye Leanza.)

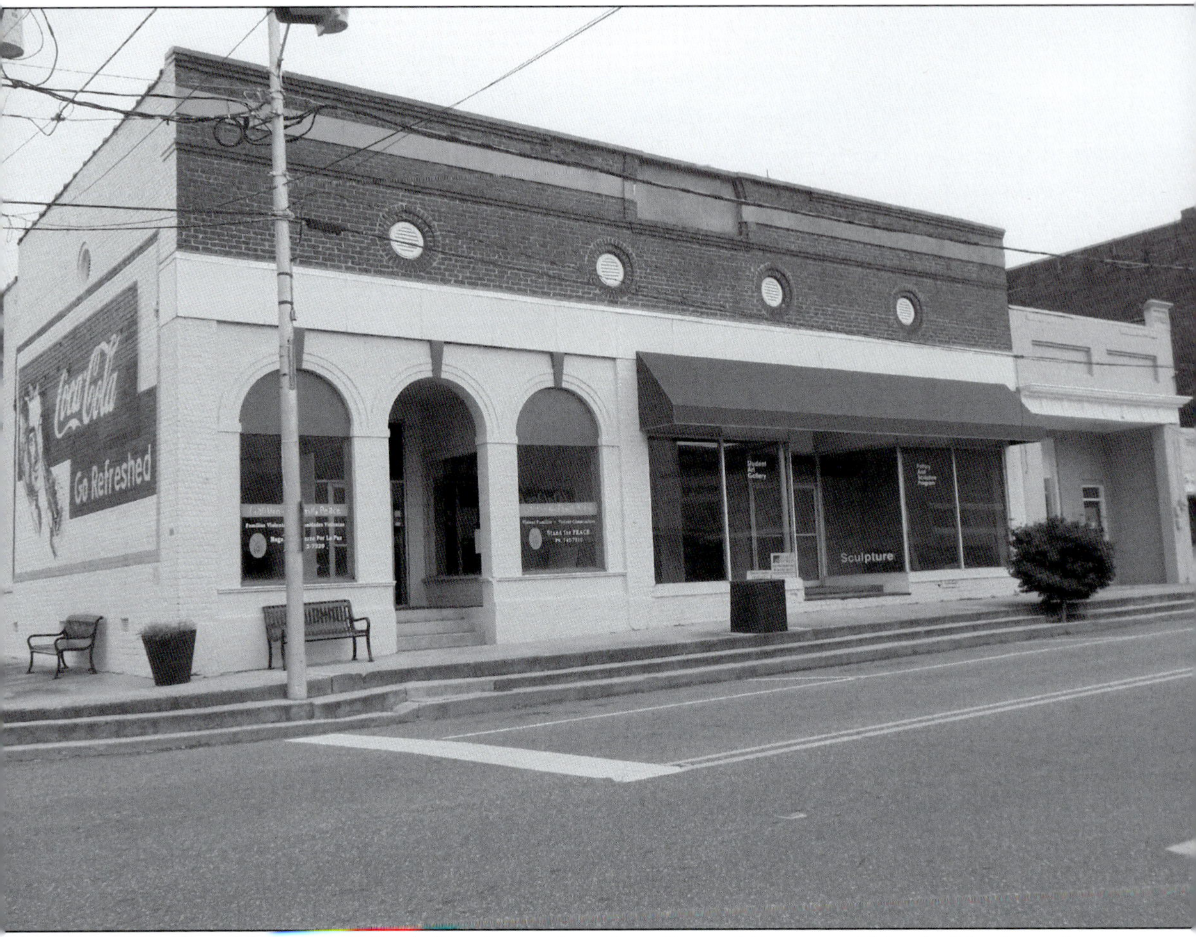

The Coca-Cola mural (far left) is located on East Second Street and North Chatham Avenue. It was originally painted in 1949 by Harold Draper, and in the 1970s a Jordan Matthews High School art class touched it up. The sign on the mural reads, "This 'Clark Gable' Coke sign was an official Coke sign designed by their artist." (Photograph by author.)

Nine

Surrounding Area Attractions

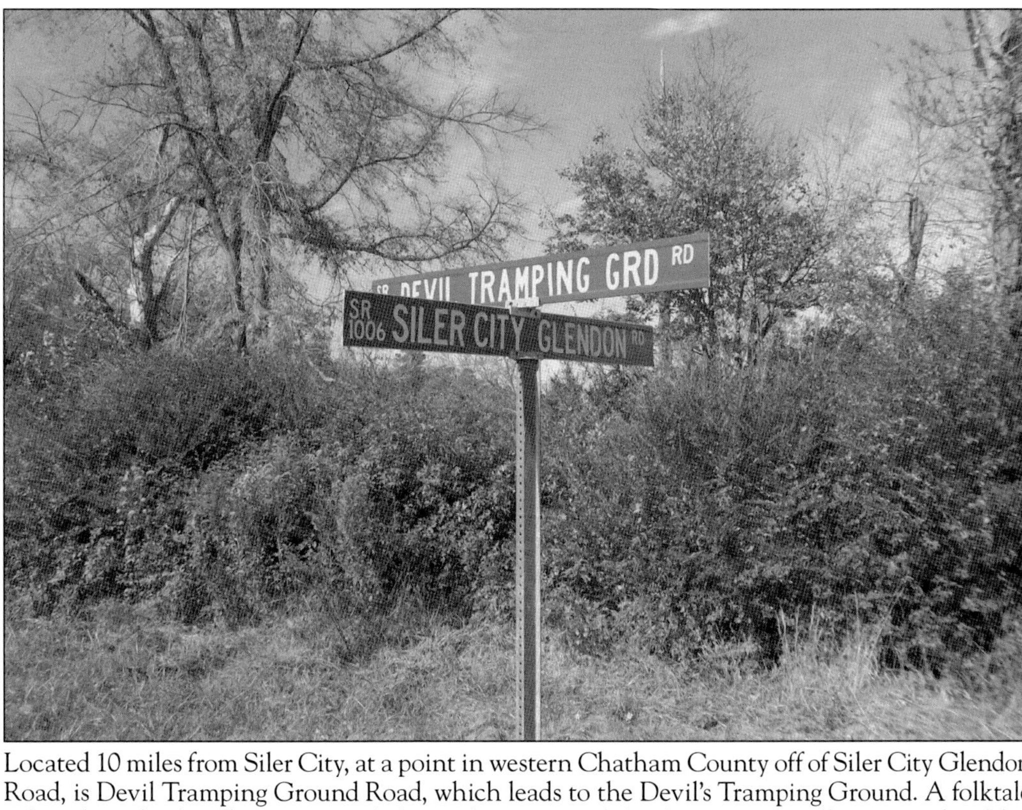

Located 10 miles from Siler City, at a point in western Chatham County off of Siler City Glendon Road, is Devil Tramping Ground Road, which leads to the Devil's Tramping Ground. A folktale is based on the fact that in a wooded area there is a path leading up to a well-worn circle of dirt that is about 40 feet in diameter with a mound of dirt in the center, built up like a large anthill, or mound. The area outside the ring is lush with grass and other plant life, but nothing grows in the ring circle. (Photograph by author.)

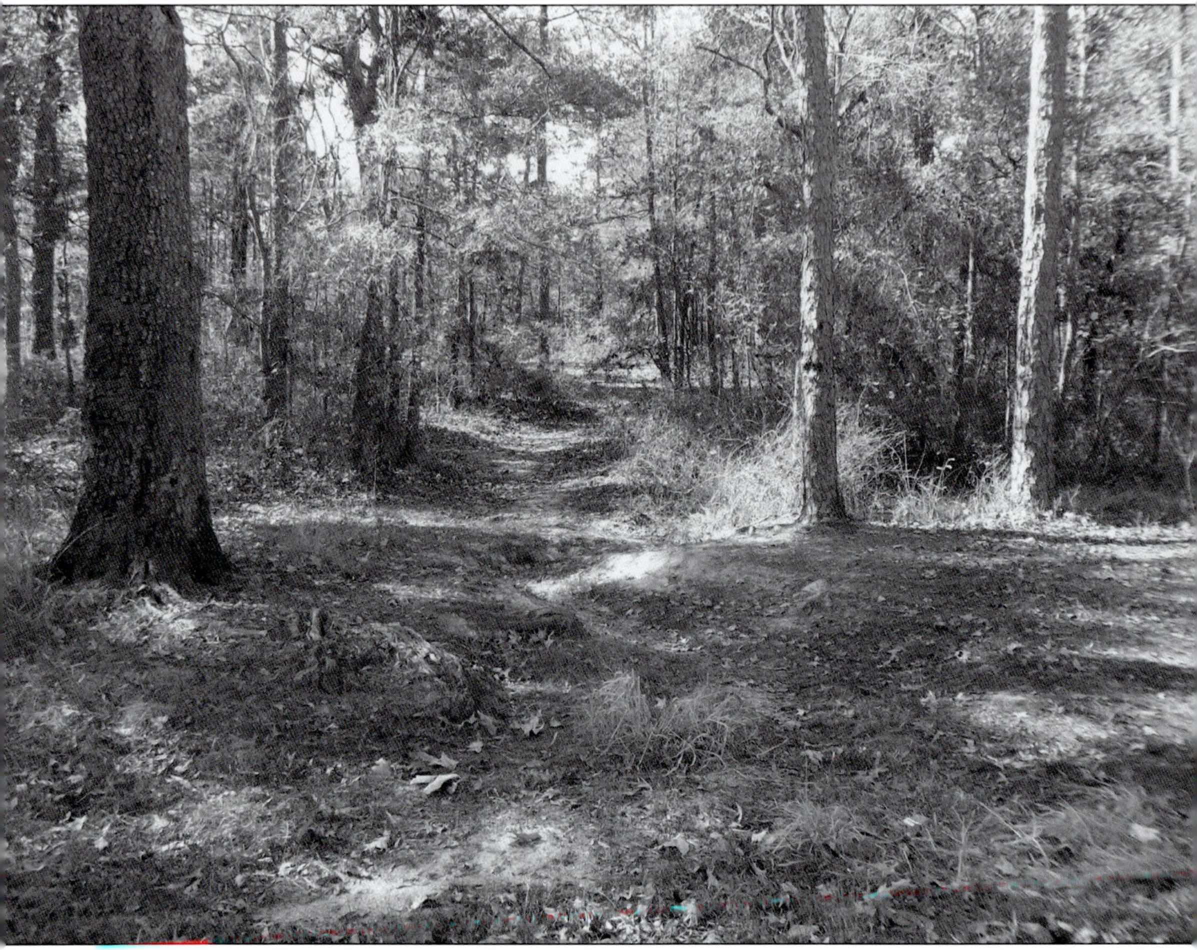

Approximately one mile down Devil Tramping Ground Road, on the right, are a half-moon graveled parking area and a path leading up into the woods that has been around as far back as anybody can remember. The path itself is about a foot wide and is barren of any obstructive growth. (Photograph by author.)

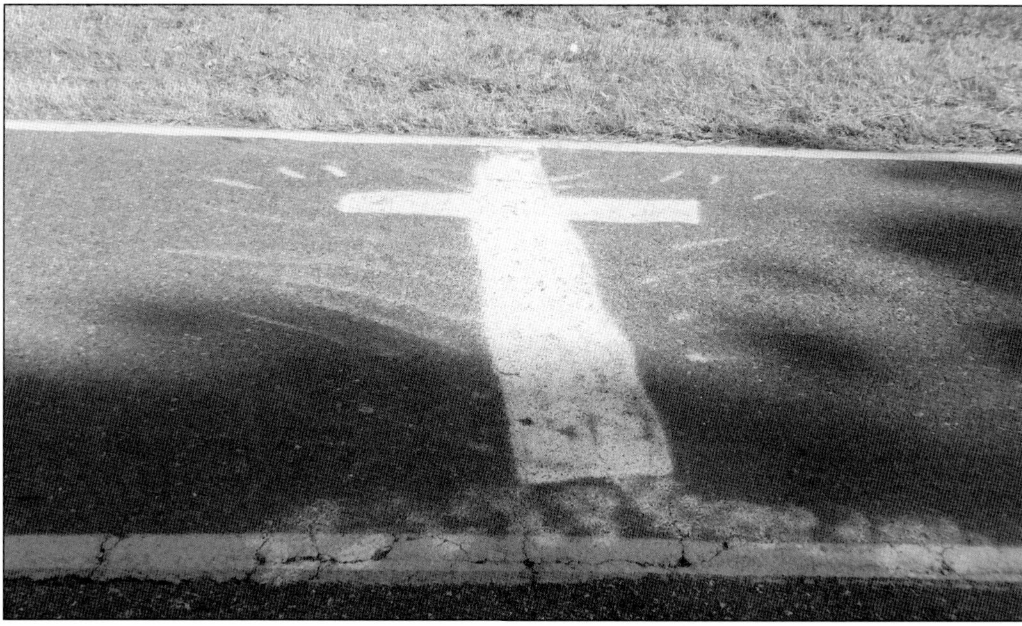

A painting of a cross on this road could have been created to ward off the Devil, similar to the hanging crosses in the trees in the area. The story goes that the Devil arises nightly to tramp around the circle as he thinks up new means of causing trouble for the human race. According to folklore, "If something is put on the mound, the next day it will not be there." (Photograph by author.)

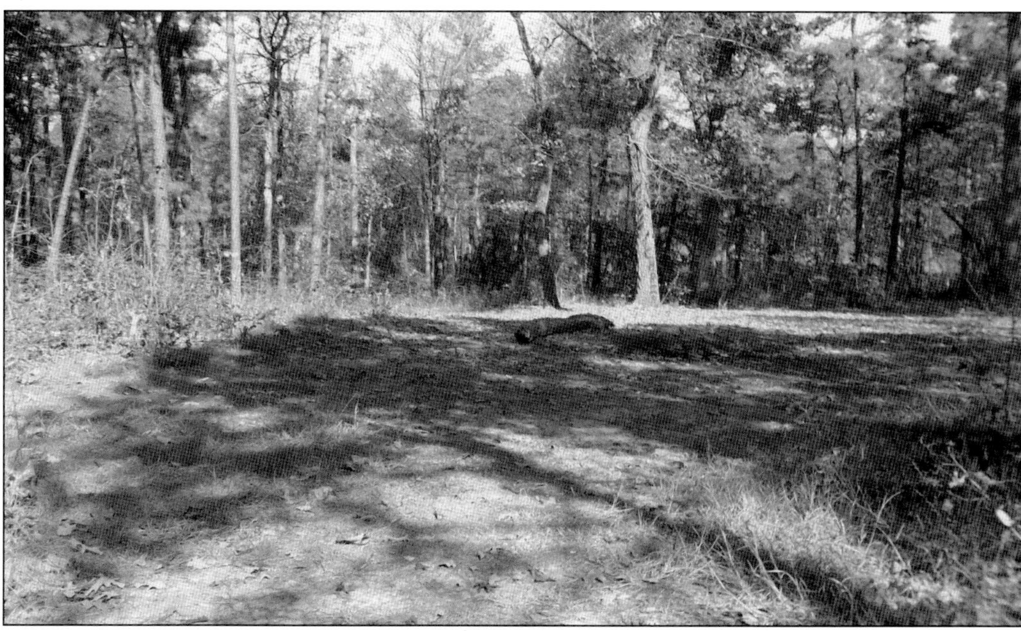

Writings may be painted on the trees, a log might be pulled up to the mound to sit on, and bottles or other objects may be found on the mound. Folklore states, "At the first light of morning the devil is gone, winging his way like a bat across the world to carry out his evil purposes." Though no one has ever seen the Devil stalking here, it still is believed to be haunted by Satan, the sinful friend of mankind. (Photograph by author.)

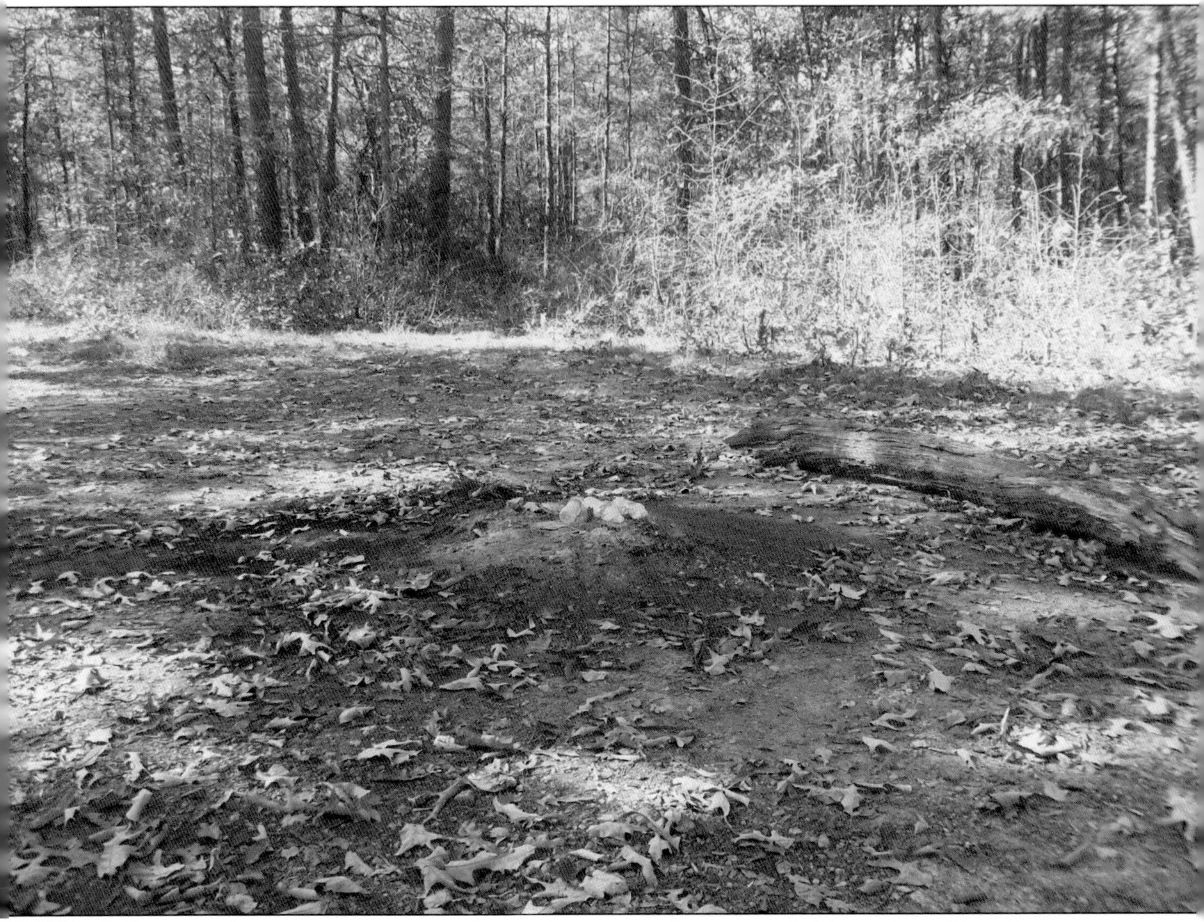

Other explanations suggest that Native American tribes roamed this section of Chatham County hundreds of years ago. The treading of their feet wore a circle in the earth as they performed dances for the Great Spirit. More information can be found in a book titled *The Devil's Tramping Ground and Other North Carolina Mystery Stories* by John Harden. (Photograph by author.)

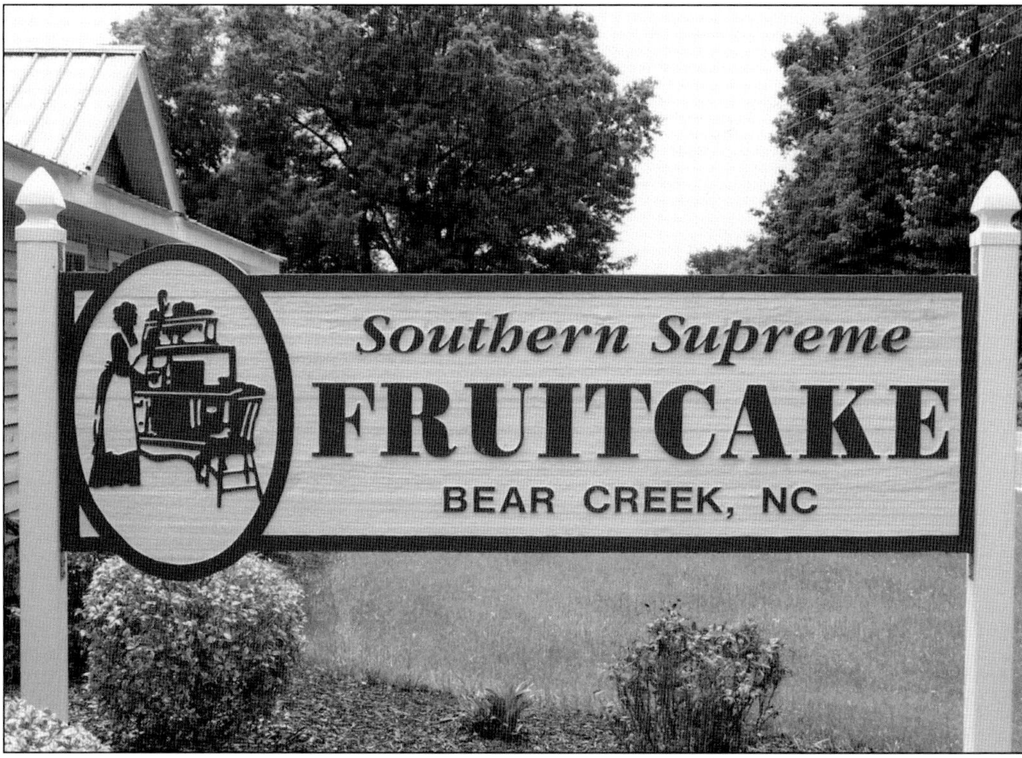

The story of Southern Supreme Fruitcake begins back in 1984 with a fruitcake recipe that the founders wanted to share with the world. Their business started in a garage that they converted into a kitchen. With help from family and friends, they launched a successful mail-order business in Bear Creek, North Carolina. (Courtesy of Southern Supreme Fruitcake Company.)

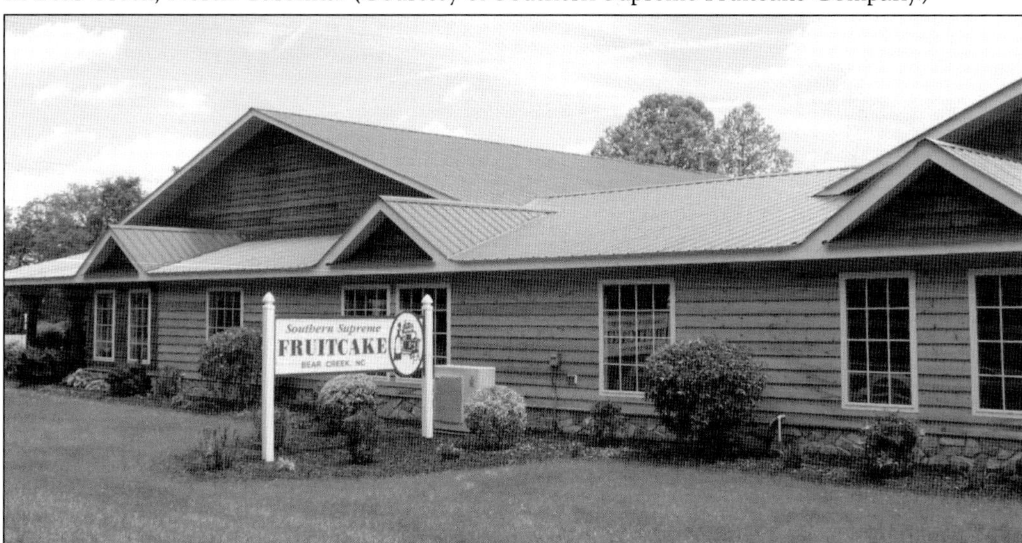

Southern Supreme Fruitcake is located at 1699 Hoyte Scott Road in Bear Creek, North Carolina, near the Harper's Crossroad community, which is 15 minutes from Siler City off of Siler City Glendon Road. The Scott family invites everyone to come by and visit their showroom and share a slice of fruitcake and coffee with them. (Courtesy of Southern Supreme Fruitcake Company.)

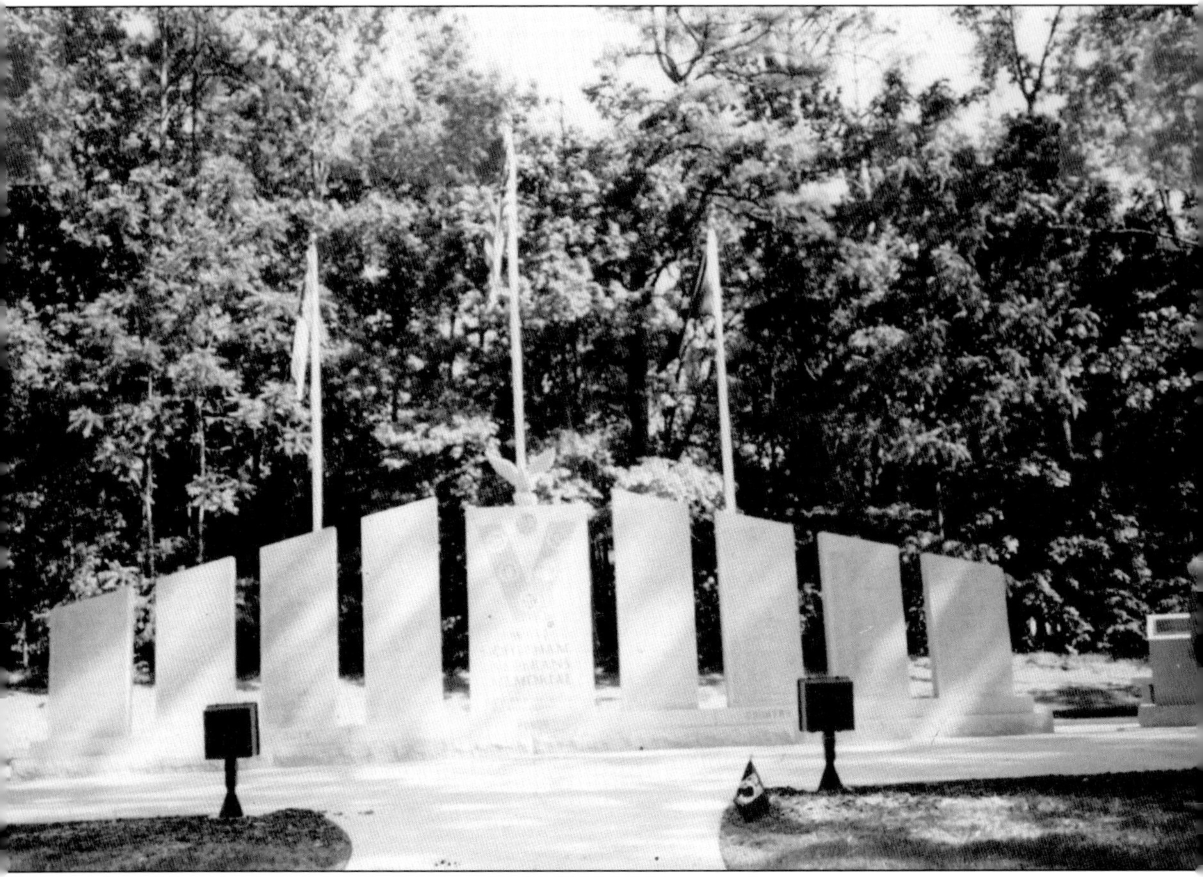

The West Chatham Veterans Memorial is located at Siler City's Bray Park on South Second Avenue. Siler City graciously provided a site for the monument, which depicts each branch of the military service, along with the Great Seal of the United States. The memorial is organized by name, branch of service, and war or conflict era. (Courtesy of Farmers' Alliance Store and Nancy Tysor.)

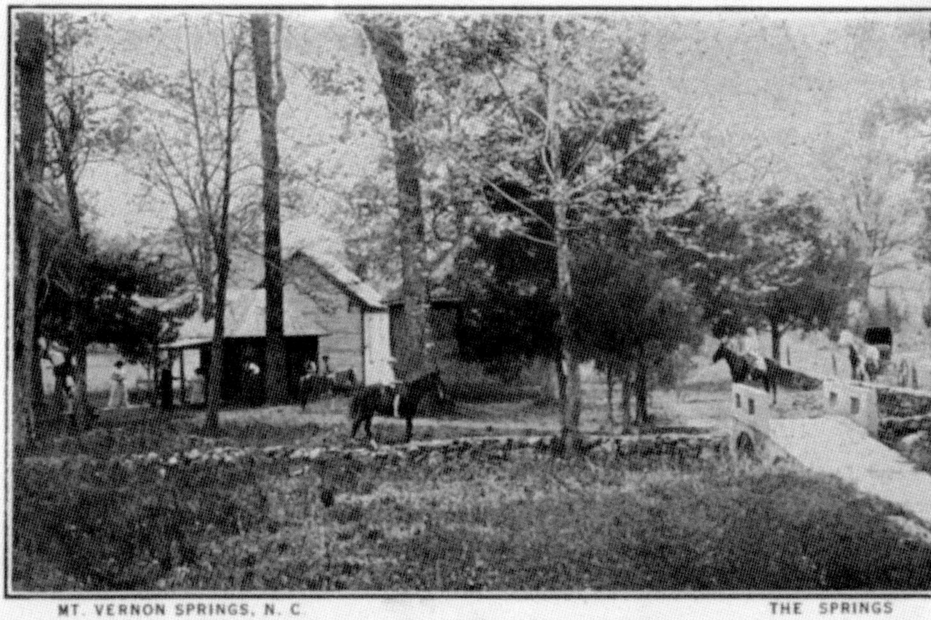

South of Siler City, off Old US Route 421 on Mount Vernon Springs Road, are two natural springs pouring clean mineral waters named Health and Beauty. The waters flow from two taps set in a concrete cistern that was built around 1907. A springhouse built around 1880 once stood at the site. (Courtesy of North Carolina Collection Photographic Archives, Wilson Library, University of North Carolina at Chapel Hill.)

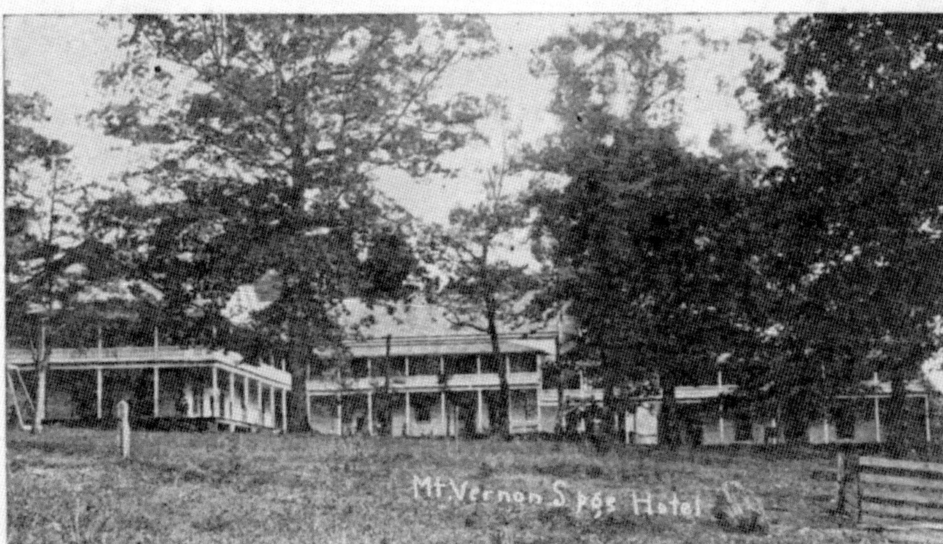

Between 1881 and 1920, Mount Vernon Springs Hotel operated as a popular summer health spa. Healing and medicinal qualities were attributed to the twin springs, named Health and Beauty, by settlers in the 1750s. Today, drinkable water still flows from two adjacent pipes. The site is listed in the National Register of Historic Places. (Courtesy of North Carolina Collection Photographic Archives, Wilson Library, University of North Carolina at Chapel Hill.)

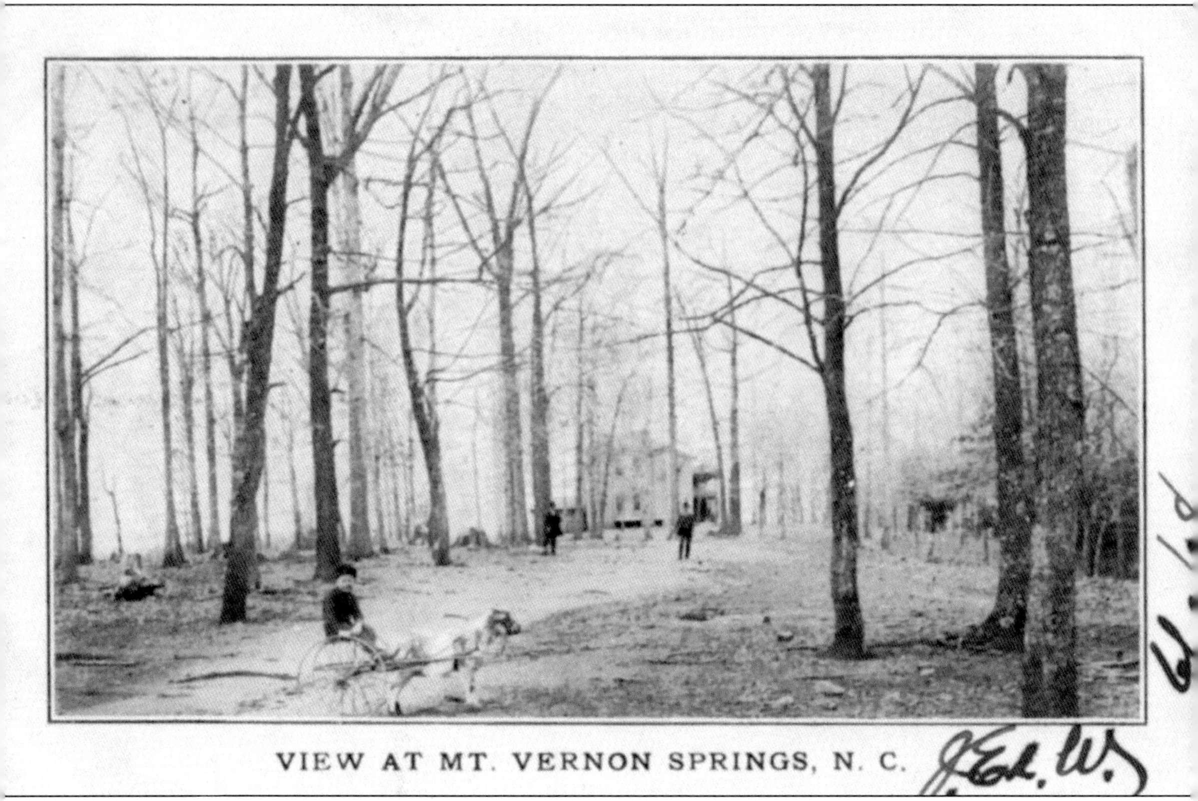

Mount Vernon Springs was once a growing community. This view is of a sparsely wooded area with a child sitting in a goat-pulled cart and two men and a large house in the distance. (Courtesy of North Carolina Postcards Collection Photographic Archives, Wilson Library, University of North Carolina at Chapel Hill.)

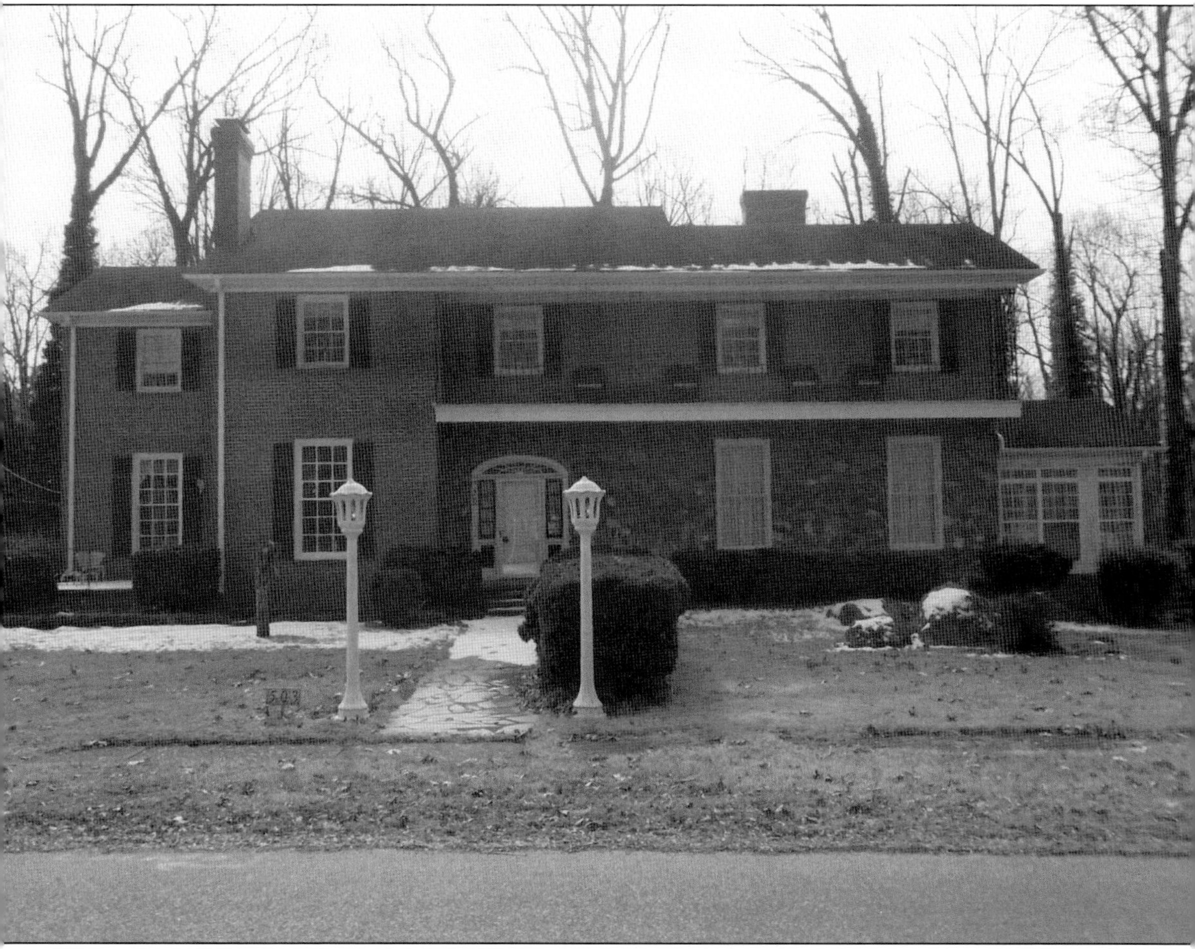

Frances Bavier was born on December 14, 1902, in New York City. She had a successful career in acting on Broadway, entertaining the troops in the USO during World War II and appearing in Hollywood movies beginning in 1951 and on various television programs beginning in the 1950s (with her most famous role being that of Aunt Bee on *The Andy Griffith Show*). She retired to Siler City, North Carolina, in August 1972. The private home, as the photograph shows, was of brick and stone. It has large rooms, hardwood floors, 11-foot-high ceilings, crystal chandeliers, and a total of 9,000 square feet (counting the basement and porches). Bavier lived here until she died in December 1989. She is buried in the Siler City town cemetery. (Courtesy of Larry Russell.)

BIBLIOGRAPHY

brookwoodfarms.com/index.php/our-story

Hadley, Wade Hampton, Jr. *Historical Buildings of the Central Business District Siler City, North Carolina*. Pittsboro, NC: The Chatham County Historical Association, 1996.

———. *Siler City, North Carolina: 1887–1987, A History for the Town's Centennial Anniversary on March 7, 1987*. Siler City, NC: Caviness Printing Service Inc., 1986.

———, Doris Goerch Horton, and Nell Craig Strowd. *Chatham County: 1771–1971*. Pittsboro, NC: Chatham County Historical Association, 1997.

library.unc.edu/services/digitalcollections/

Osborn, Rachel, and Ruth Selden Sturgill. *The Architectural Heritage of Chatham County, North Carolina*. Pittsboro, NC: Chatham County Historical Association, 1991.

www.silercity.org

www2.lib.unc.edu/dc/nc_post/

About the Organization

The Farmer's Alliance Store is a place where residents in the community can come to shop, sit a spell, and talk about the history of Siler City. There are an overwhelming number of images on display. To the best of her ability, Nancy Tysor, the current store manager, will explain to anyone when the photographs were taken and who the pictured people are. She will inform visitors that the former principal of Paul Braxton Elementary School, which was the former Siler City High School, donated most of the photographs on display in the store. The organization also supplied a large number of the images for this book. It is a place where one can feel the warmth of the community, a place that appreciates the history of the community and regularly exhibits photographs to memorialize the past. Farmer's Alliance Store has remained a strong and vibrant company that has evolved ethnically and socially by supplying the essential needs of Siler City citizens regardless of the economic landscape to serve all its patrons with a smile and a "can I help you?"